China Gold

中国金

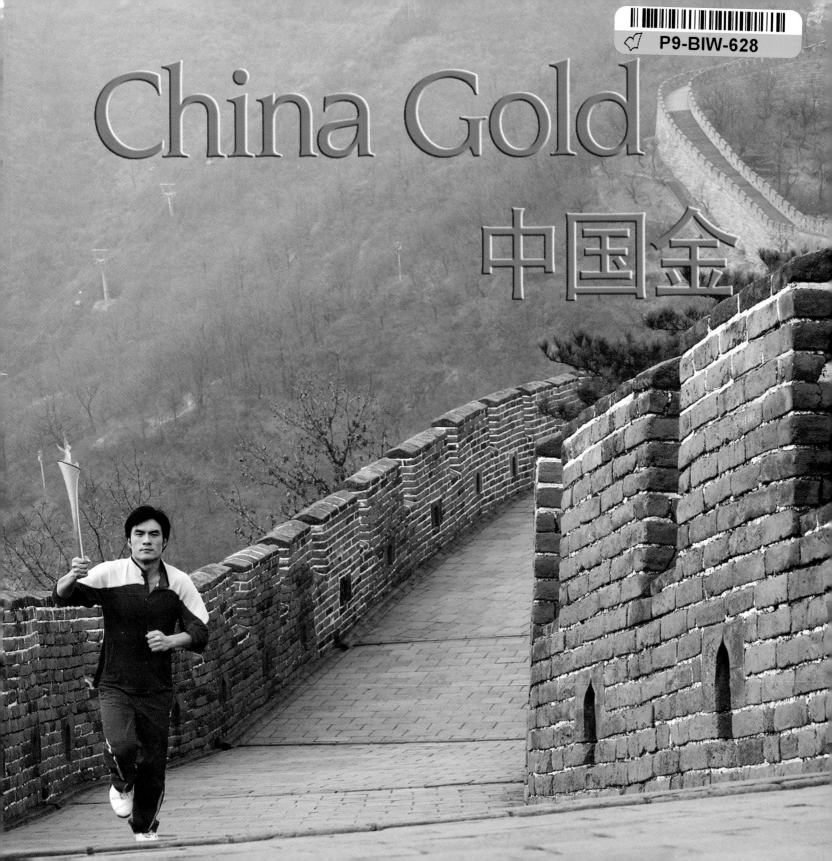

China Gold

China's Quest for Global Power and Olympic Glory

路漫漫：从辉煌奥运到世界强国

中国金

Edited by FAN Hong 凡红, Duncan Mackay, and Karen Christensen

BERKSHIRE
PUBLISHING GROUP
Great Barrington, Massachusetts

For information
Berkshire Publishing Group LLC
314 Main Street
Great Barrington, Massachusetts 01230
www.berkshirepublishing.com

Editorial Staff Elizabeth Steffey, Thomas Christensen, Marcy Ross, LU Zhouxiang (Paul)

Copy Editors Francesca Forrest and Daniel Spinella

Cover Designer Joseph DiStefano

Interior Designer Martin Lubin Graphic Design

Compositor Brad Walrod/High Text Graphics, Inc.

Proofreader Mary Bagg

Printed in China

Library of Congress Cataloging-in-Publication Data

China gold: China's quest for global power and Olympic glory/edited by
  Fan Hong, Duncan Mackay, and Karen Christensen.
    p. cm.
  Includes bibliographical references and index.
  ISBN 978-1-933782-64-5 (alk. paper)
  1. Olympic Games (29th: 2008: Beijing, China)   2. Sports—
China—History.   3. Olympics—Economic aspects—China—
Beijing.   I. Hong, Fan.   II. Mackay, Duncan.   III. Christensen, Karen.
GV7222008 .C45 2008
796.48—dc22   2008017790

Contents

Acknowledgments

CREATING A BOOK DEPENDS ON THE contributions of far more people than are evident in any acknowledgments. *China Gold* 中国金 is the result of a close collaboration between more than thirty sports experts and a publishing company that specializes in global perspectives. We are honored to be working with editor FAN Hong 凡红 and with scholars including REN Hai 任海, XIONG Xiaozheng 熊晓正 of Beijing Sport University, TAN Hua 谭华 and HU Xiaomin 胡小明 of South China Normal University, LUO Shiming 罗时铭 of Suzhou University, CAO Shuohe 曹守和 of Hangzhou Normal University, FAN Wei 樊维 of Chengdu Sport University, and JIN Yuanpu 金元浦 of the Renmin University Humanistic Olympics Studies Center. British coeditor Duncan Mackay, a well-known Olympics journalist, proudly carried the Olympic torch in London in April 2008.

Professor Allen Guttmann of Amherst College, recipient of the International Olympic Committee's first award for sports history, has been a guide and inspiration for over ten years and was instrumental in enabling us to build the global networks that have now produced three major reference works on sports around the world. He introduced us to Fan Hong when we were working on the *International Encyclopedia of Women and Sports* in 1999. Other people who helped and inspired us include Susan Brownell, Yuan Haiwang 袁海旺, and LU Zhouxiang (Paul) 吕洲翔—with special thanks to Zhouxiang for his invaluable assistance in providing the many Chinese translations for the book. We're also grateful to our designer, Joe DiStefano, who proved in the course of designing the cover that he has developed an instinct for things Chinese. The first cover included a small Chinese building. A Chinese-speaking friend looked at it and saw not a house but the character for "gold"—and indeed, it was remarkably similar! What you now see is the Chinese character *jin* 金, which seems to have come to Joe through cultural osmosis—something we're hoping readers of *China Gold* will experience as they continue to get to know Chinese culture and history and, most important, as they come to understand the hopes and dreams that Chinese people have for their country and for our world.

All the members of the editorial, design, and production team (listed on the preceding copyright page) deserve gold medals for their high professionalism, skill, dedication, and grace under pressure. Working on three continents—in English and Chinese—they, too, are champions. Special thanks to Mary Bagg, Tom Christensen, Martin Lubin, Marcy Ross, and Brad Walrod, who labored day and night (and often weekends) to complete this ambitious project.

It was no small challenge to name a book that is largely about, but not only about, the Olympics and sports. Stephen A. Orlins, president of the National Committee on U.S.-China Relations, an unreformed jock who dreamed of participating in the Olympics as a young athlete, came up with the perfect title, *China Gold*. Both English speakers and our Chinese editor and authors immediately recognized it as capturing the larger significance of a book that is not only an introduction to China in the Olympics but also to China and Chinese culture in general—and as reflecting the sense of aspiration that the Olympics symbolizes.

While the Olympics are a creation of Western civilization, the 2008 Beijing Games give China a chance to integrate the Olympic ideals into its perspective on global leadership and an opportunity to influence an event that has unique meaning around the world. We dedicate this book to the organizations and individuals committed to building international understanding, promoting respect for diverse perspectives, and solving social, environmental, and political challenges peacefully and cooperatively.

Note: To ensure that Western readers understand the correct order of Chinese names, we have followed a new international convention of capitalizing family names.

Foreword

MY FIRST MEMORY OF CHINA includes the sight of thousands of fragile green and silver saplings bending in a strong April wind. They had been planted along the airport freeway as part of efforts to win the 2008 Olympic Games. Only a few months later, in July 2001, the Games were awarded to Beijing.

I knew then that soil erosion and sandstorms were a significant problem, and that China's astonishing economic development of the past decade, while welcome, had come at an environmental price. As my taxi sped by mile after mile of new trees, I thought of the lasting benefits the Olympics could bring to China and of the importance of a Green Olympics in a developing country with huge population, a country that would clearly influence the twenty-first century in myriad ways, and one that Western nations hoped to influence as well.

China Gold 中国金 was conceived in the offices of a publishing company in western Massachusetts, a rural region of the northeastern United States where three of the world's most popular sports—basketball, volleyball, and baseball—originated. Our main hallway has been lined with Beijing Olympics bid posters since 2001, and during the intervening years, our China-related publishing has expanded, as has our publishing on international sports. *China Gold* is an inevitable alchemy, in the sense of the word as defined by Hugh Page, professor at the University of Notre Dame: "a way of thinking about the relationship of humanity and nature that accentuates the importance of transformation in both."

And its aim is alchemy, in the broadest sense: not to find the philosopher's stone or to create a precious metal but, as Page says, to "uncover those forces governing unity, diversity, stasis, and flux in the world." In the West, alchemy is the quest for a substance that "has the power to perfect that which is incomplete and make noble that which is base." In that sense, there is something alchemical about the Olympics themselves, which, at their best, provide an opportunity for nations to strive for excellence not through economic or military domination, but through athletic prowess.

Our goal has been first to provide unique information for the sports obsessed, yes, but we've also prepared a book for anyone and everyone intrigued by China, full of background history and facts you won't get anywhere else. The 2008 Beijing Games (only the third to be held in Asia) give us a new perspective on a fascinating story, that of a 5,000-year-old civilization once again taking up a position of international influence after centuries of turmoil.

And there's a bigger story to sports as well. Sport is a vital aspect of the human experience, an endeavor that, perhaps more than anything else, connects people worldwide. Basketball and soccer (football) are more universally known, and loved, than any religion or food or political system. Sports tell us about who we are and who we want to be. They create a shared language, shared passions; they highlight our aspirations and values, our ways of interacting with one another, and our appreciation of competition, achievement, and adventure.

Sports are about fame and fortune, too; some are among the world's biggest businesses. Sports can also be an agent of social change. Title IX, the U.S. law that opened college sports to women, also promoted greater participation by women in other aspects of society, while the success of African athletes in the Olympics has called attention to African achievement and potential in other areas.

While the Beijing Games have some harsh critics, most people see them as holding more promise than peril. Will China change the Olympics, or will the Olympics change China? Perhaps neither to the extent that some people may hope, but there's no doubt that the ideals of the Olympics—of fellowship and good sportsmanship, of athletic prowess and determination, and of a global community united in working toward a common future—will influence people inside and outside China in this year of China Gold 中国金.

■ KAREN CHRISTENSEN

China's Olympic Dream

中国奥运梦

IN AUGUST 1908, THE FOURTH modern Olympic Games took place in London, and it was there—in the city that will host the 2012 Games—that the first steps were taken to set China on the path to Olympic glory. Even though China was not yet a member of the International Olympic Committee and Chinese athletes did not compete, an influential Chinese educator ZHANG Boling 张伯苓, the principal of Nankai University 南开大学, was in London, on his way to visit several schools and universities in Britain.

He was impressed by the principle of the Olympics—fair play 公平竞争. He returned to China in October and introduced the idea—and ideal—of the Olympic Games to his students in Tianjin 天津.

After Zhang's introduction, students of Nankai University held a seminar that would become famous for asking the "Three Questions about the Olympics." These questions were: When would China send its first athlete to participate in the Olympic Games? When would Chinese athletes win their first gold medal at the Olympic Games? When would the Olympic Games be held in China?

It took the Chinese twenty-four years to answer the first question. In 1932 China sent LIU Changchun 刘长春, a sprinter, to participate in the Olympics in Los Angeles. He was eliminated in the earliest of the preliminary heats. It was another seventy-six years before the second question was answered. On 29 July 1984, sharpshooter XU Haifeng 许海峰 won China's first gold medal, in another Los Angeles Olympics. And it took a full century to provide an answer to the final question—"When would the Olympic Games be held in China?"—as the Games at last came to China.

Chinese people will never forget the moment on 13 July 2001 in Moscow when Juan Antonio Samaranch, then president of the International Olympic Committee, announced that Beijing would host the Twenty-ninth Olympic Games in 2008. A century after the "Three Questions" were asked, China's Olympic dream has finally come true. The Games of 2008 not only provide billions of Chinese with a chance to witness China's success in sports firsthand, but also to participate in an event that marks a crucial milestone on China's road to modernization. Hosting the Olympic Games is a symbol of China's "linking up with international standards" 与世界接轨—the biggest event in China since the Communist revolution of 1949.

The Meaning of the Olympic Dream

Acclaimed Chinese filmmaker ZHANG Yimou 张艺谋—the director of the lavish opening and closing ceremonies at the 2008 Beijing Olympics—spoke for the nation when he said: "It is not just an opening ceremony for the

Is It Not a Great Joy to Have Friends Coming From Afar?

This well-known question—answered in the affirmative, naturally—comes from the Analects of Confucius (551–479 BCE), written by the philosopher and moralist who has had great intellectual and cultural influence. While his ideas were dismissed during the early decades of the Communist period, today Confucius Institutes supported by the Chinese government, similar to the UK's British Council, have been established at universities around the world to encourage learning about Chinese language and culture. The Chinese are known for their hospitality and for their belief in the importance of building personal relationships. The chance for the Chinese nation to welcome the world makes the 2008 Olympic Games of unprecedented importance.

Olympics—it is a way of showing China to the world and what is happening today."

Some may wonder why the Olympics mean so much to the Chinese, but if we look at the history of the last two centuries it is easy to understand. China, one of the world's oldest civilizations, cherishes the memory of its long supremacy at the center of the world and the knowledge that China has contributed greatly to global scholarship, philosophy, and scientific innovation. In consequence, the Chinese people feel abiding pain and deep chagrin over what can only be described as repeated humiliations at the hands of the Western and Eastern imperialist powers in the late nineteenth century and early twentieth century.

Modern Chinese history is one of struggle and striving to restore national pride. Since the late twentieth century, China, the once "sleeping giant," has amazed the world by the pace of its economic growth and social change. Determined to catch up with the developed countries, it has taken every possible opportunity to restore the nation's confidence and achieve international recognition in many areas.

The Olympic Games, the largest sport event and one of the biggest social and corporate enterprises in the world, has become a stage upon which China can achieve some of its political, social, and economic objectives. Since the establishment of the People's Republic of China in 1949, sport has been a powerful tool, and in the Maoist era between 1949 and 1976, sport was for China, as well as other nations, right at the center of politics and diplomacy—a way to demonstrate the superiority of socialism over capitalism.

Since the 1980s China's sporting success has been regarded not only as evidence of ideological superiority and economic prosperity, but also a powerful symbol of national revival. The government and most of the Chinese people believed that Chinese athletes' excellent performances on the Olympic stage would be the best proof of China's great achievements in economic reform and modernization. Brilliant victories achieved by Chinese athletes at the Olympics not only show China's ability to stand proudly and independently among the other nations of the world, but will also strengthen the national spirit and confident vision of its citizens. To most Chinese people, the Olympic Games is where they can witness the glory of China, feel proud of being Chinese, and experience unity as a great nation.

China's Influence on the Olympics

More so than other host countries, China's culture and character has deeply influenced the 2008 Games. The Chinese have defined the Beijing Games as "humanistic Olympics" 人文奥运, "green Olympics" 绿色奥运, and "technological Olympics" 高科技奥运. These core concepts derive from shared international principles, of course, but have also been influenced by Chinese cultural understandings about social interaction, environmental protection, and modernization.

The perception of some Western people and the Western media of what the Games should bring about is likely to be different from what the majority of ordinary Chinese people might hope for. For the Chinese, especially the 94 percent of Beijing citizens who voted to support the Games, the Olympics provide the best opportunity to show the world that the identity of the Chinese culture and people is uniquely different. The Games provide the opportunity to invest in programs to control air and water pollution, while raising awareness of environmental issues. They provide job opportunities for many people, and will contribute to raising living standards. At the same time, neighborhood streets have become cleaner and public transportation has improved. New construction and upgrades to the city's infrastructure will help make Beijing a first-class world city after the Games. "One World, One Dream" 同一世界, 同一梦想 is not just a slogan but the desire and wish of Chinese people.

There is no doubt that the Chinese flag and the American flag will be raised side by side at the Games. However, China's determination goes beyond just winning Olympic gold. What next? Overtaking the United States economically by 2039 and becoming the largest economic power in the world, as some economists predict? Whether or not that occurs, the Beijing Olympic Games is seen as a milestone in China's progress toward becoming a leading economic and political power in the twenty-first century.

■ FAN HONG 凡红

The Olympic Games, the Asian Games, and China's National Games

奥运会、亚运会、全运会

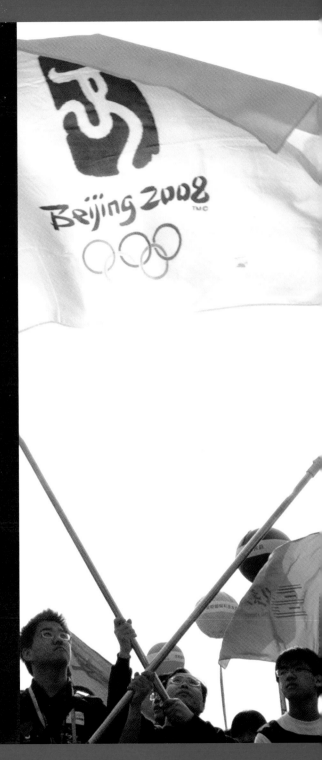

Beijing lost its first bid for the Olympics to Sydney, but in 2001 the International Olympic Committee voted to award the Games to China. At last, said a student to a BBC reporter, "The world is embracing us." As the Games approached, controversies broke out and that embrace seemed at times to change into crossed arms and mutual recriminations. Bringing the Olympics Games to Beijing was first discussed in China one hundred years ago, and Part One of *China Gold* tells the story of a century of development and challenge, of war and revolution, and of an enduring commitment to build (and rebuild) a nation that could participate on the global stage with stunning athleticism, as well as politically and economically. The Olympics of 2008 have great symbolic importance, and to understand this, we look at China's participation in the Asian Games, as well as the Olympics, and at the National Games which have been an essential proving ground for Chinese athletes.

How China Rose to Be a Sporting Giant

中国体育崛起起之路

A JOURNEY OF A THOUSAND MILES, the Chinese philosopher Lao-tzu 老子 said, begins with a single step. And so does a race of 100 meters and a nation's journey to the Olympic spotlight.

In 1932 a young man named Liu took that step when he moved into his starting position for the Olympic 100-meter race. As he did, he must have felt the great burden of the moment's historical significance; he must have withered under the weight of the expectations of a whole nation. LIU Changchun 刘长春 was at that moment the first Chinese ever to participate in the Olympic Games, and he was th single representative of the young Chinese Republic at the Olympics in Los Angeles.

Seconds later—11.1 seconds, to be exact—the first chapter of Chinese Olympic history was over. Liu Changchun had been eliminated in the first preliminary heat, finishing well behind most of his competitors.

Liu's failure became yet another open wound in the long history of defeats and humiliation that China had suffered at the hands of foreign powers. Humiliation had been a constant of Chinese history for almost a century, starting with the defeats during the Opium Wars of the mid-1800s at the hands of a technologically superior Western power. The 1895 Sino-Japanese War, lost to an up-to-then inconsequential neighbor, was even more devastating to China's self-image. Finally, only a month before the Olympic Games in Los Angeles, the Japanese had overrun a helpless Chinese army in Manchuria. Liu Changchun's failure in the preliminary heats seemed just another sign of Chinese backwardness and weakness.

More than seventy years later, another young Chinese man, again named Liu, moved into his starting position for an Olympic sprinting competition, the 110-meter hurdles. Again the expectations of a whole nation weighed on a young man's shoulders. However, this time, when the starting shot was fired, the hopes of his people did not drag the young man down. Indeed, he seemed

Chinese children learn sports such as table tennis at a very young age.

to be buoyed by those hopes. He flew over the hurdles. Exactly 12.91 seconds later, equaling the world record time, LIU Xiang 刘翔 had won China's first Olympic gold medal in a track-and-field competition and was about to become one of China's greatest sports heroes.

Liu's gold medal was China's crowning achievement at the 2004 Athens Olympics, placing the Chinese team second only to the U.S. team in the gold medal count. The special significance of Liu's victory, however, was the fact that he won in a sport in which the Chinese were traditionally not considered to be serious competitors because of their smaller and less-muscular physique. Liu Xiang's victory marked the beginning of the end of the assumption that Chinese athletes are able to excel in only a narrow field of sports. Liu, interviewed after his victory, said before bursting into tears: "I proved that Chinese people, Asian people, and yellow-skinned people are able to do well in track events."

These words expressed not only Liu Xiang's pride and happiness over his victory, but also the frustrations that past generations of Chinese had endured. His emotional statement echoed a feeling that remains important today: the joy, and the relief, that China feels at finally having overcome an era of weakness and isolation. China, during a short period of time, has risen from being in athletic terms a developing country to being one of the foremost sports powers in the world. This rise, mirroring China's overall rise to new economic and political power, has left many experts baffled and begs

XU Haifeng

In taking the first gold medal of the 1984 Summer Olympics in Los Angeles with a steely performance, sharpshooter Xu Haifeng also became a Chinese icon—he was not simply a winner, but the first winner of gold for his country since its return to the Olympic Games after a thirty-two-year absence due to controversy over the recognition of Taiwan.

Xu was an unlikely Olympic hero; he'd been training in the sport for just two years, becoming a champion sharpshooter in Anhui Province in 1982 and winning his first national title in 1983. His previous formal experience at shooting consisted of a week of military training in high school—although he reputedly was a crack shot with a slingshot during his childhood in Fujian Province.

Before joining the national shooting team, which was coached by a former high school teacher and would set him on the path to the Olympics, Xu had been farming and selling chemical fertilizer in rural Anhui Province. Xu went to Los Angeles as the rookie on a team of six—expecting merely "to take part," he later said. In the pistol events, attention gradually shifted from the Swedish world champion, Ragnar Skanaker, to the focused young man from China. Xu's victory in the 50-meter free pistol shooting final, at age twenty-seven, changed his life.

The absence of strong contenders from Eastern Europe due to the Soviet and Eastern bloc boycott of the Los Angeles Games certainly worked to the advantage of unknowns like Xu, but his win was no fluke, and he went on to prove his mettle in subsequent world competitions. In 1988, he won a bronze medal at the Summer Olympics in Seoul. Other wins accumulated over the years included three golds at the Asian Games in Seoul in 1986, four golds at the Asian Games in Beijing in 1990, and five golds at the 7th Asian Championships in 1991 as well as the World Air Pistol Championship that year.

Xu Haifeng's Los Angeles feat was commemorated in a Chinese television play, "Shots over Prada"—a reference to the name of the city's Olympic shooting range. He donated that first Olympic gold medal to China's National Museum. Retiring from competition in 1994, Xu became the coach of the gold-medals teams in the 1996, 2000, and 2004 Olympics. In anticipation of the 2008 Beijing Summer Games, Xu took over supervision of China's modern pentathlon team. A quarter century since the event that catapulted him to fame, Xu Haifeng remains a household name in China.

■ JUDY POLUMBAUM

the question that is asked so frequently: How did the Chinese do it?

Ingredients of Success

The foundation of athletic success is, in China as in every other country, athletic talent embedded within the population. Being the most populous country in the world, China obviously has the advantage of a vast number of people from which to extract athletic talent. However, this extraction of talent requires a sophisticated and highly organized sports system that identifies and fosters talent. The development of the Chinese elite sports system, which

The Chinese Ping-Pong team in front of the Statue of Liberty in New York during the 1970s.

Organizational Infrastructure

The Chinese elite sports system, adopted during the period of reform and opening up during the 1980s, is based on the *Juguo tizhi* 举国体制 approach—the support of the whole country for the elite sports system. This approach, which gives priority to the task of elite sports development, assures that all available sports resources are channeled into elite sports.

The organizational infrastructure of Chinese elite sports follows many of the principles of the old Soviet sports system. It features a state-led and tightly controlled, highly centralized, and strictly hierarchical system that relies almost entirely on state funding. Efforts to transform the organizational system established during the 1950s into a more decentralized system promoting self-supporting and less-government-dependent sports development have largely failed to produce significant results so far.

One core element of the organizational infrastructure of elite sports in China is the far-reaching, effective system of talent scouting and advancement, frequently called the "pagoda system." The basis of this system is mandatory physical education in the regular schools and in spare-time sports schools.

Only through an extensive scouting system on this basic level can the potential of the large Chinese gene pool be used and athletic talent identified across the country. Sports scouts travel the country, visiting regular schools in their search for students with athletic

made an unprecedented leap forward during the last two decades, required the carefully managed interplay of two largely different ingredients: the organizational infrastructure to detect and accommodate athletic talents, and the financial and human resources to provide adequate sports facilities and training technology.

In order to provide these two ingredients, China developed a distinctive elite sports system that combines potent characteristics of the Western-style approach with the old Soviet-style approach.

potential. They discover talented athletes who sometimes are as young as five or six years of age. If children show exceptional talent, they might be offered entry to the multilevel elite sports education system, consisting of a network of specialized sports schools. Depending on their age, such children will be sent to one of almost five hundred elite sports primary schools or more than two hundred elite sports middle schools and high schools.

Currently, approximately 400,000 young athletes are being trained in these schools. Their potential for different sports will be examined, and their training will be individualized accordingly. If they distinguish themselves during competitions against their peers, they will be promoted to the upper levels of the pagoda system at the municipal- and provincial-level sports schools, where they will be in full residency and extensively trained. From there they will have the chance of being called to the national teams and to compete in international competitions. China trains about three thousand world-class athletes on the national level—almost three times as many as the United States.

Financial and Human Resources

However, organizational infrastructure alone does not explain the extraordinary rise of Chinese sports. For many decades the Chinese sports system suffered from a lack of material resources—hardly surprising in a developing country—which translated into inadequate training facilities and backward training technology. The organizational system to detect and accommodate athletic talent might have been in place, but China did not have the monetary means to transform talented children into world-class athletes.

China's astonishing economic improvement after the reform of its economy during the 1980s provided the necessary second ingredient for athletic success: financial and human resources.

Ratomir Dujkovic, a famous Serbian footballer and coach, was brought to train China's team for the Olympics.

After the initiation of economic reform, sports facilities and equipment for elite sports education in China experienced a massive upgrade. Since then, more money has been channeled into the improvement of sports facilities and into the introduction of foreign, state-of-the-art training technology.

Also, training methodology has become more scientific. The traditional training method based on the "three unafraids" 三不怕 (unafraid of hardship, difficulty, and injury) and the "five toughnesses" 五过硬, (toughness of spirit, body, skill, training, and competition) still plays an important role in Chinese training methodology, but it has been complemented by more scientific coaching, sports psychology, and sports medicine techniques. To facilitate this transformation, China has imported foreign expertise in training methodology by hiring successful foreign sports coaches from all over the world.

Legendary Yugoslavian soccer coach Bora Milutinovic, who led the Chinese national team into the 2002 World Cup finals and enjoyed enormous popularity in China, is only one of many examples. With this flow of material resources into its sports system, China combines the most potent features of two different worlds: the strictness and meticulousness of the Soviet-style sports system and the sophistication and innovativeness of Western-style training, technology, and methodology. By the mid-1980s all the ingredients for China's ascent as a global sports power were present.

Driving Force, and Political Dividends

However, ingredients alone do not bake the cake. Important as they are, an organizational infrastructure as well as financial and human resources do not produce a highly successful sports system by themselves: it takes an intense interest in athletic accomplishments on the part of people in power to channel resources into elite sports. In China's case the prerequisite is the political will of the Communist Party of China (CPC). The enthusiasm and determination that the party displays for the advancement of Chinese athletes suggest that the political benefits deriving from athletic success is particularly high for China's political leadership. In particular athletic success yields three forms of political dividends: the strengthening of international esteem, the intensification of national unity, and the demonstration of systemic strength.

A significant factor in China's unparalleled economic development, which to an extent is based on foreign direct investment, is the Western image of China as a land of limitless economic growth and opportunity. However, most investors are nervous by nature, and capital is increasingly mobile, even

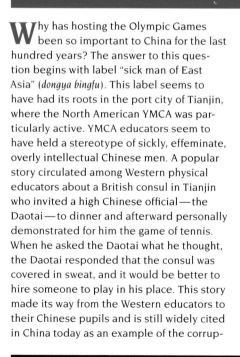

The Scholarly Stereotype

Why has hosting the Olympic Games been so important to China for the last hundred years? The answer to this question begins with label "sick man of East Asia" (*dongya bingfu*). This label seems to have had its roots in the port city of Tianjin, where the North American YMCA was particularly active. YMCA educators seem to have held a stereotype of sickly, effeminate, overly intellectual Chinese men. A popular story circulated among Western physical educators about a British consul in Tianjin who invited a high Chinese official—the Daotai—to dinner and afterward personally demonstrated for him the game of tennis. When he asked the Daotai what he thought, the Daotai responded that the consul was covered in sweat, and it would be better to hire someone to play in his place. This story made its way from the Western educators to their Chinese pupils and is still widely cited in China today as an example of the corrup-

tion of the "old society." Also bolstering the stereotype of the sickly Chinese was the publication in 1911 of *The Changing Chinese* by Edward Ross, a prominent U.S. sociologist. In that book, Ross complained that young men imitated the stooped shoulders of the scholar and wore broad-rimmed glasses even when they didn't need them, so they could look like scholars. He decried what he perceived as a lack of admiration for martial virtues. And perhaps most damning of all, he said that the young men played tennis like girls.

Of course the notion of the effeminate, intellectual Chinese is strongly contradicted by the martial arts tradition. Indeed, one can argue that kung fu films, more than anything else, have erased the perception of the effeminate Chinese among young Westerners, who admire Bruce Lee, Jackie Chan, and Jet Li.

■ SUSAN BROWNELL

Under protest, the Taiwan delegation to the 1948 Olympic Games had to accept being renamed as Formosa to avoid diplomatic disagreements.

in China. Therefore, the narrative of China's ascent needs to be fed constantly with new successes, and winning Olympic gold medals is one way to do this. Achievements of Chinese athletes in international sports, especially in events that are the focus of intense public attention, are a compelling way of asserting China's power and earning international esteem. International esteem is also a prerequisite for claiming a more influential position within the international political system. Therefore, the success of Chinese athletes does indeed yield a great political dividend on the international stage.

The athletic arenas of the modern world are the cradles of the national heroes of our time. The rise of Chinese sports has created many national sports heroes, such as Liu Xiang in track and field, YAO Ming 姚明 in basketball, and GUO Jingjing 郭晶晶 in Olympic women's diving. These heroes have become a focal point of national sentiment that bridges the deep socioeconomic, ethnic, and cultural rifts that divide today's China. In a country as vulnerable to fragmentation as China, whose national coherence is constantly threatened by deeply entrenched divisions running through society, all-embracing symbols of national unity are of great political value. When Chinese spectators watch a Chinese athlete achieve victory, it does not matter if those spectators are poor farmers from Guizhou or rich businessmen from Guangdong, veterans of the Communists' Long March of 1934–35 or their grandchildren who spend their days online gaming in an Internet cafe, Mongols from Hohhot or Han Chinese from Beijing.

When such spectators witness Chinese athletes outclassing their competitors, these unbridgeable differences are forgotten, and all of these people are, at least for the moment, mainly one thing: Chinese. Sports have an extraordinary ability to create a feeling of national connectedness that overcomes the divisions of class, age, and ethnicity. Success in sports is a powerful source of national pride and unity. For China's political leadership, whose power is directly connected to the susceptible unity and coherence of the People's Republic of China, this effect of sports obviously yields an enormous political dividend, creating a strong political incentive to allocate resources to the elite sports system.

A third important political dividend lies in the power of association. International competitiveness in sports is the privilege of wealthy and powerful nations. China's rise in the athletic arena can therefore be utilized as a symbol of the strength of the Chinese political system and its leadership, as a symbol of the competence of the Chinese Communist Party. The glow of the gold medals around Chinese athletes' necks also shines a positive light on the performance of the Chinese political elite. And most Chinese athletes are indeed well versed in stressing that their success is owed to the Chinese state and the party. During a time when the Chinese Communist Party faces enormous political challenges to its power, when its legitimacy is no longer measured by revolutionary heritage but rather by tangible political performance and success, the party looks for new ways to prove its capability. Producing successful athletes is one way for the political leadership to demonstrate its capacity and to strengthen its assertion that the current political leadership can successfully lead China into a future full of challenges.

From the beginning of the period of reform in the 1980s, the political dividends of sports success have been high. The organizational structure necessary for the creation of a superlative sports power was already in place, and the material means began to be readily available. Subsequently, virtually all the stars were aligned for the ascent of China as a global sports power—and that is why five equally aligned stars, in bright yellow on red ground, will certainly be seen many times as the national flags are raised at the medal ceremonies of the 2008 Beijing Olympics.

■ BJOERN CONRAD

China in the Olympic Games

中国金 与奥运会

TWO THOUSAND YEARS AGO, QU Yuan 屈原 (340–278 BCE), a famous Chinese poet, wrote, "The road toward the destination is very long. I will search heaven and earth to get there." This quotation aptly describes the journey China undertook to bring the Olympic Games to Beijing. The history of China's participation in the Olympic Games can be divided into three periods: the Qing dynasty 清 (before 1911), the Republic (1911–1949), and the People's Republic (1949–present).

Long before the Olympic Movement spread to China, a few Western sports existed there. Some were military exercises imported from Europe and the United States, which were in accord with the Chinese martial spirit and could be used to support the traditional Chinese ideal of a unified regime known as the "Central Kingdom" Zhongguo 中国. This regime, the Qing Dynasty, had been deteriorating gradually in authority since the

end of the eighteenth century, but still dominated the nation culturally as well as militarily. In addition, a number of Western sports that are now contested at the Olympics came to China in the nineteenth century, usually due to educators at missionary schools and universities, or under the auspices of the Young Men's Christian Association (YMCA). The British brought modern soccer to to Shanghai in 1856. Basketball, which originated in 1891 at the YMCA in Springfield, Massachusetts, arrived in China only four years later.

The first modern Olympic Games were held in 1896, thanks to the work of Pierre de Coubertin. Coubertin had traveled widely in England and the

United States to learn about sport and physical education in private and public schools as well as in colleges and universities and then convened a conference in Paris to discuss the revival of the ancient Olympic Games. The first modern Games were a huge success, with over 60,000 people attending in the restored grand marble stadium at Olympia, Greece. Coubertin told the world that he had revived the Games with these goals: 1) as a cornerstone for health and cultural progress; 2) for education and character building; 3) for international understanding and peace; 4) for equal opportunity; 5) for fair and equal competition; 6) for cultural expression; 7) for beauty and excellence;

Gold-Medal Fever

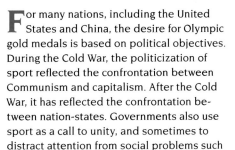

For many nations, including the United States and China, the desire for Olympic gold medals is based on political objectives. During the Cold War, the politicization of sport reflected the confrontation between Communism and capitalism. After the Cold War, it has reflected the confrontation between nation-states. Governments also use sport as a call to unity, and sometimes to distract attention from social problems such as corruption and unemployment.

Among ordinary Chinese people, the Olympic gold-medal fever springs from feelings unique to China: a sense of great pride and also crushing inferiority. Chinese people cherish the knowledge that China was once the cultural center of the world and are nostalgic for the glorious prosperity of the Tang dynasty (618–907 CE). They are pained by the more recent history of humiliation at the

hands of the West and Japan, and are united today in a desire to restore national prestige and gain international recognition.

The Games are simultaneously a ritual of international cohesion and a battlefield on which to beat economically advanced nations and restore China's confidence. The Chinese, who suffered significantly in the conflicts of the twentieth century, long to triumph in the Olympic Games. It was less than twenty-five years ago when, in 1984, China reemerged on the Olympic stage after an absence of thirty-two years. A poor nation, it nonetheless won fifteen gold medals, and came in fourth in total gold medals. The nation's success excited the entire Chinese population. "Break through Asia and Charge the World" became both a slogan and a dream for the Chinese.

and 8) for independence of sport as an instrument of social reform, rather than government legislation.

It is generally agreed that when the French envoy forwarded an invitation to the Chinese government to participate in the first modern Olympic Games, officials showed no interest in taking part. In 1904, when the Third Olympic Games took place in St. Louis, the Chinese media began to report it. In 1907, before the Fourth Olympics took place in London, a few Chinese educators suggested that China should participate in the games. However, there was no response from the Qing government. There was no other impetus sufficient to take China into international sporting competition. But the notion of such an event clearly intrigued some outward-looking Chinese educators.

The Qing dynasty, which had ruled China since 1644, was overthrown in the Republican revolution of 1911. During that year the YMCAs of the Philippines, China, and Japan proposed that an Asian Olympic Games among Asian countries be held every two years. In 1913 the first Asian Olympic Games took place in Manila, Philippines. It was an imitation of the Olympic Games including all the regulations, rules, ceremonies, and even the use of the English language. It was called the Far Eastern Olympiad. The International Olympic Committee (IOC) welcomed the games but suggested that the word *Olympiad* should not be used in the future. Therefore, in 1915 when the games took place in Shanghai, the name was changed to "Far Eastern Championship Games" (FECG). The IOC sent a telegram of congratulations to the games.

The relationship between the IOC and China grew. In 1922 the IOC invited WANG Zhenting 王正廷 (1882–1961), former Chinese foreign minister and architect of the FECG, to be the first member of the IOC from China. In 1939 KUNG Xiang-xi 孔祥熙 (1880–1967), minister of finance, and in 1947 DONG Shouyi 董守义 (1895–1978), general secretary of the China Athletic Association, became members of the IOC successively.

China Enters the Olympics

In 1928, when the Ninth Olympic Games took place in Amsterdam, China sent one observer, SONG Ruhai. Then, in 1932 China participated in the Tenth Olympics in Los Angeles by sending a single athlete, LIU Changchun 刘长春, a sprinter and national champion, and his coach to the games. After twenty-five days at sea, when Liu finally arrived in Los Angeles, he was too exhausted to perform well and was eliminated

Supporters of Beijing's 1993 bid to host the 2000 Olympics flood the Great Wall to demonstrate their enthusiasm.

Liu Changchun, China's first Olympic athlete, competed as a sprinter in the 1932 Olympics in Los Angeles.

over China, and established the People's Republic of China (PRC). The Nationalists fled to Taiwan. Both Communists and Nationalists claimed that they were the legitimate government of China. Thus began the era of the "two Chinas " in political and sports history.

The Communists lost no time in recognizing the importance of the Olympic Games as an international stage on which China's identity could be asserted. In 1952, when the Fifteenth Olympic Games took place in Helsinki, the IOC invited both Beijing and Taiwan to participate. Taiwan claimed that it could not "compete with Communist bandits on the same sports field" and withdrew from the games in protest.

China is said to have received the invitation from the IOC just one day before the opening ceremony. They managed, nonetheless, to send a delegation of forty to Helsinki one week later to raise the national flag at the Olympic Village and watch the last few events.

in the heats. Four years later, China sent its first substantial contingent: 141 Chinese athletes traveled to Berlin to compete in the Eleventh Olympic Games. They did not win a medal, but after World War II, when the Games resumed in London in 1948, China sent forty athletes. There was still no medal to take home, in the last of the Games before the establishment of the People's Republic of China. In 1949 the Chinese Communist Party, under the leadership of MAO Zedong 毛泽东, defeated the Nationalists (Kuomintang) led by CHIANG Kai-shek 蒋介石, took

Beijing prepared to participate in the Melbourne Olympics in 1956. However, when it was informed that Taiwan would attend, Beijing withdrew, despite the fact that the qualifying events had taken place and more than fourteen hundred Chinese athletes from twenty-seven provinces, cities, and autonomous regions had attended the preparatory competitions in China, and ninety-two athletes had been selected for the PRC sports delegation and were waiting to go to the Olympics. Instead, Taiwan participated.

Ma Yanhong won gold in the 1984 Olympics.

Huge celebrations broke out across China late at night when the news came that Beijing had been selected as the host for the 2008 Olympics.

Two years later, in August 1958, disappointed with the IOC's ambiguous attitude toward the "two Chinas," the PRC withdrew its membership from the IOC. Therefore, between 1958 and 1980, Taiwan represented China at six Olympics.

The situation started to change in the 1970s. In 1972 Lord Killanin became the new president of the IOC. He felt that the IOC should not continue to ignore Red China and exclude one-fourth of the world's population from the Olympic Movement and the games. He visited Beijing in 1977. The famous "Olympic formula" was produced in 1979 and China renewed its membership in the IOC. Taiwan, according to the Olympic formula, would change the name of its Olympic committee from the "Chinese Olympic Committee" to

"Chinese Taipei Olympic Committee" and change the name of its team from the "Chinese Olympic Team" to "China Taipei." In this way both Beijing and Taiwan would be able to participate in the Olympics.

In 1984 at Los Angeles, the PRC reemerged at the Olympics after an absence of thirty-two years. It won fifteen gold medals and finished fourth in the gold medal tally. Although the good showing in Los Angeles was partly attributed to the absence of the Soviet Union and the Democratic Republic of Germany, it excited the Chinese—from government officials to ordinary citizens. "Develop elite sport and make China a superpower in the world" became both a slogan and dream for the Chinese.

TABLE 1 ■ China's Participation in the Summer Olympics 1984–2004

GAMES	YEAR	HOST CITY	GOLD MEDALS	SILVER MEDALS	BRONZE MEDALS	TOTAL MEDALS	GOLD MEDAL RANKING
23	1984	Los Angeles	15	8	9	32	4
24	1988	Seoul	5	11	12	28	7
25	1992	Barcelona	16	22	16	54	4
26	1996	Atlanta	16	22	12	50	4
27	2000	Sydney	28	16	15	59	3
28	2004	Athens	32	17	14	63	3

However, for the Chinese the 1988 Olympics in Seoul, South Korea, were a nightmare. When two sport superpowers, the Soviet Union and the Democratic Republic of Germany, returned to the Olympics, China's gold medal tally shrank to five. China had slipped from fourth to eleventh in gold medals.

In 1992 China fought back at the Barcelona Olympics. Although the Soviet Union had broken up into several countries, it still took part as a unit under the name of the "Commonwealth of Independent States" (CIS). The two Germanys had reunited, and the country was even more powerful than before. Nevertheless, China won sixteen gold medals and returned to fourth place in the gold medal count.

In Atlanta in 1996, the Chinese again won sixteen gold medals and remained fourth on the gold medal count. But in Sydney in 2000, China achieved a historical breakthrough. It increased its gold medal count to twenty-eight and finished third.

In Athens in 2004, the Chinese competed in 203 events and won thirty-two gold, seventeen silver, and fourteen bronze medals. Among thirty-two gold medals, four were won in events

The IOC and the "Two China Question"

With the triumph of Mao Zedong's Communists over the Nationalist followers of Chiang Kai-shek in China's drawn-out civil war of the 1930s and 1940s, still another vexing problem presented itself. Which was the real China in the eyes of the International Olympic Committee (IOC)? Mainland Communists? Or Nationalists who had retreated to Formosa, an island off China's coast that eventually became known as Taiwan? Because the prewar national Chinese Olympic Committee had been in the hands of the Nationalists, the IOC recognized Taiwan, which in turn insisted upon being called the Republic of China. In a series of arguments and angry rebuffs, the People's Republic failed to move the IOC toward their point of view: the argument that with a population fifty times that of Taiwan, indeed a population figure that represented nearly one-third of the world's total numbers, it was the real China; Taiwan was but an obscure offshore province. Stubbornly, the PRC remained aloof from the Olympics until changes in political times prompted their appearance at the 1984 Games in Los Angeles."

■ ROBERT BARNEY

traditionally dominated by Western athletes: track and field, swimming, rowing, and canoeing. With sixty-three medals in total, China finished third in the medal rankings after the United States and Russia. With thirty-two gold medals China beat the Russians and finished second to the United States. Furthermore, Chinese athletes established six world records, and they broke Olympic records twenty-one times.

After their triumph in Athens, the Cable News Network (CNN) commented: "In the six Olympic Games they have competed in, China has moved up the medal tally in world record time." China has become one of the three superpowers, with the United States and Russia, in the Summer Olympics.

The moment that the Athens Olympics ended the world media turned its attention to Beijing, home of the 2008 Olympics, and the next gold medal confrontation between China and the United States.

■ FAN HONG 凡红

Asian Games
中国金 中国与亚运会

IN 1911, WHEN THE NEWS REACHED Baron Pierre de Coubertin, the president of the International Olympic Committee, that the YMCAs of the Philippines, China, and Japan had established the Far Eastern Olympic Association to host games that were to be an imitation of the modern Olympic Games, he was reputedly pleased. He demanded, however, that the Far Eastern Olympic Association should not use the term *Olympiad* because that term should be used to refer only to the modern Olympic Games, which had begun under Coubertin's leadership in 1896. Accordingly, the name of the fledging association was changed to the "Far Eastern Games Federation," and the name of the games changed to the "Far Eastern Championship Games" in 1915.

In 1913 the first such games took place in Manila, Philippines. The purpose of the games, according to the directors of the YMCAs, was to promote athletic ability among the Asian youth and to unite the Asian countries through sport. The Far Eastern Championship Games were staged ten times from 1913 to 1934, before being terminated by political conflicts resulting from the rise of militarism in Japan.

After World War II, the Asian Games Federation (AGF) was established in 1949 in New Delhi, India, to unite Asian countries through sports in the "New Era." Collectively, the events would be called the Asian Games. The First Asian Games were staged in New Delhi, India, 4–11 March 1951, with only eleven nations sending athletes and only six events (all Western in origin): Japan was the major contender. Since then, Western sports have dominated the program, although attempts have been made to add indigenous Asian sports including martial arts and the Indian pursuit sport of *kabbadi*. The People's Republic of China (PRC), which had been established in 1949 under MAO Zedong 毛泽东, while the Nationalists fled to Taiwan and set

Asian Ties

The strengthening of intra-Asian ties, like the development of the European Union, is a natural evolution for China and its neighbor nations, given ties of geography and culture. Asian organizations tend to be inclusive, with some trade and political associations including Latin American countries, Australia, New Zealand and India, and sometimes giving extra-regional observer status to countries such as Mongolia, India, Pakistan and Iran. The Asian Games, too, draw participants from across the full span of the continent.

up their government in exile, sent no sports team but did send a group of nine observers.

The federation decided to follow the Olympics pattern and hold the games every four years. Taiwan and Hong Kong participated in the Second Asian Games, hosted in Manila, Philippines, 1–9 May 1954, and finished sixth and

伊拉克
I R A Q

A young girl introduces the Iraqi delegation to the Far Eastern Championship Games in 1927.

twelfth, respectively, in the medal tally (see table 1). At this point, the Communist People's Republic of China stopped its participation in the Asian Games to avoid the controversy arising from the "two Chinas" situation—both Communists and Nationalists claiming that they were the legitimate government of China.

At the Third Asian Games, hosted in Tokyo, 24 May–1 June 1958, 173 athletes from Taiwan competed and won six gold medals, finishing fourth. This was the best ranking for Taiwan in the Asian Games. CHUAN-KWANG Yang 杨传广, a decathlete, won a gold medal in the second and third Asiads, thereby earning the nickname "Asian Iron Man" 亚洲铁人. At the 1960 Olympics in Rome, he broke an Olympic record and won China's first Olympic silver medal. Hong Kong participated in the Third Asian Games as well (see table 2).

The Fourth Asian Games were hosted in Jakarta, Indonesia, 24 August–4 September 1962. The Indonesian government refused the entry of the delegation from Taiwan, so only athletes from Hong Kong participated. They won one bronze metal (see table 3).

The Fifth and Sixth Asian Games were staged in Bangkok, Thailand, 9–20 December 1966, and 24 August–4 September 1970. Taiwan and Hong Kong sent teams to both games but performed poorly. Taiwan's ranking dropped to eighth and then twelfth among the participants (see tables 4 and 5).

China's participation changed dramatically in the Seventh Asian Games in Teheran, Iran, 1–16 September 1974. About a year before the games, the

TABLE 1 ■ China's Participation in Second Asian Games					
RANK	PARTICIPANT	GOLD	SILVER	BRONZE	TOTAL
6	Taiwan	2	4	6	12
12	Hong Kong	—	—	1	1

TABLE 2 ■ China's Participation in Third Asian Games					
RANK	PARTICIPANT	GOLD	SILVER	BRONZE	TOTAL
4	Taiwan	6	9	10	25
16	Hong Kong	—	—	1	1

TABLE 3 ■ China's Participation in Fourth Asian Games					
RANK	PARTICIPANT	GOLD	SILVER	BRONZE	TOTAL
12	Hong Kong	—	—	1	1

TABLE 4 ■ China's Participation in Fifth Asian Games					
RANK	PARTICIPANT	GOLD	SILVER	BRONZE	TOTAL
8	Taiwan	5	9	10	24
16	Hong Kong	—	—	1	1

TABLE 5 ■ China's Participation in Sixth Asian Games					
RANK	PARTICIPANT	GOLD	SILVER	BRONZE	TOTAL
12	Taiwan	1	5	12	18

TABLE 6 ■ China's Participation in Seventh Asian Games					
RANK	PARTICIPANT	GOLD	SILVER	BRONZE	TOTAL
3	China	33	45	28	106

TABLE 7 ■ China's Participation in Eighth Asian Games					
RANK	PARTICIPANT	GOLD	SILVER	BRONZE	TOTAL
2	China	51	55	45	151
17	Hong Kong	—	2	3	5

council of the Asian Games Federation had voted to accept the People's Republic of China as a member and to withdraw recognition of Taiwan. The PRC sent its first team to the Asian Games: 269 athletes competed in fourteen sports and won 106 medals, finishing third after Japan and Iran in the medal tally (see table 6). Chinese athletes performed well in shooting, diving, gymnastics, and badminton.

At the Eighth Asian Games in Bangkok, Thailand, 9–20 December 1978, China participated in fifteen of the nineteen sports and raised its ranking to second behind Japan (see table 7).

The Ninth Asian Games, in New Delhi, India, 19 November–4 December 1982, were the last Asiad to be held under the authority of the AGF. China sent its largest team—444 athletes—since its return to the Games. Although China

中国与亚运会

and Japan won the same number of medals, China won sixty-one to Japan's fifty-seven gold medals, taking first place in the medal tally (see table 8). The young Chinese high jumper ZHU Jianhua 朱建华 cleared the bar at 2.33 meters, not only breaking the Asian record but also setting the best record in the year.

At the Tenth Asian Games, in Seoul, South Korea, 20 September–5 December 1986, China participated in twenty of the twenty-five sports (see table 9). The Chinese gymnast LI Ning 李宁 won four gold and two silver medals. Later he became president of the Li Ning Company, a well-known sportswear company in China. At this Asiad, China, Japan, and South Korea were triumphant, winning 90 percent of the competitions.

The Tenth Asian Games was the first organized by the Olympic Council of Asia (OCA), which succeeded the Asian Games Federation in 1981. The General Assembly of the OCA adopted the International Olympic Committee's way of dealing with China's participation in the Olympics. As a result, Taiwan returned to the Asian Games with the name "Chinese Taipei" 中国台北. An agreement between the Chinese Olympic Committee and the Chinese Taipei Olympic Committee in 1989 paved the way for athletes of Taiwan to take part in the next Asiad, hosted in Beijing.

The Eleventh Asian Games were the first hosted in Beijing, 22 September–7 October 1990. They were also the first international multisport megaevent staged in China. These games improved China's international relations and national integration. These games were also the first participated in by athletes from China's mainland, Taiwan, Hong Kong, and Macao. For this reason the OCA declared this Asiad one of the best in history. Ninety-eight Asian records were broken—a record number! Preparing for the games, Beijing built twenty stadiums and gymnasiums and renovated thirteen others. As the host country, China demonstrated its pride and strength by winning nearly 60 percent of the gold medals (183), securing its standing as the Asian superpower in sports (see table 10). It was at this Asiad that DENG Yaping 邓亚萍, who later dominated world tournaments in table tennis, at-

TABLE 8 ■ China's Participation in Ninth Asian Games

RANK	PARTICIPANT	GOLD	SILVER	BRONZE	TOTAL
1	China	61	51	41	153
20	Hong Kong	—	—	1	1

TABLE 9 ■ China's Participation in Tenth Asian Games

RANK	PARTICIPANT	GOLD	SILVER	BRONZE	TOTAL
1	China	94	82	46	222
10	Hong Kong	1	1	3	5

TABLE 10 ■ China's Participation in Eleventh Asian Games

RANK	PARTICIPANT	GOLD	SILVER	BRONZE	TOTAL
1	China	183	107	51	341
16	Chinese Taipei (Taiwan)	—	10	21	31
17	Hong Kong	—	2	5	7
23	Macao	—	—	1	1

TABLE 11 ■ China's Participation in Twelth Asian Games

RANK	PARTICIPANT	GOLD	SILVER	BRONZE	TOTAL
1	China	125	83	58	266
7	Chinese Taipei (Taiwan)	7	12	24	43
21	Hong Kong	—	5	7	12
26	Macao	—	1	1	2

TABLE 12 ■ China's Participation in Thirteenth Asian Games

RANK	PARTICIPANT	GOLD	SILVER	BRONZE	TOTAL
1	China	129	78	67	274
6	Chinese Taipei (Taiwan)	19	17	41	77
13	Hong Kong	5	6	6	17
29	Macao	—	1	—	1

The opening ceremonies of the Sixth Asian Winter Games.

tracted attention by winning three gold medals and one silver medal.

At the Twelfth Asian Games in Hiroshima, Japan, 2–16 October 1994, five former republics of the Soviet Union in central Asia competed for the first time, bringing the number of participating national Olympic committees to forty-two. Although China won only 125 gold medals, in contrast to 183 at the previous Asiad, China remained in first place in the medal tally (see table 11). The outstanding athlete in this Asiad was Chinese gymnast MO Huilan 莫慧兰. She won five gold medals and one silver medal. The International Federation of Gymnastics later named a movement she originated in her routine after her.

At the Thirteenth Asian Games in Bangkok, Thailand, 6–20 December 1998, China kept its top ranking in the

medal tally with 129 gold medals (see table 12). The largest Games to date, with 9,469 athletes and officials from

Politics and the Asian Games

The Asian Games are a major Olympic "tune-up" festival—a chance for world-class athletes to prepare for the Olympics—and like the Olympics they have been affected by political conflicts. Israel has often been excluded because of its ties to the West; Taiwan suffered the same fate in 1962. Mainland Chinese athletes did not compete until 1974, and Iraq was barred in 1990. The Games have been used by political leaders to enhance their own and their nation's power in Asia and beyond. In 1962,

President Sukarno of Indonesia used the Jakarta Games to assert Indonesian leadership in the third world, and angering both rival India and the International Olympic Committee. Similarly, for the 1982 Games, India spent nearly $1 billion to construct new sports facilities, and South Korea's hosting of the 1988 Games helped to make it a legitimate power in several sports. At the same time, Korea was criticized for its repression of student protestors during the Games.

Guangzhou—Trading Center through the Centuries

Guangzhou, the trading hub of the Pearl River Delta and the main point of entry to China from the Hong Kong Special Administrative Region, is the home of the biannual Chinese Export Commodities Fair, more commonly known as the Canton Trade Fair, which was founded in 1957. As far back as the eleventh century, foreign traders lived in Guangzhou, trading ivory and spices for silk and tea. In recent years, Guangzhou has played a pivotal role in China's modernization effort, attracting foreign capital and investment.

The Canton Trade Fair has grown from the attendance of 1,223 businesspeople from 19 countries in 1957 to over 80,000 businesspeople from 180 countries in 2005, while trade volume has soared from US$17.54 million in 1957 to over $30 billion.

over forty-one nations, the Bangkok Games were free of major political problems in the spirit of its motto: Friendship Beyond Frontiers.

This Asiad marked the first that Hong Kong participated in after its unification with China in 1997. Hong Kong athletes won five gold medals. The sailor LAI-SHAN Lee 李丽珊 of Hong Kong, a gold medalist at the Olympics in Atlanta, Georgia, in 1996, won her first Asiad gold medal at these games.

The Fourteenth Asian Games were hosted in Pusan, South Korea, 2–16 September 2002. They were the first Asian Games participated in by all members of the OCA. China won 150 gold medals (see table 13), and the Chinese weightlifters and shooters did especially well. Six weightlifters broke world records, and the Chinese women's shooting team broke a world record that had stood for thirteen years.

The Fifteenth Asian Games were hosted in Doha, Qatar, 1–15 December 2006. These games were the last major event similar to the Olympics before China hosts the Olympics in 2008. Therefore, China used these Asian Games to prepare its athletes for the 2008 Olympics. More than 60 percent of the Chinese athletes were new faces. Even though they were less experienced in the international arena, they performed well and kept China in first place in the medal tally for the seventh straight Asiad. Of the five world records broken in these games, four were broken by Chinese women weightlifters. CHEN Yanqing 陈艳青, a twenty-seven-year-old woman gold medalist at the Athens Olympics in 2004, broke three world records at Doha. Hong Kong sent the largest delegation in its history with 320 athletes. Their performances were quite good (see table 14).

The Sixteenth Asian Games will be staged in Guangzhou (Canton), a southern city on the Pearl River Delta, in November 2010. Guangzhou is China's third-largest city, a major hub for international commerce, and the location of the second Asiad China has hosted since 1990. The city regards the preparation for the Asian Games as an opportunity to accelerate the city's development and enhance its prestige.

■ REN HAI 任海

TABLE 13 ■ China's Participation in Fourteenth Asian Games					
RANK	PARTICIPANT	GOLD	SILVER	BRONZE	TOTAL
1	China	150	84	74	308
7	Chinese Taipei (Taiwan)	10	17	25	52
16	Hong Kong	4	6	11	21
29	Macao	—	2	2	4

TABLE 14 ■ China's Participation in Fifteenth Asian Games					
RANK	PARTICIPANT	GOLD	SILVER	BRONZE	TOTAL
1	China	165	88	63	316
10	Chinese Taipei (Taiwan)	9	10	27	46
15	Hong Kong	6	12	10	28
30	Macao	—	1	6	7

THE NATIONAL GAMES OF THE
People's Republic of China have been regarded as mini-Olympic Games in China. Take the recent National Games, which took place in 2005, as an example. It had almost ten thousand elite athletes competing in 357 events in thirty-two sports, most of which are Olympic events, following the rules and regulations used in the Olympics. In addition, all the Olympic rituals were practiced at the games: the torch relay, lighting of the flame, logo, mascot, athlete's oath, playing of the games and national anthems, raising of the games and the national flags, and opening and closing ceremonies. The National Games, the largest and highest level comprehensive sports event in China, have prepared Chinese athletes for international competitions and have played an important role in China's achievements in international sports. Between the PRC's First National Games in 1959 and the Tenth National Games in 2005, Chinese athletes have won 1,899 world titles (world cups, world championships) and Olympic medals. The National Games, like the Olympics, demonstrate China's determination to forge boldly ahead, economically and politically, in the twenty-first century.

Early Competitions

Before the founding of the People's Republic of China in 1949, the first sports meet was held in 1890, during the Qing dynasty, in Shanghai, when St. John's College hosted a track-and-field meet. St. John's College was a U.S. missionary college in Shanghai and was among the first missionary schools and colleges to promote modern sports in China. Influenced by such missionary schools, state-run schools also began to organize sports competitions at the beginning of the twentieth century. Thereafter, collegiate sports competitions took place in major Chinese cities, such as Beijing, Shanghai, and Tianjin. It was from these beginnings that a national sports meet developed.

In 1910, at the eve of the birth of the Republic of China (in 1911), the Shanghai YMCA initiated the first of an earlier series of National Games and held them in Nanjing. One hundred and forty athletes from North and South China, Shanghai, Wuning, Nanjing, and Suzhou took part in track and field, soccer, basketball, and tennis. After the establishment of the republic, six National Games were held at irregular intervals: Beijing, 1914; Wuchang, 1924; Hangzhou, 1930; Nanjing, 1933; Shanghai, 1935; and again in Shanghai, 1948.

Some of the games in this period served the function of selecting elite athletes for major international sports events and so were held before each of the Far Eastern Championship Games and the Berlin and London Olympic Games. They also promoted sports participation in Chinese society in general and in schools and universities in particular.

In 1949 the People's Republic of China was established by the Chinese Communist Party. The new government continued to hold the National Games because they were a tool for social

Where the Athletes Come From

In China, almost every province has its own top sports. For example, there are many first-class badminton players in Hunan Province, and Hebei Province is famous for shooting. However, among all the provinces Liaoning Province has contributed most to the miraculous performance of Chinese elite athletes in the Olympic arena. Among the Olympic champions hailing from Liaoning are Yuan Hua (women's judo, Sydney), WANG Junxia (women's 10,000 meter, Atlanta), WANG Yifu (men's shooting, Athens), WANG Nan (women's table tennis, Sydney and Athens), and ZHANG Ning (women's badminton, Athens.)

Liu Xiang waves the flag of the Shanghai delegation to the 2005 Chinese National Games.

cohesion and national unity. Since 1959 the National Games have been held ten times. (See table 1.)

The games are generally organized and financed by the central and regional governments. Nevertheless, since the Sixth National Games in 1987, funding has come from government, sponsors, and advertisements.

PRC's First National Games, 1959

The First National Games took place in Beijing in 1959, after the celebration of the tenth anniversary of the founding of the People's Republic of China. The games were intended to show the superiority of the socialist system, the high spirit of the Chinese people who were building a socialist country, and the progress that had been made in the past ten years. The Workers' Stadium in Beijing was especially built and became one of the ten biggest buildings in China. More than seven thousand athletes from twenty-nine provinces and autonomous regions as well as from the People's Liberation Army (PLA) participated in thirty-six competition sports and six performance sports.

The Communist Party leaders attached great importance to the games, and Party leaders including Chairman MAO Zedong 毛泽东, President LIU Shaoqi 刘少奇, and Premier ZHOU Enlai 周恩来 attended the opening ceremony. HE Long 贺龙, vice premier and head of the national sports ministry, gave the opening speech. Zhou Enlai awarded a sports merit medal to those athletes who broke world records and had won

TABLE 1 ■ National Games of China			
NATIONAL GAMES	YEAR	PLACE	ATHLETES
First	1959	Beijing	7,707
Second	1965	Beijing	5,922
Third	1975	Beijing	12,497
Fourth	1979	Beijing	15,189
Fifth	1983	Shanghai	9,697
Sixth	1987	Guangdong Province	7,518
Seventh	1993	Beijing and Sichuan Province	10,510
Eighth	1997	Shanghai	7,647
Ninth	2001	Guangdong Province	12,314
Tenth	2005	Jiangsu Province	9,986

world championships during the past ten years. Four world records, in swimming, parachuting, shooting, and aeromodeling, were broken at the games. Swimmer MU Xiangxiong 穆祥雄 was one of the games outstanding athletes.

Second National Games, 1965

In 1965 the Second National Games were also held in Beijing, six years after the first games. In that period Chinese sports had made significant progress. In 1961 the Twenty-sixth World Table Tennis Championships had been held in Beijing, and China had won the men's team title for the first time. The training principle of assiduity and obedience became the guiding principle of the Chinese elite sports training system.

Almost six thousand athletes from twenty-nine provinces, municipalities, autonomous regions, and the PLA took part. There were twenty-two events, and martial arts was listed as a performance event for the first time. Nine world records were broken, in weight lifting, archery, parachuting, and shoot-

ing. Following the People's Republic's success at the Twenty-sixth World Table Tennis Championships in 1961, table tennis became the most popular sport event at the National Games.

Together, more than sixteen thousand people performed a set of group calisthenics entitled "Ode to Revolution" 革命赞歌 at the opening ceremony in front of Chairman Mao Zedong and other Communist Party leaders. This display indicated that the Chinese people were going all out to conquer difficulties and achieve success in all aspects of socialist society.

Third National Games, 1975

The Third National Games were held in Beijing in 1975. There were twenty-eight competition sport, and six performance sports in the games. A total of 12,497 athletes from thirty-one delegations from all over the country competed. Winter sports made their first appearance, and they included speed skating, ice hockey, figure skating, skiing, and short-distance speed skating, Three shooting world records were bro-

ken, and NI Zhiqin 倪志钦, competing in the high jump, became the star of the games. He broke the world record with a jump of 2.25 meters. Competitors from Guangdong, Beijing, and Shanghai won gold medals.

In April 1975, various events emphasized the growing importance of mass sports in China. With the approval of the State Council, the National Sports Ministry released the "Notice on the Nationwide Implementation of the National Physical Exercise Standards Regulations," 国家体育锻炼标准 requiring physical education in school and in the army. At the games awards were presented to three hundred outstanding work units. At this time more than twenty-three thousand people performed the mass group calisthenics "Ode to the Red Flag" 红旗颂 at the opening ceremony.

Fourth National Games, 1979

In 1979 Beijing was again the site for the National Games. More than fifteen thousand athletes from thirty-one provinces (including Taiwan), municipalities, autonomous regions, and the PLA competed in thirty-two adult events and two junior events. The 25,000-li (1 li = 500 meters) New Long March torch relay appeared at the games for the first time. The touch relay route followed in the footsteps of the famous Long March of 1935, a critical event in Chinese Communist Party history. The torch relay symbolized that in the 1980s China, led by the Communist Party, would begin another Long March that would lead the country toward modernization in the new era. DENG Xiaoping 邓小平, the new leader of the Communist Party, attended the opening ceremony.

Athletes broke 5 world records and equaled 3 more. They also broke 8 Asian records and 102 national records. The games awarded the Medal of Honor in Sports to fifty-one athletes who had won world titles and to coaches who had made significant contributions since 1979.

LUAN Jujie 栾菊杰 became the women's foil champion with victories in all five outings and was the outstanding female athlete at the games. Before the games in 1978, she had competed at the Youth Fencing Championships in Madrid, Spain, and had won the silver medal to become the first Asian woman to step into the upper echelons of world fencing. She was regarded as the top foil in Asia.

Fifth National Games, 1983

In 1983 the Fifth National Games were held in Shanghai, the first time that the games had been held outside Beijing. Guided by the policy of

opening China up to the outside world and catching up with the Western countries, Chinese sports had begun to enter the international arena. China had renewed its membership in the International Olympic Committee (IOC) in 1979 and it had participated in the Asian Games in 1982. China placed first in both the gold medal count and total medals won to establish its dominant position in the Asian sports world.

On 9 September 1983, President LI Xiannian 李先念 lit the torch for the Revitalizing China Torch Relay for the games. On 15 September, Deng Xiaoping provided the games with the instruction: "Improve the Competition Standard, Win Glory for the Country." 提高水平, 为国争光 International Olympic Committee president Juan Samaranch attended the opening ceremony.

Almost nine thousand athletes from twenty-nine provinces, municipalities, autonomous regions, the PLA, and the Locomotive Sports League took part in twenty-five competition sports and one performance sport. Chinese athletes broke two world records and equaled three others. The best performance was that of ZHU Jianhua 朱建华, who broke the high-jump world record at 2.38 meters. XU Haifeng 许海峰 won two silver medals in the men's free pistol and air pistol competitions. He later became China's first Olympic gold medalist at the Los Angeles Olympic Games in 1984.

The opening ceremonies of the 2005 Chinese National Games.

The first commercial donation, 113,600 Renminbi (RMB) (US$14,000), was made to these games, accounting for 1.16 percent of the total budget.

Sixth National Games, 1987

The Sixth National Games took place in Guangdong in 1987 as 7,518 athletes participated in forty-four competition sports and three performance sports. The Guangdong provincial sports commission and the organizing committee made these games an artistic and cultural event as well as a sports competition, as evidenced by opening show ("Soaring Aspirations" 凌云志) the China Olympic Philately Exhibition, and the adoption of the concept of a mascot and emblem for the games. The emblem represented the ambition and energy of the city (Guangzhou) in the forefront of reform and opening up of the new China.

Chinese athletes broke fifteen world records and equaled four others. They also broke forty-eight Asian and eighty-two national records. The Guangxi provincial delegation featured the games' stars: HE Zhuoqiang 何灼强 who broke the snatch and total world records in the 50-kilogram class weight lifting, HE Yingqiang 何英强, who broke the snatch world record in the 56-kilogram class weight lifting, and LIN Ning 李宁, the "Prince of Gymnastics," 体操王子 who made his last National Games appearance.

Statistical Snapshot of China

Capital	Beijing
Government type	Communist state
Area	9,596,960 sq km; slightly smaller than the US
Population	1,321,851,888 (July 2007 est.)
Population below poverty line	8% (2006 est.)
Infant mortality rate	*male*: 20.1 deaths/1,000 live births *female*: 24.47 deaths/1,000 live births (2007 est.)
Life expectancy at birth	*male*: 71.13 years *female*: 74.82 years (2007 est.)
Unemployment rate	4% (2007 est.)
Literacy	*male*: 95.1% *female*: 86.5% (2000 census)
Internet users; % of population	162 million (2007); 12%
Languages	Standard Chinese or Mandarin (Putonghua, based on the Beijing dialect), Yue (Cantonese), Wu (Shanghaiese), Minbei (Fuzhou), Minnan (Hokkien-Taiwanese), Xiang, Gan, Hakka dialects, minority languages

Seventh National Games, 1993

The Seventh National Games were co-hosted by Beijing and Sichuan Province in 1993. There were forty-three competition sports at the games. Twenty-six competitions took place in Beijing and fifteen in Sichuan. However, sailboat and sailboard events took place in Qinhuangdao, Hebei Province. More than ten thousand athletes in forty-five delegations from all over China took part. The new Chinese president, JIANG Zemin 江泽民, opened the games.

The games saw 4 world records broken, 3 world records equaled, and 34 Asian records and 117 national records broken. The Liaoning middle-distance running team, "Ma's Army" 马家军, (named for their coach, MA Junren's 马俊仁, strict discipline) broke the 1,500-meter, 3,000-meter, and 10,000-meter world records. These games helped accelerate the momentum of China's reform and opening up and also encouraged the Chinese people to support the bid for the Olympic Games. The Seventh National Games also took place shortly before the outcome of China's Olympic bid was announced and were staged as a showcase of China's capability to host the Olympic Games.

Eighth National Games, 1997

The Eighth National Games were held in Shanghai in 1997. These were the largest national sports event in China with 319 events in twenty-eight sports.

Liu Xiang leads the Shanghai delegation to the 2005 Chinese National Games.

More than seven thousand athletes representing forty-six delegations took part. Hong Kong sent a delegation for the first time after it had become a special administration region. President Jiang Zemin and IOC president Juan Antonio Samaranch attended the opening ceremony. A cultural gala entitled the "Era of Progress" highlighted the commitment of the Chinese people to realize the goal of national rejuvenation through peaceful development with high spirit and passion in the new era.

Chinese athletes broke forty-one world records, equaled three other world records, and broke fifty-five Asian records and sixty-six national records. The stars were female athletes from Liaoning Province: JIANG Bo 姜波 broke the women's 5,000-meter world record; in swimming CHEN Yan 陈妍 broke the women's 400-meter individual medley relay world record. Female athletes also performed well in weight lifting. When the Eighth National Games were held, women's weight lifting had already been listed in the program of the 2000 Sydney Olympics. At the Chinese

National Games, women weight lifters broke most of the world records and even a few Chinese records! (Some Chinese records were higher than the world records, and some of the Chinese records were later recognized as world records.)

During these games seven sports cultural exhibitions were held. Sports cultural exhibitions on such a large scale were unprecedented. In particular the China Sports Art Exhibition was held at the Shanghai Museum. The 497 exhibits there were selected from ten thousand from all over China. IOC president Samaranch selected eighteen exhibits to be included in the collection of the IOC.

Ninth National Games, 2001

At the Ninth National Games, held in Guangdong in 2001, more than twelve thousand athletes from forty-five delegations participated in 30 major and 345 minor events. The Macao Special Administration Region was represented for the first time. President Jiang Zemin and new IOC president Jacques Rogge were present at the opening ceremony. Competition was on a world-class level in China's strong Olympic sports, such as gymnastics, shooting, weight lifting, badminton, table tennis, and diving. Most impressive were the women weight lifters. They broke six world records. The shooters, including men's and women's air rifle, men's and women's 10-meter running target, and women's sports pistol, also gave world-class performances.

Anti-doping enforcement at these games was the most stringent in the history of the National Games. A total of 1,349 tests were conducted, more than the total at the seventh and eighth games together. A blood test also was used for the first time. It exposed eight violators, who were penalized. One athlete who did not take the test on time was disqualified. Six athletes who had excessive amounts of the hormone erythropoietin (EPO) in their bodies withdrew from the games.

Tenth National Games, 2005

The Tenth National Games were held in Jiangsu Province in 2005. This marked the first time in the history of the games that the hosting venue was determined by bidding. The sacred fire of the tenth games was composed of the Flame of Scientific Advancement, the Flame of Chinese Civilization, and the Flame of China's Renaissance. The "Millions with But One Heart" 我们万众一心 torch relay further raised awareness of nationwide fitness. Almost ten thousand athletes competed in 357 events in thirty-two sports.

Unlike past National Games, the tenth games played a special role: a rehearsal for the Beijing Olympic Games in 2008. As China's president HU Jintao 胡锦涛 stated: "I hope the preparation for the Olympic Games can be evaluated through this Games so that the preparation for the Olympic Games could be done better." The setup of the events of the tenth games conformed with that of Olympic events. One sport and twelve events were added. Most athletes who had participated in the Athens Olympic Games in 2004 participated in the tenth games.

At these games China's three traditional sports powers—Beijing, Shanghai, and Guangdong—did not dominate the events. The games saw a more even distribution of medals among eight other delegations, marking the overall improvement of the level of competitive sports in the country. Six world records were broken. LIU Xiang 刘翔 was the star of the games, partially because he had tied the world record in the men's 110-meter hurdles at the Athens Olympics.

The National Games show the unity of China; they also are a window through which to view China's economic and sporting progress and a training ground to prepare Chinese athletes for international competition.

■ LUO SHIMING 罗时铭 AND CAO SHOUHE 曹守和

PART TWO

Olympic Sports

奥运体育

C hina is known for its successes at table tennis, diving, and gymnastics, and it has been particularly successful in badminton, weight lifting, and shooting. Beyond these key sports, much effort has been made in recent years to develop boxing, tennis, baseball, canoeing and kayaking, and athletics—there's even considerable effort going into the development of cricket, a sport of mind-boggling importance in India and other British Commonwealth countries, many of which have close economic ties with China. The next chapters take an in-depth look at several of China's most popular sports, their origins and cultural significance, and provide insight into Chinese history; they look as well at some of today's top athletes. Sports that are not covered in separate chapters are nonetheless mentioned in sidebars and tables. China's first gold medalist, for example, was sharpshooter XU Haifeng, and his story has been told in a sidebar on page 3.

中国金 Athletics 田径

ATHLETICS, ALSO KNOWN AS track and field, is probably the most basic and universal of physical competitions. The name of the sport originated from the Greek word *athlon*, meaning "contest," and it describes a collection of sports that include running, throwing, and jumping events.

In ancient China, as elsewhere around the world, athletics were often related to military training. During the Spring and Autumn period 春秋 (770–476 BCE), soldiers would be trained in running, leaping and wrestling, riding, jousting, and the use of weapons. It's no surprise that the first athletic event in the ancient Olympics was a foot race known as the stade. The earliest records of this event can be dated back to 776 BCE. Events such as longer foot races, a race in armor, and the pentathlon (consisting of the stade, long jump, discus throw, javelin throw, and wrestling) were also included in the ancient Olympic Games, as well as in the Isthmian, Nemean, Roman, and Pythian Games, collectively known as the Panhellenic Games.

The earliest recorded athletic meeting of the modern era was organized at Shrewsbury, Shropshire, England, by the Royal Shrewsbury School Hunt. In 1896 athletics was an official men's event in the first modern Olympic Games. But it was not until 1928 that women were allowed to participate in track-and-field events in the Olympic Games.

The athletics events in the modern Olympic Games can be divided into four areas: track, field, road, and combined events (see table 1).

The International Association of Athletics Federations (IAAF) was founded in 1912. The IAAF established separate outdoor World Championships in 1983. There are a number of regional games as well, such as the European Championships, the Pan American Games, and the Commonwealth Games. In addition there is a professional Golden League circuit, culminating with the IAAF World Athletics Final, as well as indoor championship meets, such as the World Indoor Championships.

Modern Athletics Comes to China

In the late nineteenth century, Western missionaries introduced modern athletics to China and started to organize athletic meetings at missionary schools and colleges. In 1890 China's first modern athletic meet was held at St. John's College in Shanghai. A few years later, athletic sports such as race walking, running, jumping, and throwing were introduced to Chinese schools in big cities. Some schools in Tianjin held athletic meetings in 1902. The initial National Athletics Meeting took place in Nanjing, the capital of the republic, in 1907, and more than eighty schools participated.

After the establishment of the People's Republic of China in 1949, the central government considered athletics as

TABLE 1 ■ Track and Field Events in the Olympic Games	
AREA	**EVENTS**
Track events	Sprints (100m, 200m, 400m)
	Middle-distance running (800m, 1,500m)
	Long-distance running (5,000m, 10,000m)
	Hurdling (100m and 400m for women, 110m and 400m for men)
	Relays (4x100m and 4x400m)
	3,000m steeplechase
Field events	Long jump, triple jump, high jump, pole vault, shot put, discus, javelin, and hammer throw (for both men and women)
Road events	Men's and women's marathons
	Men's 20km and 50km race walking
	Women's 10km race walking
Combined events	Heptathlon for women
	Decathlon for men

a valuable sport for the nation and started to promote it. Beginning in 1953 China has held the National Athletics Meeting each year.

The government's support of athletics was rewarded when ZHENG Fengrong 郑凤荣, a female athlete from Shandong Province, was crowned the champion in women's high jump at the International Athletics Championship in Berlin in 1957. In the same year, she set a new world record for the women's high jump with a leap of 1.77 meters at the Beijing Athletic Meeting. This victory made her the first Asian athlete to break an athletic world record since 1936.

In the 1960s athletes in Taiwan performed very impressively on the international stage. For example, in 1960 YANG Chuanguang 杨传广 from Taiwan Province won a silver medal in the men's decathlon at the Seventeenth Olympic Games in Rome. In 1963 the records of more than fifty Chinese athletes met the entrance requirements for the Tokyo Olympic Games (held in 1964). In 1968 JI Zheng 纪政 from Taiwan won a bronze medal in the women's 80-meter hurdles at the Nineteenth Olympics in Mexico City. In 1969 and 1970, at the international athletic matches held in Munich, she also broke the world records of the 100-meters, 200-meters, 100-meter women's hurdles, and 200-meter women's hurdles.

In the 1980s, when China opened up to the outside world, Chinese athletes began to appear on the international sports stage. ZHU Jianhua 朱建华 broke the world record for the high jump three times in 1983 and

TABLE 2 ■ Chinese Olympic Medals, 1984–2004				
YEAR	LOCATION	MEDALS	ATHLETE	EVENT
1984	Los Angeles	Bronze	Zhu Jianhua	Men's high jump
1988	Seoul	Bronze	Li Sumei	Women's shot put
1992	Barcelona	Gold	Chen Yueling	Women's 10,000m race walking
1992	Barcelona	Silver	Huang Zhihong	Women's shot put
1992	Barcelona	Bronze	Li Chunxiu	Women's 10,000m
1992	Barcelona	Bronze	Qu Yunxia	Women's 1,500m
1996	Atlanta	Gold	Wang Junxia	Women's 5,000m
1996	Atlanta	Silver	Wang Junxia	Women's 10,000m
1996	Atlanta	Silver	Sui Xinmei	Women's shot put
1996	Atlanta	Bronze	Wang Yan	Women's 10km race walking
2000	Sydney	Gold	Wang Liping	Women's 20km race walking
2004	Athens	Gold	Liu Xiang	Men's 110m hurdles
2004	Athens	Gold	Xiang Huina	Women's 1,0000m

1984, with jumps of 2.37, 2.38, and 2.39 meters. XU Yongjiu 徐永久 and YAN Hong 阎红 were crowned champions in 10-kilometer race walking in 1983 and 1985. HUANG Zhihong 黄志宏 won the women's shot put world championship in 1989. Chinese athletes won twenty-nine (men 11, women 18) gold medals at the Eleventh Asian Games held in Beijing in 1990. Their brilliant victory demonstrated China's dominance in athletics in Asia at the time.

Chinese athletes also achieved victories at the Olympic Games and world championships. In 1988 LI Sumei 李素梅 won the bronze medal of the women's shot put with a record of 21.06 meters at the Twenty-fourth Olympic Games in Seoul. In 1991 HUANG Zhihong 黄志红 and XU Demei 徐德妹 won the gold medals in the women's shot put and javelin throw respectively at the Third IAAF World Championships. In 1992 CHEN Yueling 陈跃玲 won the gold medal in women's 10-kilometer race walking at the Twenty-fifth Olympics in Barcelona. In 1993

JIANG Bo 姜波 set a new world record in the women's 5,000 meters. In 2001 HUANG Yanmei 董艳梅 ranked fourth in the women's 5000 meters at the IAAF World Championships in Canada. GAO Shuying 高淑英 ranked fifth in the women's pole vault.

The most distinguished victory for the Chinese was LIU Xiang's 刘翔 gold medal in men's 110-meter hurdles at the Athens Olympic Game in 2004. His brilliant victory made him the first Chinese male athlete to win a gold medal in a men's track-and-field event at the Olympic Games. It broke the myth that "yellow-skin people could not jump and run fast." It also made him a hero in China and throughout Asia.

From 1984 to 2004 China participated in six Olympic Games. Table 2 shows China's progress in the medal count.

In twenty-first-century China, new training bases have been built to meet the needs of athletes and coaches. For example, a new training facility located at Shangrila Mountain in Yunan

Province was established in 2007. The altitude of this training base is above 3,200 meters. Altitude-training programs for the Chinese national race-walking team will be carried out there.

In addition, China has sent dozens of athletes abroad for advanced training programs. For example, China sent eight elite athletes to the United States for a five-month training program in

2007. All the costs for such training are covered by the government. The General Administration of Sport of China has spent more than 500 billion RMB on training programs for elite athletes.

Eyes on Beijing 2008

The starting point of the 2008 Olympic marathon event is at Tiananmen Square with the race finishing in the National Stadium. The start/finish point of the race-walking event is also the National Stadium. The race will be a round trip on a 2-kilometer course at the boulevard on the Olympic Green. Eleven hundred male athletes and nine hundred female athletes will participate in the athletic events of the Beijing Olympic Games and forty-seven sets of medals will be awarded.

Traditionally, the United States has dominated the men's and women's 100 meters, 200 meters, and 400 meters. For the men's 100 meters, Tyson Gay from the United States and Asafa Powell from Jamaica are the most capable competitors. For the women's 100 meters, Allyson Felix from the United States may win the gold medal. For the men's 110-meter hurdles, the war for the gold medal may break out between Liu Xiang from China, Terrence Trammell from the United States, and Dayron Robles from Cuba.

For the long-distance events, the dominance of Ethiopia and Kenya seems unchallengeable. Tirunesh Dibaba, the current world record holder of women's 5,000 meters from Ethiopia will be the most capable competitor in that event. For the women's marathon, ZHOU Chunxiu 周春秀, the cham-

Racewalking is a complex Olympic sport that was hugely popular in Victorian Europe and is increasing in popularity in China.

pion of the London Marathon in 2007, will face strong opponents from Kenya and Japan. For the men's walking race, twenty-eight-year-old HAN Yucheng 韩玉成 from China is a capable competitor for a medal.

China's Athletes in the Lead

WANG Junxia 王军霞 (b. 1973) has been regarded as one of the best long-distance runners in China's sports history. In 1992 Wang won the world junior champion in the 10,000 meters (32:29.90) in Seoul. In 1993 she won the title in the women's 10,000 meters at the Stuttgart World Championships. In 1994 she was awarded the prestigious Jesse Owens Prize. She was the first and only Asian woman to win that prize. She won the gold medal in the women's 5,000 meters and a silver medal in the 10,000 meters (31:02.58) at the Atlanta Olympic Games in 1996.

LIU Xiang (b.1983) 刘翔 is the most outstanding 110-meter hurdler in China. Liu participated in the world junior championships in 2000 and ranked

The First China-born Olympic Medalist

Eric Liddell, the runner portrayed in *Chariots of Fire* who refused for religious reasons to run on a Sunday, was the first Olympic gold medalist born in China.

Liddell, known in China as Lee Airui, was the son of Scottish missionaries and grew up in Tianjin, a city southwest of Beijing. At the 1924 Olympics in Paris, Liddell, a devout Christian, found himself unable to participate in the preliminary heats for his own event, the 100-meter race. Instead, he made a last minute switch to the 400-meter contest. He not only won the race but set a new world record, and became a symbol of personal faith as well as athletic brilliance.

Returning to China, he became a coach at the Xinxue School in Tianjin, a mission school that is now Tianjin's Middle School #17. During World War II he was imprisoned by the Japanese in North China. He died there, in the land where he was born, and today a plaque in Tianjin commemorates the home of Lee Airui, China's first Olympic medalist.

fourth in the 110-meter hurdles. In 2002 he won a silver medal in Lausanne in the 110-meter hurdles at the IAAF Grand Prix. In 2003 he won a bronze medal in 110-meter hurdles at the IAAF World Championships in Paris. In 2004 at the Athens Olympic Games, Liu Xiang won the gold medal in the same event. This brilliant victory made him the first Chinese male athlete to earn a gold medal in a men's track-and-field event at the Olympic Games. In

2006, at the IAAF Super Grand Prix in Lausanne, he set the men's 110-meter hurdles world record at 12.88 seconds. Liu is the first Chinese athlete to achieve the "triple crown" of athletics: world record holder, world champion, and Olympic champion.

■ CHANG SHENG 常生 AND LU ZHOUXIANG 吕洲翔

田

径

31

Badminton

中国金 羽毛球

羽毛球

32

BADMINTON, LIKE MANY OTHER racket sports, has a long history. In the fifth century BCE, Chinese started to play a ball game called *ti jian*, 踢毽 which can be translated as "shuttle kick." As the name suggests, the object of the game was for players to keep a shuttle from hitting the ground without using their hands. Regardless of whether *ti jian* had anything to do with badminton, it was the first sport to use a shuttle.

Centuries later, a ball game named "battledore and shuttlecock" was played in India, Siam (Thailand), and Japan. In that game people use a battledore (paddle) to hit the shuttlecock (a small feathered ball) back and forth.

A net was introduced, and the game became a competitive sport called *poona*. By the 1860s some British army officers had learned the sport in India and took it back to England. Years later, the game was played among the upper class in England. In 1873, guests of the Duke of Beaufort played the game at his country place, Badminton House in Gloucestershire, and it thus became known as "the badminton game" among guests, who introduced it to other friends. In 1877 the Bath Badminton Club was established and developed the first official set of rules, which was similar to the modern rules for the game.

In 1899 the first all-England championship for men was held, and in 1900 came the pioneer tournament for women. However, these tournaments were regarded as "unofficial," and it was not until 1904 that the first of-ficial all-England matches took place. Badminton's popularity in Britain grew so fast that by 1920 there were nearly three hundred badminton clubs; the number had reached five hundred by 1930.

Badminton quickly spread from England to the United States, Canada, Australia, and New Zealand and made big strides in Europe. At the 1972 Olympics, badminton was staged as a demonstration sport event. In 1992 the game became an official Olympic sport at Barcelona, Spain, with singles and doubles competitions for men and women. After its appearance there, the game became more and more popular around the world.

In 1948 the first world-class tournament, the Thomas Cup (world men's team championships), was held in Scotland. Malaysia won the title and became the first country to inscribe its

A coach trains young students in the intricacies of badminton.

name on the Thomas Cup. International tournaments include the Surdiman Cup, the Uber Cup, and the World Individual Championships. After all these years, badminton is neither so different from its Indian predecessor nor the game played by the European elite society in the mid-1800s except for the speed and technique of the sport.

Badminton Introduced in China

Badminton was introduced to China by the British in the late nineteenth century. In 1910 staff and students in YMCAs and schools in big cities such as Beijing, Guangzhou, Tianjing, and Chengdu started to play the game. In 1931 the first Chinese badminton team was established. In 1932 the first China Open was held in the city of Tianjin.

In 1945 the first badminton association in China, the Shanghai Badminton Association, was established. In the same year, this association organized the first Shanghai Championship Tournament.

During the 1950s badminton became more popular in big cities. In 1954 several overseas Chinese coaches from Indonesia came back to China and promoted the game in terms of tactics and training techniques. In 1963 and 1964, the Indonesia Badminton National Team visited China and competed with China's national team. Competitions between the two national teams

Hospital workers in Beijing play a casual game of badminton during their lunch hour.

offered a chance for Chinese to study and learn advanced techniques from their opponents. When the Chinese team beat Denmark and Sweden in friendship matches in 1965 and 1964, it marked another turning point in the team's growing mastery.

When China's Cultural Revolution (1966–1976) began, badminton teams were disbanded in each city and province. It was not until 1971 that the national badminton team was reorganized by the central government. In 1974 the first Youth Badminton National Championships took place in Kun Ming and twenty-one provincial badminton teams participated in the matches. These championships have been held each year since 1974 with the goal of discovering talented young athletes.

In 1982 China won the men's team championship title at the Thomas Cup

with a brilliant victory against Indonesia; the score was 5–4. In 1986 China won both the Thomas Cup and the Uber Cup in Djakarta, Indonesia. These two victories shocked the sports world. The following year, Chinese players won all the gold medals at the Fifth Individual World Badminton Champion in Beijing. By then China had become the only country that held all seven world titles (men's and women's team and five singles sets). This record was unprecedented.

However, when badminton became an official Olympic sport at Barcelona in 1992, none of the seven gold medals was won by China. In the 1990s Indonesia and Malaysia recaptured all the world titles from China.

The 1996 Olympic Games in Atlanta saw Chinese badminton reach another milestone, when GE Fei 葛菲 and GU Jun 顾俊 took the gold for the

Yang Yang,
the 1987 Male
Badminton
Champion.

(BWF), the positions of Chinese shuttlers in the world rankings remain unchallenged; it will be possible for this formidable team to win all five gold medals at the Beijing 2008 Olympic Games (see table 2).

TABLE 2 ■ Badminton World Federation World Ranking (2007)			
WORLD RANK	NATION	NAME	POINTS
Men's Singles			
1	China	Lin Dan	78,161
2	China	Chen Jin	61,111
3	China	Chen Yu	59,020
4	China	Chen Hong	57,871
5	China	Bao Chunlai	55,991
Women's Singles			
1	China	Xie Xingfang	70,701
2	China	Zhang Ning	69,821
3	China	Zhu Lin	57,261
4	Germany	Xu Huaiwen	54,910
5	China	Lu Lan	53,821
Men's Doubles			
1	China	Fu Haifeng Cai Yun	71,631
2	Korea	Jung Jae Sung Lee Yong Dae	55,460
3	Indonesia	Wijaya, Candra Gunawan, Tony	55,430
Women's Doubles			
1	China	Zhang Yawen Wei Yili	70,221
2	China	Gao Ling Huang Sui	64,271
3	China	Yang Wei Zhang Jiewen	63,891
Mixed Doubles			
1	China	Xie Zhongbo Zhang Yawen	59,701
2	Thailand	Prapakamol, Sudket Thoungthongkam, Saralee	59,341
3	Indonesia	Widianto, Nova Natsir, Lilyana	55,581

women's team and DONG Jong 董炯 was awarded the gold for men's singles (see table 1). Two years later, in 1998, China recaptured the Uber Cup from its South Asian competitors at Hong Kong. Chinese also had won the Surdiman Cup in 1995 (Lausanne), 1997 (Glasgow), and 1999 (Copenhagen).

Chinese athletes have dominated badminton for a decade, but the sport is developing strongly in Indonesia, Malaysia, South Korea, Britain, and some Scandinavian countries.

Olympic Leaders

Five sets of medals will be awarded at the Beijing Olympics: men's and women's singles, men's and women's doubles, and mixed doubles.

According to information released by the Badminton World Federation

TABLE 1 ■ China's Olympic Medal Tally (1992–2004)				
YEAR	HOST CITY	GOLD	SILVER	BRONZE
1992	Barcelona	0 (out of 4)	0	5
1996	Atlanta	2 (out of 4)	1	2
2000	Sydney	4 (out of 5)	1	3
2004	Athens	3 (out of 5)	1	1

Source: International Olympic Committee's website.

Source: Badminton World Federation website.

In men's singles Chinese player LIN Dan 林丹 and Taufik Hidayat from Indonesia are the favorites for the gold medal. Lin Dan, "China's Super Dan" 超级丹 (b. 1983), is China's top seed in 2008. Since 2004 he has been ranked number one in the world. In 2006 Lin won against his teammate BAO Chunlai 鲍春来 in the finals of the World Badminton Championships held in Madrid, Spain. He also won the gold medal at the 2007 World Championships in Kuala Lumpur, Malaysia. Taufik Hidayat (b. 1981) is a former world champion and the 2004 Olympic champion in the men's singles. He is the only first-rung player who retains the fifteen-point style of play in the revised twenty-one-point system. Hidayat is known for his relaxed, smooth playing style and is one of the best all-around players in the world. He is perhaps the world's most spontaneously innovative badminton singles player today. To date, no competitors are strong enough to challenge the domination of China (see table 3).

Leading Athletes and Coaches

ZHAO Jianhua 赵剑华 (b. 1965) is 1.83 meters tall and left-handed. He entered a sports school at the age of twelve and was selected for the Jiangsu badminton team (provincial level) at the age of thirteen. Jianhua joined the Chinese national team at the age of eighteen in 1983. One year later, he defeated Morten Frost and won the Scotland Open. This was the first time he was noticed on the international stage. In 1985 Jianhua defeated four world-class players within three months. This

TABLE 3 ■ Favorite Gold Medal Competitors in 2008		
EVENT	**MEN**	**WOMEN**
Singles	Hidayat, Taufik (Indonesia)	Zhan Ning (China)
	Lin Dan (China)	Xie Xingfang (China)
	Bao Chunlai (China)	
Doubles	Fu Haifeng, Cai Yun (China)	Gao Lin, Huan Hui (China)
		Yang Wei, Zhang Jiewen (China)
		Wei Yili, Zhang Yawen (China)
Mixed Doubles	Xie Zhongbo, Zhang Yawen (China)	
	Widianto Nova, Natsir Lilyana (Indonesia)	
	Lee Kyung Won, Lee Hyo Jung (Thailand)	

achievement shocked the badminton world, and soon he was recognized as one of the four "Heavenly Kings" (so named because they were the top four Chinese badminton players.. In 1986 he recovered from a lung disease that had forced him to rest for one year. And he soon won the Malaysia Open,

Li Lingwei, the 1987 Female Badminton Champion.

China Open, and Thailand Open. He won the 1987 Badminton World Cup, 1988 Thomas Cup, 1990 Thomas Cup, 1991 All-England World Championship, and 1991 World Badminton GP Finals Championship. In 1994 Jianhua retired from the national team and entered a management college in Singapore to study economics. Now he works as an image ambassador for a sports brand in China.

YANG Yang 杨阳 (b. 1963) is the only badminton player in the world who has won consecutive World Badminton Championships men's singles titles. He played a major role in China's early win of the coveted Thomas Cup and belonged to China's golden generation of badminton players of the 1980s. As a member of that generation, Yang Yang played an important role in making China a world badminton superpower. Players of his generation set the foundation for current Chinese world-class badminton players.

ZHANG Ning 张宁 (b. 1975) won the gold medal for China in the women's singles at the 2004 Summer Olympic Games. She also won the 2003 World Badminton Championships (women's singles) in Birmingham, England. By 2007 she was at the top of women's world rankings and was targeting the gold medal at the 2008 Olympic Games.

Lin Dan 林丹 (b. 1983), "China's Super Dan," is China's top seed in 2008. Since 2004 he has been ranked number one in the world. In 2006 Lin won against his teammate Bao Chunlai in the finals of the World Badminton Championships held in Madrid, Spain. He also won the gold medal at the 2007 World Championships in Kuala Lumpur, Malaysia.

LI Lingwei 李玲蔚 (b. 1964), the "Badminton Queen" 羽毛球皇后 of China, was the champion at the 1983 and 1989 World Badminton Championships. She won the 1984, 1985, 1986,

and 1987 Badminton World Cup and the 1984, 1986, and 1988 Uber Cup. She dominated world badminton during the 1980s and was unquestionably the most outstanding female badminton player in China. Li Lingwei retired in 1989 and became a coach of the Chinese national badminton team in 1995.

TANG Xianhu 汤仙虎 (b. 1941) was born in Indonesia and lived there for many years. Xianhu came back to China in the late 1960s and brought advanced badminton techniques to China and developed his own style. In 1978 Tang Xianhu won the gold medal in the mixed doubles at the Bangkok Asian Games. Tang Xianhu is considered a pioneer of Chinese badminton. He is also the most successful badminton coach in China, and is today responsible for the national badminton team and in charge of the men's mixed doubles team.

■ FAN WEI 樊维 AND LU ZHOUXIANG 吕洲翔

Basketball

中国金 篮球

BASKETBALL WAS INTRODUCED TO China in 1895, just four years after James Naismith, secretary and physical education instructor of the Young Men's Christian Association (YMCA) in Springfield, Massachusetts, nailed a fruit basket to a wall at Springfield College (then the YMCA training school). Naismith probably never imagined that his invention—basketball—would have such an impact on the world of sports. Today, the teams and players of the National Basketball Association (NBA) have won the hearts of many basketball fans throughout the world with their performances. The Dow Jones stock index rose when Michael Jordan returned to the NBA in 1995. And since Jordan first set foot

on a professional basketball court, the fee for broadcasting NBA games has increased tenfold. Chinese schoolchildren who idolize Jordan proudly choose his name as their "English name."

Basketball at first was called "Naismith ball." However, because points were scored by shooting soccer balls into a fruit basket, the sport became known as "basketball" and soon became popular throughout the United States. Today, although fruit baskets, soccer balls, and nine players per team have long since disappeared , some of the original rules—such as the rule setting the height of baskets at 3.05 meters—still remain as Naismith conceived them.

In 1895 basketball appeared as a competitive sport in U.S. colleges. In 1898 the first professional basketball league was formed. Beginning with the 1904 St. Louis Olympic Games, basketball was played as a display sport until the

1936 Berlin Olympics, when basketball made its debut as an official Olympic event.

The U.S. team dominated Olympic basketball for a half century before it failed to win the gold medal for the first time at the 1988 Olympics in Seoul, South Korea. That failure eventually led to a rule change that allowed professional players to play in Olympic basketball games. At the 1992 Barcelona Olympics, a team consisting primarily of NBA stars, headed by Michael Jordan and Magic Johnson, took part in the Olympics for the first time and won the title of "Dream Team" with its excellent performance. However, the progress of European basketball teams, especially the Croatian, Yugoslavian, and Lithuanian teams, brought great changes in the 1990s as more European basketball players went on to star in the NBA. At the 2004 Athens Olympics, the U.S. team failed to win the gold medal for a second time.

Basketball has exploded in popularity in recent years amongst Chinese youth.

Basketball in China

After the sport was introduced to China in at the Tianjin Zhonghua YMCA in 1895, basketball spread to YMCAs in Beijing, Shanghai, and other cities. In 1913 China sent a team made up of students from Shanghai, Nanjing, and other major cities, to participate in the first Far East Championship Games in Manila, Philippines. In 1936 China competed for the first time in the Eleventh Olympic Games in Berlin.

The Chinese men's basketball team began to dominate the sport in Asia during the 1970s and 1980s. The team swept five Asian Championship titles in succession from 1975 to 1983. The Chinese women's basketball team finished third at the 1983 World Championship.

The Chinese Basketball Association (CBA) was established in 1995. During the past ten years, the CBA has produced many basketball stars. WANG Zhizhi 王治郅 joined the NBA in 2001. Later YAO Ming 姚明, the league's most famous star, joined the Houston Rockets in 2002. Both players led Chinese basketball players onto the international professional basketball stage.

The popularization of basketball in China has been promoted aggressively by the CBA. Basketball has never been more popular than it is today: Much-favored three-men street basketball, campus basketball, and the Chinese University Basketball Association (CUBA), which has up to seven hundred teams, are all in full swing.

The Chinese men's national basketball team, headed by Yao Ming, defeated a strong European opponent, the Serbian team, and made its way into the top eight in the 2004 Athens Olympic Games.

Famous Coaches and Players

David Willard Lyon was born into a Christian missionary family in Hangzhong in southern China and received his education in the United States. After graduation from College of Wooster in Ohio, he was sent to work in China in 1895 by the Foreign Department of the International Committee of the YMCA of North America. He and his wife arrived in Tianjin on 17 November. On 8 December Lyon played a "basket and ball game" during his lecture

---

The YMCA Brings Modern Sports to China

Modern sports came to China toward the end of the nineteenth century. Britons resident in the "Middle Kingdom" established football clubs in Tientsin (1884) and Shanghai (1887), but Americans, especially those working under the auspices of the YMCA, were far more important players in the game of ludic diffusion. In its early years, Chinese basketball was nurtured almost exclusively by the YMCA. Dr. Willard Lyon, who opened the Tientsin YMCA in 1895, was a typical activist. He was not content to limit his attention to the young Chinese who frequented the YMCA. "As early as 1896," wrote Jonathan Kolatch, "the Tientsin YMCA embarked on a program of promoting athletic competition in [Chinese] schools." In 1902, when C. H. Robertson arrived to assume responsibilities in Tientsin, he followed Lyon's path and spent part of his time in the local Chinese schools. He also arranged for an American teacher of physical education to be employed, at YMCA expense, in the school system. To stimulate interest on the part of the Chinese, the Americans resident in Tientsin organized an annual athletic meet for students at the local schools.

Although the YMCA never had more than fifteen or twenty "physical secretaries" for all of China, those few were amazingly influential as coordinators of programs in Chinese and mission schools, as promoters of athletic meets, as trainers of native sports administrators, and as propagandists for increased support of physical-education programs. Basketball was, as those familiar with the game's origins might have guessed, the YMCA's favored sport. Dr. Lyon had introduced it in Tientsin, but the most energetic promoters of the game were located in Shanghai, where Dr. Max J. Exner arrived in 1908 as the Chinese YMCA's first National Physical Director.

When the YMCA organized China's first national athletic meet, at Nanking in October of 1910, basketball was part of the program (along with track and field, tennis, and soccer). Although the officials were Americans, all the athletes on the one hundred forty competing teams were Chinese. A symbolic moment occurred during the meet when high-jumper SUN Baoqing snipped off the queue of hair that had knocked the crossbar from its support and made his first attempt a failure. He tried again, shorn, and became the national champion.

■ ALLEN GUTTMANN

A young basketball player in Beijing goes for a lay up shot.

at Beiyang Medical School. In March 1896 he organized the first basketball game at the Tianjin YMCA. Thus, Tianjin became the birthplace of Chinese basketball.

DONG Shouyi 董守义 is known as the "father of Chinese basketball" 中国篮球之父. After graduation from Beijing Tongzhou Xiehe College (later merged into Beijing University) in 1916, he became sports secretary of the Tianjin YMCA. He participated in the Far East Championship Games several times as a member and later captain of the Chinese basketball team. In 1923 he studied at Springfield College in Mas-

sachusetts. After his return to China in July 1925, he coached the men's basketball teams of Tianjin Nankai University and Beijing Normal University. The Chinese men's national basketball team consisted mainly of members of these two teams. Between 1936 and 1952, he took part in the Olympic Games three times as a coach and as the head coach of the Chinese team. Between the 1920s and 1960s, he coached a number of basketball stars and other coaches in China. He was a member of the International Olympic Committee between 1947 and 1958.

Yao Ming 姚明 may be the most outstanding player in the history of Chinese basketball. Born in Shanghai in 1980, Yao Ming received his first basketball as a gift on his fourth birthday from his parents, who were both basketball players. He joined the Chinese national team at age eighteen and led the team to the Asian Championship title many times. In June 2002, as the NBA's number one draft pick, Yao Ming signed a three-year contract worth $10.8 million with the Houston Rockets. Soon, Yao Ming attracted public attention in the United States and throughout all of Asia. Some people

Baseball in China

Japan may be considered Asia's premier baseball nation, but China was the first Asian country where baseball (*bangqiu*) was introduced. In 1863 the Shanghai Baseball Club was established by American medical missionary Henry William Boone. Boone, born in Java, spent his early years in China. As a teenager he moved to New York City, then the hub of baseball. After medical school and a brief stint as a surgeon for the Confederate States of America, Boone returned to China to become director of the General Hospital for Europeans in Shanghai. A sports enthusiast, Boone organized baseball teams in Shanghai schools. From there the game spread throughout China. School-centered tournaments were the primary venue for competition, but the Chinese also sporadically organized teams for international games. In 1913, for example, during the presidency of YUAN Shikai, China finished third in the Far East Games.

Baseball remained popular in China for over fifty years, but its heyday came during the late 1920s and 1930s when China was ruled by CHIANG Kai-shek and the Guomindang. Then the Shanghai Pandas were China's most powerful team. The popular team was founded by LIANG Fuchu, the "grandfather of Chinese baseball," who learned to play baseball while studying in Japan. In 1934 Liang organized a game in Shanghai against an American all-star team, featuring Babe Ruth.

After the Communist victory in 1949 Liang Fuchu taught Chinese sailors in Qingdao how to play baseball. A 1950 Communist Party decree required People's Liberation Army soldiers to learn the game. Liang Fuchu coached the winning team from Shanghai in the 1956 national competition. Baseball peaked in China in 1959 when twenty-three teams comprised a national league and thirty provincial, military, and city teams participated in a national tournament. Within a few years, however, MAO Zedong decided to disband the league claiming it was a remnant of Western impe-

rialism. During the height of anti-Western Cultural Revolution (1966–1976), former coaches and players were often targeted for abuse. Chinese were forced to hide gloves, bats, and other equipment for fear of attack by overzealous Red Guards.

With the opening of China and the coming to power of reform-minded DENG Xiaoping, the Chinese were reintroduced to baseball. By the 1970s the China Baseball Association was formed and in the 1980s Liang Fuchu's sons worked as baseball coaches for city teams. The Los Angeles Dodgers made the first overtures for international cooperation by sponsoring Chinese developmental leagues. In 1986 the Dodgers financed a new modern baseball facility in Tianjin called "Dodger's Stadium." Today the China Baseball League has six teams that play a thirty-game season. Major League Baseball International maintains close ties with the China Baseball Association.

■ JUNE GRASSO

---

called him China's "biggest export" ever. However, the biggest gainer from Yao Ming's signing might just be the NBA itself because the increased interest of Asian fans has contributed to the NBA's policy of expanding overseas, especially in Asian markets.

Basketball in the Beijing Olympics

In order to realize its goal of ranking sixth in the 2008 Olympics, the Chinese men's basketball team in April 2007 began a six-month train-

ing program, playing more than thirty practice games. The Chinese men's team faced problems such as a relatively weak guard play, a loose defense, and tendency to miss shots at crucial moments. Only if these problems were solved during training could the Chinese men's team, led by Yao Ming, Wang Zhizhi, and YI Jianlian 易建联, be a match for the strong teams fielded by the United States, Argentina, and Spain in the Beijing Olympics. The team's prospects were further weakened by a foot injury Yao Ming sustained in February 2008. The stress fracture side-

lined him from the rest of the Houston Rockets season, and his Olympic teammates had to cope with the possibility that Yao would have to sit out the Beijing Games.

The Chinese women's basketball team set fourth place as its goal in the Beijing Olympics. Led by MIAO Lijie 苗立杰 and SUI Feifei 隋菲菲, in the spring of 2008, the eighteen-woman team began five months of intensive training and practice games to prepare for the Olympics.

■ ZHANG LING 张玲

中国金 Diving

跳水

PEOPLE HAVE BEEN TAKING THE plunge—jumping off cliffs and rocks into water to amuse themselves—since ancient times. Historical evidence suggests that diving dates back at least to Greece's ancient games. In Naples, Italy, a 2,500-year-old tomb depicts a man diving from a narrow platform.

The world's earliest competitive diving may have taken place over a millennium ago in ancient China. During the Song dynasty 宋 (960–1279 CE), people performed a kind of fancy diving called "aquatic trapeze." 水秋千. Participants took off from a rolling trapeze, turned somersaults in the air, then dived into the water. Aquatic trapeze-diving competitions were held in palaces and cities. Techniques included the "starting dive," "somersault," "body opening," and "entry work." Aquatic trapeze closely resembled modern competitive diving.

The first official diving competitions in the world took place at the aquatic palace in Dongjin, the capital of Song dynasty of ancient China between 1082 and 1125. ZHAO Jie 赵佶, king of the Song dynasty, watched these competitions. Diving developed further as an athletic discipline in seventeenth-century Europe as gymnasts practiced their acrobatics over water.

Although swimming and diving are commonly linked, diving has more in common with gymnastics. In the early 1800s Swedish and German gymnasts practiced their somersaults and twists over water. Their practices became known as "fancy diving," a term that stuck until the early 1900s.

Male divers competed in the modern Olympic Games for the first time in 1904; their goal was to swim the farthest underwater after a dive. At the 1908 Olympic Games in London, the pool was 100 meters long, and the diving tower was removable. In 1908 springboard diving was added to the original platform-diving event. Four years later, at the 1912 Olympic Games in Stockholm, Sweden, fancy diving was introduced, and women were allowed to compete in their own platform event.

In the 1920s divers grew tired of the slow rotation from rigid takeoffs starting with a straight position, and the pike and tuck positions began to dominate, making multiple somersaults possible. From then on, the United States, instead of Sweden and Germany, began to dominate the sport. In 1924 the United States won all Olympic diving events except the bronze medals in the women's platform event. In 1932 divers from the United States occupied every

跳水

41

A group of young divers are instructed in proper technique.

space on the Olympic medals podium in both the men's and women's events.

The 1928 Olympics included compulsory and voluntary dives. The compulsory dives were selected after each Olympics and were trained for during the four years before the next Olympics. This form of competition continued for twenty years. From 1949 to 1956, all dives on platform and springboard were voluntary, so with competitors opting for more difficult dives, the basic dives were rarely seen in competition. The conditions were then revised to include five required basic dives from the springboard, and restrictions on women's diving were removed.

Several divers have won gold medals in both the springboard and the platform events at the same Olympics. American Albert White was the first in 1924, followed by American Peter Desjardins in 1928 in Amsterdam. He was the first diver to score a perfect 10.00. In the 1948 London Olympics, Victoria Draves of the United States was the first woman diver to win a gold medal in two diving events. Only Pat McCormick from America won gold in both the springboard and the platform diving events in 1952 and 1956 successively. In recent years diving has evolved rapidly, and great advances have been made in improving techniques and the complexity of dives.

A coach trains his student in proper diving form.

Off the Springboard

Diving stages in China were first erected at coastal cities such as Hong Kong, Shanghai, and Tianjin in the late nineteenth century. In 1935 the Shanghai International Aquatic Games were held. England, United States, Germany, and China participated. The diving events involved standing and running plain dives from firm boards, and they were for men only. The United States took first place. At that time modern competitive diving in China was restricted by many factors, including politics, economics, and culture (few citizens were interested in diving).

At the Second Far Eastern Games in 1915, held in Shanghai, the scores of diving competition were determined by the distance of a dive. That kind of dive is now called a "forward dive straight." Twelve years later, at the Eighth Far East Games in Shanghai, fancy dives from platform and springboard were performed, and China ranked first. In the same year the first Chinese book on diving (translated from English) was published by Shanghai Diligence Publishing Group. The book introduced techniques, training methods, and diving rules. But between 1937 and 1949, during civil war in China and World War II, the development of diving in China, understandably, declined.

The People's Republic of China was established in 1949 and there was a new effort to promote physical education and sporting competition. The national swimming/diving championships took place in 1952 and the event attracted an audience of thousands. After the

Chinese diver Guo Jingjing in mid-dive.

championships diving became a popular sport in some big cities.

The Soviet Union diving team visited China in 1954. It demonstrated complex platform diving skills for Chinese coaches and athletes. Chinese athletes began to develop their techniques. At the 1955 National Aquatic Games, many athletes performed a forward somersault 1.0 twist dive. By 1958 some divers executed even the forward somersault 3.5 twist dive. From then on

"difficult," "beautiful," "skillful," and "accurate" became the aims of diving in China.

When the Cultural Revolution began in 1966, many swimming pools became fish ponds; most swimming and diving teams were dismissed. The national diving team, however, was spared. It trained at a Beijing indoor swimming pool along with the national swimming team until 1974, when the construction of a separate diving center was finished. In that year, the Chinese diving team won four gold medals at the Seventh Asian Games. Four years later, at the Eighth Asian Games in Thailand, China won all the gold and silver medals in diving. China's diving team indisputably has been the dominant team in Asia since then.

Between 1973 and 1979 Chinese divers improved their skills and acquired clean-entry techniques. In the 1980s the Chinese diving team impressed many people with victories at international diving competitions, such as the London Diving Invitational in 1980, the U.S. Diving Invitational in 1981, the Eleventh International University Games in Bucharest in 1982, and the Second FINA Diving World Cup in Mexico in 1981. Between 1989 and 1992, the Chinese diving team won twenty gold medals at the FINA Diving World Cup.

TABLE 1 ■ China's Olympic Medal Tally (1992–2004)

YEAR	HOST CITY	GOLD	SILVER	BRONZE
1988	Seoul	2 (out of 4)	3	1
1992	Barcelona	3 (out of 4)	1	1
1996	Atlanta	3 (out of 4)	1	1
2000	Sydney	5 (out of 8)	5	0
2004	Athens	6 (out of 8)	2	1

Source: Organizing Committee for the Olympic Games.

China's diving team has been called the "Dream Team" since the Sydney Olympic Games in 2000. The team won five gold medals at Sydney, six gold medals in Athens later in 2004, and won all ten gold medals at the Fifteenth FINA Diving World Cup in 2006 (see tables 1 and 2). It is predicted that the "Dream Team" would win all eight gold medals at the Beijing Olympics in 2008.

Platform Beijing

Events at the 2008 Beijing Olympics include the 3-meter synchronized springboard (men and women), the 10-meter synchronized platform (men and women), the 3-meter springboard (men and women), and the 10-meter platform (men and women).

Alexandre Despatie of Canada has been considered the main threat to China in the men's 3-meter springboard. At the age of thirteen, Despatie

TABLE 2 ■ Fifteenth FINA Diving World Cup (2006)

RANK	COUNTRY	GOLD	SILVER	BRONZE
1	China	10	4	1
2	USA	0	3	2
3	Russia	0	2	1

Source: Féderation Intermantionale de Nanation Amateur (FINA).

Diving Champion Shi Meiqin helped establish China as a diving powerhouse.

Games and won three gold medals and one bronze. That success carried on to the 2004 Olympics in Athens, where he won the silver medal in the 3-meter springboard event. At the 2005 FINA World Championships, cheered by the hometown Montreal crowd, Despatie became the first diver to be world champion on all three boards.

China, however, has a new generation of diving stars, notably HE Chong 何冲 and LUO Yuton 罗玉通. As a world champion rookie, He Chong won the gold in the men's synchronized 3-meter springboard at Montreal in 2005 and won the gold medal in the 3-meter springboard at the Champions Diving Tour in 2006.

In the women's 3-meter springboard, the greatest chance of winning gold has been with either GUO Jingjing 郭晶晶; and WU Minxia 吴敏霞. Guo Jingjing was the gold medalist at the 1999, 2000, 2002, and 2004 FINA World Diving Cup; and the 2001, 2005, and 2007 World Diving Championships. In 2004 Guo Jingjing won the Olympic gold medal in the 3-meter women's springboard in Athens and another gold medal in the 3-meter women's synchronized springboard with Wu Minxia. Wu Minxia joined the national team in 1998; she was the gold medalist at the 2003 FINA Diving Grand Prix, 2003 FINA Diving Grand Prix, 2003 World Diving Championships, and 2004 and 2006 FINA Diving World Cup. These two outstanding Chinese divers are not only opponents but partners, and may cooperate to win for China the gold medal in the women's 3-meter synchronized springboard.

captured the hearts of Canadians when he won a gold medal in the 10-meter platform diving event at the 1998 Commonwealth Games and became an overnight celebrity. He won the gold medal in 3-meter springboard events in the 2002 Commonwealth Games in

Manchester, England, and gold at the 2003 World Championships in Barcelona in the 10-meter platform diving event. That year he also won his first world championship in the 10-meter platform diving event and then traveled to Santo Domingo for the Pan Am

Diving Duos at the Olympics

Olympic synchronized diving (diving in pairs) began at the Sydney 2000 Games. Here's how the International Olympic Committee's website (www.olympics. org) explains the competition and judging.

Competitors perform a series of dives and are awarded points up to 10, depending upon their elegance and skill. The points are then adjusted for the degree of difficulty, based on the number and types of manoeuvres attempted, such as somersaults, pikes, tucks and twists. A reverse 1.5 somersault with 3.5 twists, for example, is among the most difficult.

A panel of seven judges traditionally scores a dive, judging such elements as approach, take-off, execution and entry into the water. Nine judges assess synchronised diving. Four judge the execution of individual dives, and five assess synchronization—how the pairs mirror height, distance from the springboard or platform, speed of rotation and entry into the water.

platform and a gold medal in women's 10-meter synchronized platform. The seventeen-year-old Jia Tong is a new hope for China's diving team. She won the women's 10-meter platform synchronized diving gold at the Eleventh World Swimming Championships in 2005 when she was fifteen years old. She also won the gold medal of the women's 10-meter platform in the FINA World Cup in 2006.

Champions of the Plunge

GAO Ming 高敏 (b. 1970), the "Diving Queen," began her diving training at the age of nine. She joined the Sichuan provincial team when she was eleven and the national team when she was fifteen. When she was sixteen, in 1986, she won the women's springboard title in the Fifth World Swimming Championships. One year later, Gao became the women's springboard champion at the FINA Diving World Cup in Holland. She then won gold in the springboard event at the 1988 Seoul Olympics, becoming the first Chinese woman

On the other hand, Russian veteran Julia Pakhalina, one of the world's best springboard divers, undoubtedly challenges the dominance of China in the women's 3-meter springboard. She was the silver medalist at the 2006 World Championships with a score of 610.62, just 2.62 points behind Wu Minxia.

In the women's 10-meter platform, Laura Wilkinson of the United States is the most capable opponent of the Chinese divers. She was the gold medalist at the 2000 Olympic Games, and the champion of the 2004 FINA Diving World Cup and the 2005 World Diving Championships. She is also the only woman in history to earn all three titles on the platform. She upset the heavily favored Chinese divers in the 10-meter platform dive at the 2000 and 2004 Olympics. She is expected to perform well in 2008. Another powerful challenger is Émilie Heymans, a Canadian diver. She won a silver medal at the 2000 Summer Olympics in 10-meter platform synchro and a gold medal at the 2003 World Championships in Barcelona in the 10-meter platform.

However, the Chinese athletes, LAO Lishi 劳力诗 and JIA Tong 贾童, will fight for the gold medal in the women's 10-meter platform against Laura Wilkinson and Émilie Heymans (see table 3). Lao represented China at the 2004 Summer Olympics, earning a silver medal in the 10-meter women's

TABLE 3 ■ Gold Medal Competitors in 2008 Olympics		
EVENT	MEN	WOMEN
3-m springboard	Alexandre Despatie (Canada)	Guo Jingjing (China)
	Dmitriy Dobroskok (Russia)	Wu Minxia (China)
	He Chong (China)	Julia Pakhalina (Russia)
	Luo Yutong (China)	
10-m platform	Lin Yue (China)	Laura Wilkinson (USA)
	Huo Liang (China)	Jia Tong (China)
	Hu Jia (China)	Émilie Heymans (Canada)
		Lao Lishi (China)
		Cheng Ruolin (China)
Synchronized 3-m springboard	He Chong, Wang Feng (China)	Guo Jinjin, Li Ting (China)
		Guo Jinjin, Wu Minxia (China)
Synchronized 10-m platform	Lin Yue, Huo Liang (China)	Jia Tong, Cheng Ruolin (China)
		Kang Li, Wang Hao (China)

Source: Author's predictions.

athlete to win titles in three successive major diving competitions.

XIONG Ni 熊倪 (b. 1974), a legendary figure in Chinese diving, participated in four Olympics within thirteen years and won five medals: three gold, one silver, and one bronze. Xiong joined the Hunan provincial team at the age of eight. Four years later, he swept four titles in the National Diving Championships, a performance that earned him a place on the national team. At the age of fourteen, he won a silver medal in men's platform diving at the Olympics in Seoul in 1988. Although his increasing weight forced him to shift from platform diving to springboard diving, Xiong went on to reach a new horizon in his career. At the Olympic Games in Atlanta in 1996, he won a springboard diving gold medal, the first for China in this event. He also won a gold medal in the men's 3-meter springboard synchronized diving at the Olympic Games in Sydney.

FU Mingxia 伏明霞 (b. 1978) won the platform-diving world championship in 1991 at the age of twelve, making her the world youngest diving champion of all time. She was also the world's youngest gold medalist in Olympic div-ing events. When she won a gold medal at the 1992 Olympics in Barcelona, she was only thirteen. Throughout the 1990s Fu dominated the sport with her picture-perfect dives. During the 2000 Olympics in Sydney, Fu won her fourth gold medal, joining Americans Pat McCormick and Greg Louganis as the world's only quadruple Olympic diving champions. With four Olympic gold medals and one silver, Fu is one of the best divers China has ever produced.

TIAN Liang 田亮 (b.1979) is one of the youngest members of the national team. He brought glory to the team by winning gold in the men's 10-meter platform in Sydney. At the Athens Olympics in 2004, he won the bronze medal in the 10-meter platform and a gold medal in the men's synchronized 10-meter platform. In 2005 Tian was temporarily demoted to a provincial squad for violating the regulations of the China General Administration for Sport, and he then retired in 2007.

Guo Jingjing (b. 1981) began her training in diving in 1988. In 1992 she was selected to dive for the Chinese national team. Guo represented China at the 2004 Olympics, winning a gold medal in the 3-meter women's syn-chronized springboard with Wu Minxia before finally winning her first individual Olympic gold medal in the 3-meter women's springboard.

Wu Minxia (b. 1985) took up diving in the second Shanghai Diving School in 1991 and joined the Shanghai municipal diving team in 1995. She joined the national team in 1998. Wu won a gold medal in the first 3-meter synchronized springboard at the 2003 FINA World Championships in Barcelona, Spain. One year later, at the Athens Olympics, with Guo Jinjin, she won a gold medal in the 3-meter synchronized springboard diving event.

ZHOU Jihong 周继红 (b. 1965) was the first Chinese woman to win an Olympic gold medal in the 10-meter platform diving event as well as the first diving gold medalist for China. In 1982 she joined the national team. After retiring in 1986, Zhou Jihong became the diving coach of the provincial diving team of Hubei. Four years later, she began to coach the national diving team. Since 2000 Zhou has been a head coach of the national diving team.

■ FAN WEI 樊维 AND LU ZHOUXIANG 吕洲翔

Football/Soccer

足球

AT THE 1999 WOMEN'S WORLD CUP, one of the most famous moments of the tournament was American defender Brandi Chastain's victory celebration after scoring the Cup-winning penalty against China. She took off her jersey and waved it over her head (as men frequently do), showing her muscular torso and sports bra as she celebrated. The 1999 final in the Rose Bowl in Pasadena, California, had an attendance of 90,185, a world record for a women's sporting event.

Soccer has certainly come a long way since its origins. Ancient cultures as diverse as the Greeks, Persians, and Vikings played ball games that could have evolved into soccer. However, the Fédération Internationale de Football Association (FIFA) acknowledged in 2002 that ancient soccer first appeared in Zi Bo 淄博, China, when the Chinese began to play a game called *cuju* 蹴鞠. *Cu* means "kick," and *ju* means "ball," and the game is mentioned in the *Shiji*, an ancient Chinese text. Even LI Yu 李渔 (50–130 CE), the famed Han-dynasty poet, wrote of football.

Some three thousand years ago, *cuju* players kicked a leather ball filled with feathers and hair through an opening measuring only 30–40 centimeters wide into a small net fixed onto long bamboo canes—a feat that obviously demanded great skill and technique. In a variation of this maneuver, players were not permitted to aim at their target unimpeded but rather had to use feet, chest, back, and shoulders while trying to withstand the attacks of opponents. Use of the hands was not permitted.

Cuju was used as a military training method as well as a physical education exercise in the Han dynasty 汉 (206 BCE–220 CE). *Cuju* started to become popular as a sport in the Tang dynasty 唐 (618–907 CE) and Song dynasty 宋 (960–1280 CE). During these periods the rules, techniques, and equipment of the sport developed and the game became popular with both the upper and lower classes. The games declined in thirteenth century during a period of dynastic change and political turmoil.

Nevertheless, it is generally acknowledged that Britain is the birthplace of modern soccer. The sport was first known in Britain as "association football," a rugged, kicking team sport. This term was shortened to "a-soc" and finally to "soccer." Even though the sport was loved by ordinary people, the government did not approve of it because it took too much of people's time. Instead of practicing archery (a sport useful for warfare), they were playing soccer. This is why, some researchers say, King Edward III banned soccer in the 1300s. Other kings also tried to suppress the sport, but too many people loved the game and did not care if they were jailed or punished for playing it.

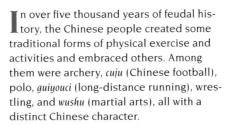

Chinese Classic Football

In over five thousand years of feudal history, the Chinese people created some traditional forms of physical exercise and activities and embraced others. Among them were archery, *cuju* (Chinese football), polo, *guiyouci* (long-distance running), wrestling, and *wushu* (martial arts), all with a distinct Chinese character.

Cuju was Chinese classic football. It started during the Warrior States Period (475–221 BCE). It was originally an aggressive, competitive game and was played by two opposing sides, each with goals. During the Han (206 BCE–220 CE) and Tang (618–907 CE) dynasties, due to its competitiveness, the game was often used by military mandarins to train soldiers in order to cultivate their fighting spirit and improve their physical conditioning. However, as time passed, two goals merged into one in the Song (960–1279 CE) and Yuan (1260–1368) dynasties. Vigorous competition was replaced by a much gentler phenomenon: less competitive and primarily exhibitive.

■ FAN HONG

Soccer began to spread from England to other countries in the late 1800s. The first official Olympic men's soccer match took place at the 1900 Paris Games, where Britain defeated France to claim the first soccer gold medal. Since then soccer has been an official Olympic sport. Women's soccer became an Olympic sport in 1996 in Atlanta, where the U.S. team defeated the Chinese team and won the gold medal.

In 1904 the FIFA was founded in Paris, and by 1930 there were professional leagues in many European countries. FIFA established its own world professional soccer championship—the World Cup—playing the first one at the Centenary Stadium in Montevideo, Uruguay, on 18 July 1930.

With increased television coverage of the sport, soccer grew in popularity during the 1960s. The champion of the FIFA World Cup is considered the "real" champion in the soccer world. For players the Golden Boot Award, which belongs to the leading goal scorer(s) of each championship, is the highest honor (see table 1).

Besides the Olympic Games and the FIFA World Cup, another leading world soccer tournament is the European Cup, also known as the "Champions

Bora Milutinovic led China's National Team in the 2002 FIFA world cup, and remains a popular figure in China today.

League." In 1955 the European Cup was established as a competition for league champions of European countries. The competition have has been a driving force in the development of soccer in Europeand a festival for soccer fans all over the world.

Modern Soccer in China

It has been recorded that the British brought modern soccer to China, first to Shanghai, then to big cities such as Beijing, Tianjin, and Guangzhou, in 1856. In 1879 the first documented match took place in Shanghai. In 1887 the Shanghai Football Club was formed. Twenty years later, in 1907, the first soccer league was established in Shanghai, with Thomas Dewar—a whiskey distiller—providing a trophy to the winners. Although the sport was initially dominated by British expatriates, other nationalities soon joined in, notably the Portuguese.

In 1923 the South China Club in Hong Kong represented China on a tour of Australia. In 1936 China participated in the Olympic soccer events in Berlin. Between the 1920s and 1940s, under the supervision of the Chinese Athletic Association, soccer matches took place in Shanghai, Beijing, and Guangzhou between a variety of clubs, including Union, Korean SC, Tung Hwa, Tsong

TABLE 1 ■ FIFA World Cup and Golden Boot Award Winners since 1986		
YEAR	WORLD CUP	GOLDEN BOOT AWARD
1986	Argentina	Gary Liniker (England) 6 goals
1990	West Germany	Toto Schillaci (Italy) 6 goals
1994	Brazil	Hristo Stoichkov (Bulgaria) 6 goals; Oleg Salenko (Russia) 6 goals
1998	France	Davor Suker (Croatia) 6 goals
2002	Brazil	Ronaldo Luis Nazário de Lima (Brazil) 8 goals
2006	Italy	Miroslav Klose (Germany) 5 goals

Source: Fédération Internationale de Football Association website.

Peh, plus European teams Sokol, Italiano, and Jewish Recreation.

In 1951, just two years after the People's Republic of China was founded, the National Football Federation was formed and the initial League Championship was held. In many cases teams represented regions rather than cities. Within a few years, sports institutes were developed, attended by the most promising players from factory and school teams. These institutes, along with the formation of a National Class A Tournament, enhanced the level of play. During the 1950s, Chinese teams built their skill levels through matches with foreign teams—primarily from other Communist countries.

In the mid-1960s, the Cultural Revolution (1966–1976) brought a halt to the game's progress, since all competitive sports were banned until 1972. Two years later, through the efforts of Henry Fok, FIFA executive and long-time supporter of soccer in China, FIFA member teams were permitted to play the Chinese. Then, in 1976, China was allowed to join the Asian Football Conference. That ushered in a wave of international activities. Pele and the New York Cosmos visited China to play, followed by teams from twenty-nine countries. In turn, some forty-seven national teams welcomed the Chinese team. By 1980, China was accepted as a full member of FIFA, which allowed its national team to play in qualifying matches for the World Cup, the Asian Cut, and the Olympics.

Sun Jihai is one of the most famous Chinese football players playing outside of China.

奥运体育

Members of the Chinese women's national team.

In 1984 China won the silver medal at the Asian Cup. In 1987 China qualified to play at the Twenty-fourth Olympic Games, in Seoul, South Korea, by defeating its strong opponent, Japan, in the qualifying round. This event became a landmark in China's soccer history.

In 1994 the Chinese Professional Soccer League (CPSL) was established. Under the supervision of the Chinese Football Association's (CFA) Professional League Committee, this nationwide league was divided into Divisions 1 and 2: Division 1 was subdivided into Divisions Jia 甲 A and Jia B (*jia* is a Chinese word for "top" or "first"). Division 2 was subdivided into regional divisions. As the twenty-first century began, the CPSL attracted countless soccer fans in China and made soccer

the country's most popular sport. This period was the golden age in China's soccer history. However, during the last ten years, soccer fans have lost their patience and passion and finally abandoned the CPSL. According to an online survey, which was carried out with cooperation between the television network of the People's Republic of China (CCTV) and sina.com, soccer fans questioned the credibility of the results of more than half of the first division matches in the 2003 season. In many cities soccer enthusiasts boycotted live games in a wave of silent protest.

Beyond a doubt a decade's worth of professional soccer has lined the pockets of Chinese players, club managers, and even referees. However, this activity has taken place in the absence of

commensurate improvements in skills either on the pitch or in club administration. Systematic difficulties have worked against the promotion of the professional sport. The Chinese first division soccer league is jointly operated by the Chinese Football Association and the Football Sport Management Center of the State General Administration of Sports. This dual system has for ten years headed up the richest sport in China. However, the system has been beset with crises and seems destined to issue regulations that are full of loopholes. The ups and downs of Chinese soccer over the past decade can perhaps be explained by a management system that has not yet been fully reformed.

In 1996 China's women's national soccer team stunned the world by winning a silver medal at the twenty-sixth Olympic Games in Atlanta. This victory was China's unique achievement in soccer and brought China a new hope in the sport.

Olympic Soccer/Football

Soccer matches in the Olympic Games in Beijing take place in five cities: Beijing, Tianjin, Shanghai, Qinhuangdao, and Shenyang. The men's title game will be held in Beijing at the National Stadium. Twenty-eight teams (twelve women's teams and sixteen men's teams) will compete against each other.

According to the latest FIFA/Coca-Cola World Ranking established by FIFA, in the men's events the finals may be between traditionally strong teams such as Argentina, Brazil, Italy, Spain, Germany, France, and Portugal. In the women's events the United States, Germany, Sweden, Norway, and Brazil stood out as leaders. (See table 2.)

Leading Athletes and Coaches in China

LEE Huitang 李惠堂 (b. 1905) is considered one of the greatest Asian footballers in the pre–World War II period. During the 1930s, there was an old saying in Shanghai about Lee Huitang: "If you want to see the Beijing Opera, you should go to see the performance of Meilanfang [the famous actor at the time]; if you want to watch soccer, you must go to see Lee Huitang." He was called the "King of Asian Football."

Lee Huitang was born in Hong Kong. He joined the China National Soc-

TABLE 2 ■ FIFA/Coca-Cola Men's and Women's Teams World Ranking	
RANKING	TEAM
■ Men's Teams	
1	Argentina
2	Brazil
3	Italy
4	Spain
5	Germany
6	Czech Republic
7	France
8	Portugal
9	Netherlands
10	Croatia
■ Women's Teams	
1	Germany
2	USA
3	Sweden
4	Brazil
5	Norway
6	Korea DPR
7	France
8	Denmark
9	Canada
10	England

cer Team in 1923 and played for the national team that won the 1925, 1927, 1930, and 1934 Far Eastern Games. He became the captain of the Chinese national team that competed at the Eleventh Olympic Games in Berlin in 1936. During his professional career, Lee Huitang made 1,260 goals. He was awarded the title "The World Soccer King" by a soccer journal in Germany in 1936. He became the head coach of the Chinese national team in 1948. He coached the Chinese Taipei soccer team and led it to win the 1954 and 1958 Asian Games. In 1965 he became vice-president of FIFA. He is the first Chinese to reach that position

SUN Jihai 孙继海 (b. 1977) is well-regarded for his speed and strength and also valued for his versatility—having played several key positions in the past, including left wing, central defense, and holding midfielder. He was one of the first Chinese players in the English leagues, signing with the Crystal Palace team in 1998 then moving to the Manchester City FC. Though plagued by injuries, he is remarkably resilient and continues to be a key defender for Manchester City.

SUN Wen 孙雯 (b. 1973) is one of the most outstanding international female soccer players in China—the first woman ever nominated as the Asian Soccer Confederation's Player of the Year. She joined the China national team at the age of seventeen. In the 1999 Women's World Cup, Sun was awarded both the Golden Ball and the Golden Boot. Named in 2001 at the FIFA Woman Player of the Century (along with U.S. player Michelle Akers), Sun retired in 2003, then returned to play in 2005, before retiring again. Often sought for her opinion of China's chances at Beijing 2008, she remains an icon for female athletes around the world.

FIFA Women's World Cup 2007 was held in China from 10–30 September 2007. Originally, China was to host the 2003 Women's World Cup, but the outbreak of SARS in that country forced that event to be moved to the United States.

■ FAN WEI 樊维 AND LU ZHOUXIANG 吕洲翔

Gymnastics
中国金 体操

GYMNASTICS HAS A LONG HISTORY in China. During the Spring and Autumn period 春秋 (770–476 BCE) and the Warring States period 战国 (475–221 BCE), Chinese people practiced Dao Yin Shu 导引术 (medical gymnastics), which was similar to modern gymnastics and was practiced to heal illnesses and to keep the body healthy. Fitness gymnastics, such as Wu Qin Xi (five-animal exercise), Ba Duan Jin 八段锦 (eight fragments), and Yi Jing Jing 易经筋 (muscle-bone strengthening exercise), all practiced by the ancient Chinese, are still practiced by many Chinese today. In addition, ancient Chinese literature and paintings contain many records of such acrobatic gymnastics such as swing, handstand, somersault, and throw and catch, which were similar in execution to modern gymnastics.

The Launch of Modern Gymnastics

The word *gymnastics* comes from the Greek word *gymnos*, which means "naked." Its meaning is derived from the ancient Greek custom of exercising naked. The definition and content of gymnastics have varied throughout history. In the fifth century BCE, such activities as running, jumping, throwing, wrestling, dancing, horse riding, and military games were all classified as gymnastics, and this definition held for many centuries. Later the ancient Greeks practiced gymnastics to improve physical fitness, whereas the ancient Romans used wooden horses and other apparatuses to practice equestrian skills.

It was not until the nineteenth century, however, that modern gymnastics began to develop rapidly in Europe. The European Gymnastics Federation (EGF) was founded in 1881 and the Federation of International Gymnastics (FIG) in 1896. Gymnastics was a sport in the first modern Olympic Games held in Athens in 1896.

If people today could watch the international artistic gymnastics competitions of one hundred years ago, they would probably find some of them familiar; competitions featured not only such events as horizontal bars, parallel bars, hand-rings, vault, and pommel horse, but also long jump, rope climbing, and weight lifting. But these events were exclusively for men; not until the

Even ancient artistic styles demonstrate how gymnastics and acrobatics have long been a part of Chinese culture.

Ninth Olympic Games in 1928 were women granted the right to compete. Today men's gymnastics events include team and all-round individual events, floor exercise, pommel horse, hand-rings, vault, parallel bars, and horizontal bars. Women's gymnastics events include team and all-round individual events, vault, uneven bars, balance bars, and floor exercise.

Of all the Olympic sports, gymnastics may be the best at demonstrating the agility of the human body and at making spectators fall head over heels in love with an athletic performance. Gymnastics has become one of the Olympic sports that awards the most gold medals. Together with the men's and women's trampoline and the artistic gymnastics events, gymnastics accounts for seventeen gold medals. As a result Olympic gymnastics is vigorously contested among sports powers around the world.

After the 2004 Olympic Games in Sydney, Australia, the Federation of International Gymnastics decided to eradicate the subjective factors of the judges that affect the scores gymnasts are awarded. In 2006 new rules were adopted. The "10.0 full score" was abolished, and the Code of Points was split into more detailed parts to make the scores show the differences between gymnasts more accurately.

Famous Gymnasts

The United States, Russia, Ukraine, Romania, and China are among the most powerful countries in contemporary world gymnastics. From these countries have emerged several stars.

The Origins of Gymnastics

People performed balancing and tumbling activities in Egypt and China before 2000 BCE. During the second millennium BCE Minoan athletes on the island of Crete in the Mediterranean not only balanced and tumbled, but also grasped the horns of a charging bull and vaulted with a front handspring to a landing on the bull's back. As part of their training in skills needed in warfare, the ancient Romans used wooden horses to practice mounting and dismounting. This apparatus evolved into the vaulting and pommel horses of gymnastics. Early models were built to resemble horses with saddles or had at least one end curved upward like the neck of a horse. The three sections of the gymnastics horse still retain the names *neck*, *saddle*, and *croup* (rump).

■ RICHARD V. MCGEHEE AND RUSS CRAWFORD

The Romanian female gymnast Nadia Comaneci amazed the world at the 1976 Olympic Games as she became the first gymnast in Olympic history to earn a perfect 10 score. She earned seven perfect scores in all, a feat that seems almost unachievable by gymnasts of today.

The Chinese gymnast LI Ning 李宁 was famous for the extreme difficulty of his routines. In the Twenty-third Olympic Games in 1984, he won three gold medals in the floor exercise, pommel horse, and hand-ring events and invented two difficult hand-rings and parallel bars moves, later named after him by the Federation of International Gymnastics.

The Russian beauty Svetlana Khorkina is no doubt the queen of gymnastics. Her scores are always at the top of the field. Her elegance has enthralled audiences throughout the world.

Gymnastics in China

Modern gymnastics was introduced in China around 1860. During the late nineteenth century and early twentieth century, it became the main part of physical education activities in schools. The sport developed after establishment of the People's Republic of China in 1949, as the country began to recover from civil war and the ravages of World War II. The Chinese national gymnastics teams were formed in 1953, and China became a member of the Federation of International Gymnastics in 1956. At the end of the 1970s, the Chinese gymnastics teams started to show outstanding results in international competitions. In the 1980s the Chinese men's and women's gymnastics teams became two of the most powerful teams in the world. In 1982 Li Ning shocked the world with his six straight gold medals in the Sixth Gymnastics World Cup and won the title "Prince of Gymnastics" at the Twenty-third Olympic Games in Los Angeles. Two of his teammates won gold medals in the same Olympics. LOU Yun 楼云 won a gold medal in the vault, and MA Yanhong 马艳红 won in the uneven bars.

体
操

54

Chinese women have won more gold medals than Chinese men have in international competitions—thus, the "stronger women and feebler men" phenomenon was characteristic of Chinese sports in the 1980s and 1990s. By the year 2000, however, performance in both programs had slipped. The men's team won only one gold medal at the 2004 Athens Olympics, and the women none. After training with great determination, the Chinese gymnastics teams enjoyed a revival and won eight of the fourteen gold medals in the Gymnastics World Championship in Aarhus, Denmark, in October 2006. YANG Wei 扬威 won three gold medals in the men's team, all-round, and parallel bars events. In addition, CHENG Fei 程菲 was the most successful woman, winning three titles in the women's team, vault, and floor exercise events.

A member of the Chinese gymnastics team at the 2004 Olympics.

Twenty-first-Century Chinese Gymnasts

As the world prepared for the 2008 Olympics, the Chinese gymnastics teams received considerable attention, but knowledgeable observers were alert to the fact that it was in some ways a new, young, and untried group of athletes, and suggested that the instability of their performances might be the biggest obstacle to their winning gold. The U.S. team has been dominant in the sport, and although the prowess of the Russian and Romanian teams has declined in recent years with the retirement of a number of star gymnasts, these teams and the fast-rising Italian, Ukrainian, and Australian teams were also significant threats to the Chinese women. The Chinese gymnast Cheng Fei, with her signature "Cheng Fei Vault," has been thought to have a good chance to win gold medals in the vault and floor exercise events. Winning the balance beam gold medal is another goal of the Chinese women's team.

As for men's gymnastics, the U.S., Japanese, and Russian teams remain China's strongest opponents in the team events. YANG Wei and CHEN Yibing 陈一冰 are two particularly promising Chinese athletes, and calm and stable gymnasts such as XIAO Qin 肖钦 and FENG Jing 冯敬 almost guarantee the Chinese team a gold medal in the men's pommel horse event. CHEN Yi Bing's hand-rings performance and Yang Wei's and LI Xiaopeng's 李小鹏 parallel bars skills are known throughout the world—and likely to bring home gold.

■ ZHANG LING 张玲

Martial Arts

中国金 武术

THE CHINESE REGARD MARTIAL ARTS (wushu) 武术 as the essence of traditional Chinese sport. Wushu originated in the fighting skills that were part of military training in ancient China. These fighting skills were divided into two categories during the late Song dynasty 宋 (960–1279). The first category was entertainment: Books in the Song dynasty recorded martial arts performances such as wrestling, fighting among two or more opponents, fighting with sticks, and archery in cities and temples. The second category was self-defense: People practiced martial arts skills in secret societies for self-defense or military purposes.

During the Ming dynasty 明 (1368–1644), the techniques and postures of martial arts developed. The basic element of martial arts in this period consisted of movements concentrated on different body and foot techniques. Movements such as jumping, rolling, and rotation were organized into series. These series were applied in physical training, attacking, and defending.

During the Qing dynasty 清 (1644–1912) martial arts were sometimes discouraged by the Manchu rulers. Wushu nonetheless remained popular and continued to develop: more than sixty kinds of fist positions were developed. Each fist position feature was a series and each series consisted of several movements. That's not all. During the centuries under Qing rule there were more than twenty kinds of Chinese boxing and over ten kinds of broadswordplay, such as long-handle broadsword, short-hilted broadsword, and Shaolin double swords. Wushu had a revival, too, in the middle of the nineteenth century as nationalistic feelings were roused by the Chinese defeat in the Opium War of 1842.

Modern Western sport had a tremendous impact on martial arts. At the end of the nineteenth century, some gymnastics specialists introduced European gymnastics to the marital arts. The establishment of the Jingwu Association (1910) and the Chinese Martial Arts Academy (1927) grew out of this transformation of Chinese martial arts. The "new martial arts" were a combination of traditional martial arts and modern gymnastics.

During the early 1950s, martial arts became a formal event in China's National Games. In addition martial arts tournaments were held periodically in both urban and suburban areas in China.

China's Wong Ting Hong fought Vietnam's Phan Quoc Vinh during the Wushu competition of the 15th Asian Games.

International Martial Arts

Since the beginning of the twentieth century, martial arts have been internationally acknowledged as a sport—even though many martial arts do not meet certain Western criteria for a sport, such as rules of play that allow a winner to be determined and a primary goal of victory—and they have become more and more popular around the world. International martial arts competitions have been frequently held since that time and some martial arts have developed new forms that are easier to judge in competition and are more closely aligned with Western conventions about what a sport is.

At the Eleventh Asian Games in 1990, martial arts became a formal event. One year later, the International Wushu (Martial Arts) Federation (IWUF) was established. The IWUF was accepted as a full member of the General Association of International Sports Federations in 1994 and was recognized by the International Olympic Committee (IOC) in 1999.

To date, the World Wushu Championships consist of the following categories: long-fist boxing, southern-style fist boxing, Taijiquan 太极拳, swordplay, spearplay, broadswordplay, staffplay, southern-style broadsword, southern-style staff Taiji swordplay, and duel. The categories of free fighting for men and women are 48 kilograms, 52 kilograms, 56 kilograms, 60 kilograms, 65 kilograms, 70 kilograms, 75 kilograms, 80 kilograms, 85 kilograms, and 90 kilograms. The World Martial Arts Championships have been held eight times between 1991 and 2005 (see table 1). The World Martial Arts and Free Combat Games have been held three times. In addition Europe and America have also organized a number of international martial arts championships.

TABLE 1 ■ World Martial Arts Championships (1991–2005)		
DATE	**PLACE**	**COUNTRIES/REGIONS PARTICIPATING**
1991 (10/12–18)	Beijing, China	41
1993 (11/21–27)	Kuala Lumpur, Malaysia	53
1995 (8/17–22)	Baltimore, MD, United States	56
1997 (11/3–8)	Rome, Italy	52
1999 (11/3–7)	Hong Kong, China	61
2001 (10/31–11/4)	Yerevan, Armenia	30
2003 (11/3–7)	Macao, China	58
2005 (12/9–14)	Hanoi, Vietnam	65

Martial arts have a deep history in China, and have branched out into competitive techniques and more peaceful practices.

Wushu Styles and Genres

Martial arts had developed a large number of different techniques, characteristics, styles, and genres by the end of the sixteenth century. However, there were no uniform criteria for different genres. Generally, the genres were sorted by category, section, religion, and tactical features.

The differences between *Neijia* boxing and *Waijia* boxing are their tactical features and drilling styles. The characteristics of *Neijia* boxing are staying still, attacking while defending, and taking advantage of the opponent's strength. The characteristics of *Waijia* boxing are bravery, promptness, exerting strength, attacking forward, and with anticipatory strategy. Each genre consists of several categories, named after its style or founder.

The Shaolin 少林 genre was named after its origin place—Shaolin Temple in Henan Province, the holy land of Buddhism. The characteristics of Shaolin are rigid attack, fast break, and moving back and forth flexibly. It features exercises for one person as well as combat between two or more fighters. Nowadays, Shaolin is the most influential genre in China. Hundreds of martial arts schools are named after it. Each year, many martial arts fans from foreign counties travel to Shaolin to study martial arts.

Wudang 武当 boxing originated in the Wudang Mountains in Hubei Province, and includes Taijiquan and Taiji swordplay. Taijiquan has existed since the Ming dynasty (1368–1683). There are five styles of Taijiquan: Chen 陈, Yang 杨, Wu (Jiquan) 吴, Wu (Yu-

Tai Chi

Tai chi is a Chinese martial art that is linked to the Daoist meditative, philosophical, and medical tradition. In China invalids and the elderly often perform the soft, slow movements of the popular Yang style of tai chi to strengthen the constitution and to promote longevity. Advocates say that disciplined daily practice enhances the quality and circulation of *chi* (vital energy) within the body, improves bodily functions, tones muscles, and engenders a relaxed mental attitude. The majority of the millions of people who practice tai chi in China and elsewhere do so for these benefits, but tai chi also is a premier martial art that can be practiced even late in life.

Chinese legendary history attributes tai chi's origin to Zhang Sanfeng, a Daoist expert who was canonized in 1459, but tai chi entered recorded history centuries later as a martial art practiced esoterically by the people of Chenjiagou in Henan Province. A form of the art was first demonstrated and taught in public in Beijing by Yang Luchan (1799–1872), who had learned it in Chenjiagou. Scholars say Yang accepted all challenges from the many Beijing martial arts masters, never to be defeated and never to seriously injure an opponent. He became known as "Yang the Invincible" and was appointed martial arts instructor to the imperial court. Yang Luchan publicly taught the slow and soft performance of a lengthy sequence of patterns, but he transmitted a much larger and more varied body of lore to his private students, a practice in keeping with martial arts tradition. Popular conceptions of tai chi as an only vaguely martial exercise, although beneficial to health and longevity, are drawn from Yang's and his successors' publicly taught form. This process of simplifying and softening has made tai chi accessible to many more people than would otherwise be the case. However, the more obviously martial and physically strenuous Chen style continues to be practiced, as do the derivative Sun, Wu, and Hao styles.

■ Michael G. Davis

hsiang) 武, and Sun 孙 style. Chen style and Yang style are the most popular styles among martial arts fans. They originated in Wen County in Henan Province. Taijiquan demands a relaxed mind and relaxed abdominal respiration. It can improve respiration, increase the metabolic rate, and help people keep fit. Because of its slow and soft motion, it can be applied as a healing exercise, especially for elders and people with illness.

Southern-style fist boxing was popular in southern China. It includes Shaolin-qiaoshou 少林桥手, Wuzuquan 五祖拳, Hequan 鹤拳, and Luohanquan 罗汉拳 in Fujian Province; Zhoujiaquan 周家拳, Tulongquan 屠龙拳, and Ciaoceda 小策打 in Guangxi Province; Hongjiaquan 洪家拳, Heihuquan 黑虎拳, and JInggangquan 金刚拳 in Zhejiang Province; Hongmenquan 洪门拳, Yumenquan 鱼门拳, and Kongmenquan 孔门拳 in Hubei Province; and Wujiaquan 巫家拳, Hongjiaquan 洪家拳, and Xuejiaquan 薛家拳 in Hunan Province.

Among all the styles of Southern-style fist boxing, Hongquan 洪拳 is the most

武
术

57

popular. Hongquan originated in simulation: It generally simulates animals' movements and combines attack and defense tactics with an artistic technique. It includes mantis-style boxing, monkey-style boxing, eagle-claw boxing, duck-style boxing, snake-style boxing, drunkard boxing, and eagle boxing.

Martial Arts and the Olympic Games

In 1936 China's martial arts team performed at the Berlin Olympics, receiving an ovation from the audience. This was the first time that the Chinese martial arts were demonstrated at the Olympic Games.

When Beijing successfully bid for the 2008 Olympic Games, there was a strong intention to include the martial arts in the 2008 Games. Things did not develop, however, as China intended. Denis Oswald, executive commissioner and president of the ASOIF (Association of Summer Olympic International Federations) indicated that the main consideration in determining whether martial arts would become an Olympic event was its popularity around the world, and it was determined that the martial arts were not as popular as other modern sports.

After several negotiations between the International Olympic Committee (IOC) and Beijing Organizing Committee for the Olympic Games (BOCOG), it was agreed that a special event entitled the "Beijing Olympic Wushu Competition" would be held during the 2008 Olympic Games. Fifteen sets of medals would be awarded with three categories for men's events — 56 kilograms, 70 kilograms, and 85 kilograms — and two categories for women's events — 52 kilograms and 60 kilograms.

The Chinese national martial arts team was established in 2006 specifically to compete in the Beijing Olympic Games. The team consists of forty-eight athletes specializing in martial arts routines and fifty athletes competing in the free-fighting events, including famous fighters such as LIU Hailong 柳海龙 and CHEN Long 陈龙.

In international competitions, Malaysia, Vietnam, Japan, Hong Kong, and Macao are strong competitors. For free fighting, Russia, France, Italy, Iran, and Philippines challenge the dominance of China. European athletes are capable in heavyweight categories.

■ TAN HUA 谭华

Swimming

中国金 游泳

SINCE PREHISTORIC TIMES PEOPLE have taken to swimming like, well, ducks to water. Drawings of swimmers dating from the Stone Age have been found in the Cave of Swimmers in Egypt and references to swimming appear from 2000 BCE in the *Epic of Gilgamesh*, the *Iliad*, the *Odyssey*, the Bible, and later in the Old English epic poem *Beowulf*.

In China swimming originated along the middle and lower reaches of the Huang (Yellow) River 黄河 where people developed the skills to move through and float on water. Swimming was not only a fundamental life skill but also a hunting and warring skill. The Chinese character for bath 浴 was found on oracle bones of the Shang dynasty 商 (1766–1045 BCE), and the word *swim* 泅 first appeared in annals of the Spring and Autumn period 春秋 (770–476 CE). Drawings on bronze ware from the period 475–221 BCE show scenes of people swimming in rivers. During

the Han dynasty 汉 (206 BCE–220 CE), nobles bathed in the royal aquatic pool. During the Tang dynasty 唐 (618–907 CE), a swimming pool called the "aquatic hall" 水殿 was built for nobles' use, and a ball game similar to modern water polo came into fashion there.

Whether a swimmer chose to wade, float, or dive, in ancient China swimming was considered a practical life skill rather than a recreational activity or sport.

Competitive Swimming in China

Competitive swimming—using mostly the breaststroke—began in Europe around 1800. England was the first modern society to develop swimming as a sport. Swimming came to China later in the nineteenth century and it wasn't long before competitions were organized in coastal cities such as Hong Kong, Guangzhou (Canton), Shanghai, Tianjing, and Qindao. In 1887 the first 25 × 25 meter swimming pool was built in Guangzhou. In 1906 the Victoria Swimming Federation of Hong Kong started to hold an annual sea competition. Participants were Chinese and European residents of Hong Kong.

At the beginning of the twentieth century, swimming associations, such as the famous Nanhua Association and Dongshan Aquatics in Guangdong Province, were established in some coastal cities. Additionally, the China Swimming Research Society was founded in 1924.

Swimming competitions took place in the whole of China. However, swimming teams from the south were more

competitive than those from the east and north. For example, in 1933 the Guangdong swimming team won the men's group gold medal, and the Hong Kong swimming team won the women's group gold medal at the Fifth National Games. YANG Xiuqiong 杨秀琼, a female swimmer from Hong Kong known as the "Chinese Mermaid," won all the gold medals in the women's individual events.

Olympic Swimming

In 1896, at the first modern Olympic Games, swimming was an Olympic event for men, with the 100-meter and 1,500-meter freestyle competitions being held in open water. As swimming gained popularity, more freestyle events were included, followed by the backstroke, butterfly, breaststroke, and individual medley. In 1908 the world swimming association, Fédération Internationale de Natation (FINA), was established.

For a variety of reasons women were excluded from swimming in the early years of the modern Olympic Games. In 1896, 1900, 1904, and 1906, women could not participate because the "Father of the Modern Olympics," Baron Pierre de Coubertin of France, shared a belief commonly held during the Victorian era that women were too frail to engage in competitive sport. It was not until the 1912 Olympics that women finally got their way and were allowed into the Olympic swimming competition.

While the first modern Olympic Games had only four swimming events, three of them freestyle, the Olympics now

Welcome Home: China's Young Foreign-born Athletes

His mother sits on a wicker chair on the viewing platform, remembering the icy mornings when as a girl she pounded length after interminable length of the same open-air pool.

She had gone on to enjoy success at the national level and then found her way to the United Kingdom. Her British husband gave their baby his copper-colored hair and Western complexion. The boy's eyes, though, were a constant reminder that he was also Asian.

Even when his parents were giving his age in months rather than years, the boy was at home in water. His infant doggy paddle early changed into a breast stroke. He and his parents had a long wait before he could finally enter competition at the age of nine.

On a visit back to her hometown in China, his mother takes the boy to her childhood pool. It is an open-air, lido-style 50-meter pool beside the new football stadium. Tower blocks surround it and clanging from construction sites carries over the pool.

Some of his mother's fellow squad members from the 1980s were now coaches, treading the deck they once looked up to. Each coach looks after a small elite squad with swimmers of different ages, a system designed to encourage competition between both coaches and their charges.

The boy emerges from the changing rooms, a slight white figure blinking in the afternoon light. When the other children arrive, their sun-browned bodies are in stark contrast with his.

The boy discovers that the pool isn't heated, not even from the sub-tropical sun. But he grits his teeth and ploughs his lone 50-meter furrows. His new coach, who had herself achieved national success and then come to this province in search of opportunity, finds a way to tell him what to do. When she has seen enough, the coach joins his mother on the platform. The boy is strong, she says, and has determination, but he wastes power through poor technique.

He trains in China for three hours a day. His skin gets closer in color to that of the others and he and the Chinese children lose their shyness and began to practice each other's languages. Some of the boys begin to see him as a rival.

The boy's parents invite the coach for a meal. In the restaurant she confides that she believes him to have Olympic potential. She would like him to return on a regular basis and she will process him into the Chinese system. The mother casts her mind back to the time she went to the embassy to add her baby to her passport. The clerk had laughed and said, "He doesn't look Chinese!" One day, she thought, perhaps he will have a choice.

In reality, China's foreign-born sons and daughters are returning. Swimming coaches in Chengdu and Beijing train China's foreign-born young swimmers every Easter and summer vacation. These children come from the United States and Canada and from the United Kingdom and other European countries to compete in sports where China is especially strong—swimming, table tennis, badminton, and gymnastics—and to take advantage of facilities and training methods unavailable in their birth countries. By the Olympics of 2020, these young athletes of the Chinese diaspora may show the world what they can achieve.

■ CRAIG GILL

---

have thirty-two swimming events: sixteen for men and sixteen for women. Each event has a maximum of eight swimmers. Preliminary heats in the 50-meter, 100-meter, and 200-meter events lead to semifinals and finals based on the fastest times. In relays and individual events of 400 meters or more, the eight fastest finishers in the preliminaries advance directly to the finals.

An Aquatic Powerhouse

The People's Republic of China (PRC) was founded on 1 October 1949. Swimming was considered a valuable sport by the new government. In 1952 the first national swimming championships took place in Guangzhou. Seven teams participated. After the championships the national swimming and diving squad, consisting of twenty-five male and thirteen female athletes, was formed.

In 1953 WU Chuanyu 吴传玉 won the gold medal in the men's 100-meter backstroke at the First International Youth Friendship Games. It was the first time that the red flag of the PRC was raised at an international sporting event. As a result of participation in the Games, the Chinese sports authority realized the importance of the modern training techniques. In 1954 fifteen young swimmers were sent to the Sport University in Budapest to study for one and one-half years. The Chinese swimmers learned fast. Between 1957 and 1960 the world record in the men's 100-meter breaststroke was broken five times by QI Lieyun 戚烈云, MU Xiangxiong 穆祥雄, and MO Guoxiong 莫国雄.

In order to select and train elite swimmers at home, in 1955 three elite swimming schools were founded, one each in Beijing, Tianjing, and Shanghai. Boys and girls with swimming talent alternated a half day of study with a half day of training in these schools. By 1965 the number of such schools reached 1,800 with 150,000 young swimmers and 3,000 full-time coaches. After several years of hard training many young swimmers grew into stars.

During the initial years of the Cultural Revolution (1966–1976) competitive sports were banned. However, China rejoined the Asian Games in 1974 and participated in the swimming competitions at the Seventh (1974) and Eighth (1978) Asian Games. Despite their training program Chinese swimmers lagged behind athletes from other Asian countries, including Japan, Korea, Singapore, and the Philippines.

In 1979 China renewed its seat in FINA. In 1983 China's International Invitational Swimming Tournament took place in Guangxi Province. It was the first time in Chinese sports history that world-class swimmers from all over the world swam in China.

China participated in the Twenty-third Olympic Games in Los Angeles in 1984 after an absence from the Olympics of over twenty years. Nineteen swimmers from China competed, but none of them finished among the top twenty swimmers in the world. After the Games the coach of the German Democratic Republic's (East Germany's) swimming team was invited to become the coach of the Chinese national swimming team. He introduced altitude training to Chinese swimmers for the first time.

In 1982 China won three gold medals at the Ninth Asian Games. It was the first time that the Chinese swimming team won gold medals at these games. However, Japan continued to dominate Asian swimming, and it was not until the Eleventh Asian Games in Beijing in 1990 that China won twenty-three gold medals in swimming and defeated Japan.

In 1988 the third Asian Swimming Championships were held in Guangzhou. Yang Wenyi clocked the world's best time of 25.28 seconds for the women's 50-meter freestyle. That was only world record in swimming held by an Asian at the time.

In 1990 the eleventh Asian Games were held in Beijing. Some Chinese swimmers used a tactic called "even speed." The new tactic is more efficient than the traditional "fast, fast, fast," "fast-slow," and "slow-fast" tactics. Consequently, Zhuang Yong won gold medals in the women's 100-meter and 200-meter freestyle, the 4 × 100-meter freestyle relay, and the 4 × 100-meter medley; Lin Li won the gold medal in the women's 200-meter medley. Five Chinese became world-class swimmers.

One year later, at the sixth FINA World Championships, China won nine medals: four gold, four silver, and one bronze. At the Twenty-fifth Olympic Games in Barcelona in 1992, China won four gold medals (see table 1) and five silver medals and broke two world records. At the seventh FINA World Championships in 1994, China won twelve gold medals and broke five world records.

In the late 1990s Chinese swimming suffered doping scandals that seriously damaged China's reputation in the sports field. At the beginning of the twenty-first century, China has made progress in the fight against doping in sport, including swimming, announcing that it planned to conduct more doping tests at the Beijing Olympic Games than have been conducted at any other

TABLE 1 ■ China's Olympic Gold Medals in Individual Swimming Events			
YEAR	CITY	ATHLETE	EVENT
2004	Athens	Luo Xuejuan	Women's 100-meter breaststroke
1992	Barcelona	Zhuang Yong	Women's 100-meter freestyle
1992	Barcelona	Qian Hong	Women's 100-meter butterfly
1992	Barcelona	Lin Li	Women's 200-meter individual medley
1992	Barcelona	Yang Wenyi	Women's 50-meter freestyle
1996	Atlanta	Le Jingyi	Women's 100-meter freestyle

Source: Fédération Internationale de Natation.

Xuejuan Luo won gold in the 100-meter breaststroke at the 2004 Olympics.

Games — working around the clock and conducting 4,500 doping tests during the Games.

Primed to Win

The National Aquatics Center (NAC) provides a twenty-first-century venue for the swimming events of the Twenty-ninth Olympic Games in Beijing, held between 9 and 21 August 2008. Zhang Yadong, the head coach of the Chinese swimming squad, has primed his swimmers to swim for gold — and silver and bronze medals, too.

The Chinese male swimmers have trained with confidence. WU Peng 吴鹏, the silver medalist in the men's 200-meter butterfly at the eleventh FINA World Championships in 2005 and the gold medalist in the men's 200-meter butterfly at the Asian Games

in Doha in 2006, is regarded as the most promising male swimmer who will compete at the Beijing Olympics. OUYANG Kunpeng 欧阳鲲鹏, China's number one backstroker and the Asian record-holder in the 50-meter and 100-meter backstroke events, is also expected to win a medal in 2008.

China's female swimmers gave their best-ever performances at the FINA World Short Course Championships in

2006, winning four gold medals and one silver. QI Hui 齐晖, the twenty-two-year-old veteran swimmer, who set the world record in 2002 and won three gold medals at the FINA World Short Course Championships in 2006, after failing to win a medal at the Olympics in 2004, was eager give her best performance in 2008 in breaststroke and individual medley events. The young swimmer WANG Qun 王群 shot to fame by defeating China's breast-stroke star Luo Xuejuan in the 100-meter event at the East Asian Games in Macao in 2005. She has given consis-tent performances in recent interna-tional competitions, winning a silver medal at the FINA Swimming World Cup in Berlin in 2006.

Nevertheless, judging from the past Olympic swimming results, China's main rivals in 2008 will be the United States and Australia (see tables 2–4). However, because the five-time Olym-pic champion Ian Thorpe retired from competitive swimming in 2006, Aus-tralia's chance of beating the United States seems slim.

Michael Phelps, the first American to win eight medals in one Olympics at the 2004 Olympics in Athens, has been a likely flashpoint in swimming events

RANK	COUNTRY	GOLD	SILVER	BRONZE	TOTAL
1	United States	12	9	7	28
2	Australia	7	5	3	15
3	Japan	3	1	4	8
4	Holland	2	3	2	7
5	Ukraine	2	0	1	3
6	France	1	2	3	6

TABLE 2 ■ 2004 Olympics Swimming Medal Tally

Source: Fédération Internationale de Natation.

TABLE 3 ■ **2000 Olympics Swimming Medal Tally**

RANK	COUNTRY	GOLD	SILVER	BRONZE	TOTAL
1	United States	13	8	10	31
2	Australia	5	12	4	21
3	Holland	5	1	2	8
4	Italy	3	1	2	6
5	Ukraine	2	2	0	4
6	Romania	2	1	1	4

Source: Fédération Internationale de Natation.

in Beijing in 2008, expected to win the men's 100-meter and 200-meter butterfly, the 200-meter freestyle, the 200-meter and 400-meter medley, the 4 × 100-meter and the 4 × 200-meter freestyle relay, and the 4 × 100-meter medley relay. Phelps's teammate, Aaron Peirsol, from California, is expected to win the backstroke events in 2008. He won three gold medals in the men's 100-meter and 200-meter backstroke and the 400-meter medley relay at the Olympic Games in Athens in 2004 and broke the 200-meter backstroke world record at the Montreal World Championships in Canada in 2006.

China's Modern Mermaids (and Mermen)

LUO Xuejuan 罗雪娟 was born in 1984 in Hangzhou. She was called the "queen of the breaststroke." She began swimming at the age of seven. In 1996 Luo joined the Zhejiang provincial swimming team. She then represented China at the 2004 Athens Olympic Games and won a gold medal in the 100-meter breaststroke, setting a new Olympic record of 1 minute 6.64 seconds. She was the only Chinese swimmer to win a gold medal at Athens. At the 2001 and 2003 World

Championships, she won the world championship in the 50-meter breaststroke. As part of the team's victory in the 4 × 100-meter medley relay in the 2003 World Championship, she set the record for the fastest women's breaststroke relay split in history. She retired from competitive swimming in 2007.

ZHUANG Yong 庄泳 was born in 1972 in Shanghai. She is one of the best female swimmers in China. Like Luo she began her swimming training at the age of seven. She joined the Shanghai swimming team at the age of thirteen. At the 1988 Seoul Olympics, Zhuang won a silver medal in the women's 100-meter freestyle. In 1989 she won the 100-meter freestyle at the Pan Pacific Swimming Championships. In

1990 Zhuang swept the gold medals in the women's 100-meter and 200-meter freestyle, the 4 × 100-meter freestyle relay, and the 4 × 100-meter medley relay at the Asian Games in Beijing. In 1991 she won a gold medal in the women's 50-meter freestyle and silver in the women's 100-meter freestyle at the FINA World Swimming Championships. At the 1992 Olympics in Barcelona, Zhuang won a gold in the women's 100-meter freestyle, China's first gold medal in an Olympic swimming event. She also won two silver medals in the women's 50-meter freestyle and the 4 × 100-meter freestyle relay in Barcelona.

YANG Wenyi 杨文意 was born in 1972 in Shanghai. She began her training in swimming at the Shanghai Sports Club in 1978 and broke national records for different age groups eighteen times at the beginning of the 1980s. She was selected as a member of the Shanghai swimming team in 1984 and joined the national team two years later. She won a gold medal in the 50-meter freestyle at the 1992 Olympics in Barcelona.

TABLE 4 ■ **Most Capable Gold Medal Competitors in the 2008 Olympics**

EVENT	MALE ATHLETE	FEMALE ATHLETE
Medley	Michael Phelps (United States)	Yana Klochkova (Ukraine) Katie Hoff (United States)
Freestyle	Michael Phelps (United States) Roland Schoeman (South Africa) Crocker Ian (United States)	Jodie Henry (Australia) Lisbeth Lenton (Australia)
Breaststroke	Kosuke Kitajima (Japan) Brooke Hanson (Australia)	Leisel Jones (Australia)
Backstroke	Aaron Peirsol (United States)	Natalie Coughlin (United States)
Butterfly	Michael Phelps (United States) Ian Crocker (United States)	Schipper Jessicah (Australia) Lisbeth Lenton (Australia)

Source: Authors' predictions.

游泳

The "Chinese Mermaid"

In the 1930s YANG Xiuqiong was widely known inside and outside China as the "Chinese mermaid." A national and international champion swimmer in several events, she was a popular role model for many women in the Nationalist Chinese republic.

Yang came from a peasant family in Yangwua village, Dongwan county, Guangdong Province on the mainland. The village was in a region of rivers and lakes, and children learned to swim as soon as they could walk. Yang was no exception. She swam when she was only two years old. When she was ten years old her father was employed as a lifeguard at the swimming pool of the Nanhua Sports Association in Hong Kong. Under his supervision, Yang swam every day and her swimming improved rapidly.

Yang was a member of the Hong Kong swimming team when the Fifth National Games took place in October 1933 at Nanjing, the capital of the Nationalist government. She broke four national records and won five gold medals. CHU Minyi, the Minister of the Administration Council of the Nationalist government and the chief organizer of the Games, imitated an ancient Olympic tradition by driving her around Nanjing in a chariot. Yang's pictures and stories filled newspapers, magazines, posters, and illustrations. She became a national hero.

When the Sixth National Games were held at Shanghai in October 1935, Yang broke four national swimming records and won two gold medals. During her appearance, the price of a ticket increased twentyfold. If she did not appear in an event spectators asked for a refund. As a matter of course, she was selected as a member of China's 1936 Olympic team. Yang's outstanding performances made the Chinese proud, while her beauty and her gentle demeanor made her a focus of male desire. Her success in sport helped to construct a new femininity—fit and independent—which was radically different from the fragile and dependent women of the past. Yang was the perfect image of a modern woman for Nationalist China. After she married in 1937, Yang retired from swimming.

■ FAN HONG AND YAN XUENING

熊神種各之後泳瓊秀楊

One of the most famous Chinese swimmers of the 1930s, Yang Xiuqiong changed the image of women in China.

CHEN Yunpeng 陈运鹏 was born in 1935. He devoted his life to Chinese swimming. He was the national champion in 100-meter butterfly and 200-meter butterfly in the late 1950s and early 1960s. He became a coach of the Chinese national swimming team in 1965 and was the head coach from 1981 to 1995. Under his coaching the Chinese team won four gold and five silver medals in the Twenty-fifth Olympic Games Barcelona in 1992. He retired in 1995 and then became a member of the World Swimming Coaches Association in 1998.

ZHANG Yadong 张亚东 was born in Zhejiang Province in 1964. He graduated from Beijing Sports University in the mid-1980s. He was appointed as the head coach of the Chinese national swimming squad after the Olympic Games in Sydney in 2000. He became famous when Luo Xuejuan, under his coaching, became a world champion in 2001 and 2003 and an Olympic gold medalist in 2004.

■ FAN WEI 樊维 AND LU ZHOUXIANG 吕洲翔

Table Tennis
中国金 乒乓球

IN 1904 WANG DAOPING 王道平, manager of a stationery shop in Shanghai, bought equipment from Japan for a new indoor game. He demonstrated the game—a kind of tennis—in order to sell the tables, nets, balls, and rackets. This was the beginning of table tennis in China.

Though table tennis is widely associated with Asian nations today, Japanese and Chinese dominance in the sport did not become obvious until the 1950s when they began winning tournaments using the supposedly outdated penhold grip (European players had moved on to the shakehand grip). But the game originated on the other side of the globe. At a house party somewhere in Victorian England—where parlor games were an important part of social life—someone decided to turn the dining room table into a miniature version of the traditional lawn tennis court. The players are said to have used a line of books to serve as the net.

They carved a ball from a champagne cork, and cut rackets from empty cigar boxes and later from parchment paper stretched around a frame.

Evolution of "Flim-flam"

In the beginning the game was called "gossima," "flim-flam," or "ping-pong." The words, as can be assumed, were derived from the sound that the ball made when hit back and forth on the table and rackets. In 1901 English manufacturer J. Jaques & Son registered one of the names for table tennis—Ping-Pong—and sold this trademark to the Parker Brothers in the United States.

During the early 1900s, the table tennis racket had a long handle and a pear-shaped hitting surface, making it look like a small-size tennis racket. Around the turn of the twentieth century, the sport underwent a few changes in England as a celluloid ball and a wooden paddle with a pimpled rubber surface were introduced—the type of equipment that Mr. Wang introduced to his customers in Shanghai in 1904.

The rules and equipment have changed drastically as table tennis has achieved more widespread popularity and then became an organized competitive sport.

In 1926 the International Table Tennis Federation (ITTF) was founded in Berlin by England, Sweden, Hungary, India, Denmark, Germany, Czechoslovakia, Austria, and Wales. A year later, the ITTF established the first official world championship and table tennis began to be adopted in Japan and other Asian countries as a serious competitive sport, one in which they have excelled. The Japanese dominated the sport in

A coach instructs players in proper service technique.

Ping-Pong Diplomacy: The "Ping" Heard Round the World

Eight years before China rejoined the International Olympic Committee in 1979, the sound of a small hollow plastic ball hitting a green table — the "ping heard round the world," as *Time* magazine put it — signaled a turning point in U.S.-China relations, and the beginning of China's re-opening to the rest of the world.

That famous "ping" sounded in April 1971, when the U.S. table tennis team, visiting Nagoya, Japan, for the World Table Tennis Championship, was invited to visit the People's Republic of China and given permission to go by the U.S. government, which had broken relations twenty-two years earlier. While the invitation was ostensibly a spontaneous gesture by lively young athletes — who exchanged gifts, in Chinese fashion, that included a T-shirt with a red-white-and-blue peace emblem and the words "Let It Be" — historians now agree that it was quietly countenanced by the Chinese government.

The U.S. team's visit to China took place three months later, in July, and Chinese Premier ZHOU Enlai was quoted as saying, "Never before in history has a sport been used so effectively as a tool of international diplomacy."

While the exchange was spontaneous, it came about during a period of changing alliances. After the Soviet invasion of Czechoslovakia in 1968, MAO Zedong and Zhou Enlai, seeing the USSR was a more potent threat than the United States, decided that improved relations with the United States would increase China's international security as well as stature. Meanwhile, President Richard M. Nixon believed that ties with the People's Republic would counterbalance the Soviet Union, improve Nixon's own political standing at home, and improve the United States' position in the Vietnam War. In 1970, the Chinese offered to arrange a high-level meeting, and that offer led eventually to national security adviser Henry A. Kissinger's visit to Beijing in July 1971.

In any event, it was the young American and Chinese table tennis players, many of them teenagers, who changed the way ordinary people in their countries thought about so-called Communist China and the "decadent, imperialistic" United States. The team was treated royally. According to U.S. team member Tim Boggan, they were sometimes offered five meals a day: "no Ming emperor was treated so well." This "people-to-people" exchange, which was extolled by the press and by both governments, provided President Nixon with a backdrop for the major diplomatic shift that was in progress. During the team's visit, the United States announced the end of a twenty-year trade embargo against the People's Republic, Nixon himself went to Beijing from 20 to 27 February 1972, the first visit by an American president to China.

Richard Solomon, now president of the United States Institute of Peace and then deputy assistant secretary of state for East Asian affairs. explains, "Ping-Pong showed how sports can be a political signaling device, a way to reach out to other nations without a full commitment from the government."

Naturally, the Americans reciprocated by inviting their Chinese opponents to visit the United States. In this case, the National Committee on U.S.-China Relations (NCUSCR) stepped in to organize, along with the U.S. Table Tennis Association, what became a huge media event, broadcast by major news outlets and publicized in magazines as diverse as *Life* and *Seventeen*. The teams traveled on one charter plane; another plane was needed for reporters and camera people. The theme was "friendship first, competition second," and although the Chinese players completely dominated the matches, somehow U.S. players managed to win surprise victories when the tour landed in their hometowns. Ticket prices were kept very low so everyone could attend — an approach the 2008 Olympics organizers also took in order to ensure that Chinese people would see the Games for themselves.

The Chinese ping-pong players were able, engaging representatives of their country — which was then referred to by many Americans as "Red China." The team's escorts, some of whom were undoubtedly intelligence officers, let all the matches continue in spite of some rowdy protests that

---

the 1950s and 1960s. The Chinese had their turn in the 1960s and 1970s. As table tennis became an Olympic event in the 1980s, other nations such as

Sweden and South Korea have also joined the game's top ranks, but in many people's minds Ping-Pong remains strongly associated with China.

Ping-Pong's Early Days

In 1925, before the international association was founded, several table tennis competitions took place in Shanghai.

President Richard Nixon, who led the effort to renew U.S. ties with China, meets with the Chinese Ping-Pong team.

they clearly would have liked to have seen stopped.

Throughout the 1980s, there were many athletic exchanges that introduced Chinese athletes to huge U.S. audiences across the country, as well as trips to China by U.S. athletes, organized by the National Committee on U.S.-China Relations along with American athletic associations and their Chinese counterparts — all in the spirit of "friendship before competition."

Instead of operating at the elite policy or academic level, efforts like Ping-Pong diplomacy bring international relations into venues that attract ordinary citizens and create interest in the popular media. Indeed, beyond gold medals, the Olympics for China are about the kind of people-to-people relationship building that was at the center of Ping-Pong diplomacy. Before the Beijing Olympics, CHEN Haosu, president of the Chinese People's Association for

Friendship with Foreign Countries (CPAFFC), was quoted in the Chinese press as saying, "Meetings between leaders have to be reinforced by people-to-people contacts, which are the best way to rid mutual suspicion and keep the diplomatic momentum moving forward." As Chen put it, these efforts are, "about the attraction of your culture and the image you leave in the hearts of foreigners."

■ KAREN CHRISTENSEN

Two years later, the Chinese national team participated in the Eighth Far Eastern Championship Games in Shanghai but failed to win any medals.

Between 1937 and 1949 development of table tennis in China slowed down its pace because of World War II and the Chinese Civil War. Only after the founding of the People's Republic of China (PRC) in 1949 did table tennis enjoy a rebirth. In 1952 the first National Table Tennis Championships took place in Beijing, where sixty-two athletes competed for the medals. In the same year the Chinese National Table Tennis Federation became an official member of the ITTF, beginning a new era for Chinese table tennis.

The National Table Tennis Team was founded in 1953 and soon after participated in the World Table Tennis Championships. In 1959 Chinese player RONG Guotuan 容国团 won the men's singles gold medal at the World Table Tennis Championships in Dortmund, West Germany. This achievement was a landmark in Chinese table tennis history. Two years later, at the World Table Tennis Championships in Beijing, China swept the gold medals in the men's singles, women's singles, and men's team events. By 2002, its fiftieth anniversary, the Chinese National Table Tennis Team had won 125 world championship titles, sweeping all the table tennis gold medals three times at the Table Tennis World Cups and twice at the Olympic Games.

In 1995 the Chinese Professional Table Tennis League was established. This nationwide league was divided into three divisions: Division 1 was the Super League. Division 2 was Jia A, and Division 3 was Jia B (jia 甲 being a Chinese word for "top" or "first"). The Super League consists of the best players in China. The Chinese Professional Table Tennis League has attracted countless table tennis fans and has played an important role in the promotion of both the athletic sport and sport for all in China.

Ping-Pong's Importance

Perhaps "Ping-Pong diplomacy" can explain why table tennis held such an important place in China during the 1970s. The era of Ping-Pong diplomacy 乒乓外交 began in 1971 when the United States table tennis team, which was participating in the Thirty-first World Table Tennis Championships in Nagoya, Japan, received an invitation from the Chinese team to visit the People's Republic of China. MAO Zedong, chairman of China's Communist Party, believed that by opening a door to the United States, China could put its hostile neighbors, notably the U.S.S.R., on notice about a possible shift in alliances. The United States welcomed the opportunity. President Richard Nixon secretly sent Secretary of State Henry Kissinger to Beijing to arrange a presidential visit to China. Nixon's journey seven months later, in February 1972, became one of the most important events in U.S. postwar history. "Never before in history has a sport been used so effectively as a tool of international diplomacy," said Chinese premier ZHOU Enlai. For Nixon it was "the week that changed the world."

Olympic Leaders

In terms of international competition, table tennis is the sport that has never disappointed the Chinese. China has dominated all major table tennis competitions and shows no signs of letting up. Since 1988 China has won sixteen Olympic gold medals out of twenty (see table 1). As the defending champions, Chinese players have been well studied by all their rivals around the world. In 2008 they must stay cautious and play their own game, although there seem to be no rivals capable enough to challenge the dominance of China (see table 2).

TABLE 1 ■ Medal Tally in Olympic Table Tennis Events, 1988–2004				
YEAR	HOST CITY	GOLD	SILVER	BRONZE
1988	Seoul	2 (out of 4)	2	1
1992	Barcelona	3 (out of 4)	2	1
1996	Atlanta	4 (out of 4)	3	1
2000	Sydney	4 (out of 4)	3	1
2004	Athens	3 (out of 4)	1	2

Source: International Olympic Committee's website.

TABLE 2 ■ ITTF Top Ten Rankings (2007)		
RANK	NAME	COUNTRY
■ Top Men		
1	Ma Lin	China
2	Wang Liqin	China
3	Boll, Timo	Germany
4	Wang Hao	China
5	Oh Sang Eun	Korea
6	Samsonov, Vladimir	Belarus
7	Chen Qi	China
8	Ma Long	China
9	Ryu Seung Min	Korea
10	Hao Shuai	China
■ Top Women		
1	Zhang Yining	China
2	Wang Nan	China
3	Guo Yan	China
4	Guo Yue	China
5	Li Xiaoxia	China
6	Tie Yana	Hong Kong
7	Li Jia Wei	Singapore
8	Wang Yue Gu	Singapore
9	Niu Jianfeng	China
10	Jiang Huajun	Hong Kong

Source: International Table Tennis Federation.

In the men's singles, German player Timo Boll may be a rival to China's Ma Lin and Wang Liqin. In the women's singles, the final competition would be between Wang Nan and Zhang Yining.

The ITTF announced plans to replace the doubles events with the team competitions at the 2008 Olympics to make the matches more exciting — and perhaps to set some limits on the table tennis superpower, China.

Paddle Powerhouses

DENG Yaping 邓亚萍 (b. 1973), the "Table Tennis Queen," is considered to be one of the best female table tennis players in the world. She won four Olympic gold medals and was a participant, individually or as a team member, in ten World Table Tennis Championships titles. Between 1991 and 1998 she was ranked the number one woman player in the world. After retirement in 1998, Deng Yaping enrolled in Tsinghua University in Beijing. After graduating from Tsinghua, she went to study for her master's degree in Loughborough University in England. She is now studying for her PhD degree at Cambridge University. She is a member of the International Olympic Committee Athletes Commission and the deputy head of the Olympic Village in Beijing.

KONG Linghui 孔令辉 (b. 1975) is one of the outstanding male players in Chinese table tennis history. In 1995 he won a gold medal in the men's singles competition at the Table Tennis World Cup in France. At the 1996 Olympics in Atlanta, Kong claimed men's doubles gold with teammate LIU Guoliang. At the 1997 World Table Tennis Championships in Manchester, England, Kong was the champion in the men's doubles competition, again teamed with Liu Guoliang. In 2000 Kong claimed the gold in the men's singles and the silver

Table tennis remains one of China's dominant sports.

in the men's doubles events at the Sydney Olympic Games. He is one of the three players in the world to complete a table tennis grand slam by winning the World Table Tennis Championships, the Table Tennis World Cup, and the Olympic singles titles.

WANG Liqin 王励勤 (b. 1978) joined the national team in 1993 when he was only fifteen years old. Wang's style is probably best described as a strong forehand and backhand looper. His above-average height allows him additional leverage for acceleration and momentum, creating more powerful shots. Wang won his first World Table Tennis Championships in Osaka, Japan, in 2001. In 2005 he again became the champion at the World Table Tennis Championships in Shanghai, China. Wang won the gold medal in doubles at the 2000 Olympics in Sydney and the bronze medal in singles at the 2004 Olympics in Athens. For most of the year in 2005, 2006, and 2007, he was ranked number one among the world's male table tennis players.

WANG Nan 王楠 (b. 1978) began to play table tennis when she was seven years old. Her particular skills are her ability to change the placement of the ball during rallies and her loop drive as well as her notable speed. In 1994 Nan won the women's singles at the Sweden Table Tennis Open. The next year she was selected for the national team and began to represent China at important competitions, such as the World Table Tennis Championships, the Women's Table Tennis World Cup, and the Olympic Games. From 1997 to 1998, she won the championships in women's singles at the Women's Table Tennis World Cup twice as well as the China Open. At the 1998 Asian Games in Bangkok, Wang won all four gold medals (singles, doubles, mixed doubles, and women teams). At the 2000 Olympics in Sydney, she won two gold medals in singles and doubles. Her record made her a grand slam champion. In the 2004 Olympic Games, she failed to retain her singles crown but won the women's doubles with Zhang Yining.

ZHANG Yining 张怡宁 (b. 1981) is China's most promising player in women's singles competion. Zhang participated in the 2004 Olympics in Athens and won gold in both singles and doubles with partner Wang Nan. In May 2007 Zhang was ranked number one in the ITTF in both women's singles and women's doubles.

LIU Guoliang 刘国梁 (b. 1976) started playing table tennis at the age of six. He joined the national team in 1991. In 1994 Liu Guoliang won the gold medal in the men's singles at the Table Tennis World Cup. Two years later, he won the gold medal in the men's singles and men's doubles (with Kong Linghui) at the Atlanta Olympics. Liu Guoliang is China's first table tennis player to make a clean sweep of all titles at major world tournaments, including the World Table Tennis Championships, Table Tennis World Cup and the Olympic Games. After retirement in 2002, Liu became a coach of the national men's team and a student at Shanghai Jiao Tong University. He was appointed the director of the coaching and research group as well as the head coach of the national men's team in 2003.

CAI Zhenhua 蔡振华 (b. 1961) is generally considered one of the best coaches that China has ever produced. Cai was an international player in the 1970s. He won his first international title at age of twenty and later finished first in three other world-class competitions before becoming a coach of the Chinese national team at the age of twenty-four. Under Cai's successful guidance, the Chinese table tennis team swept the board, taking the gold medals in the men's, women's and mixed events at the world championships and the Olympics in the 1990s and early twenty-first century.

■ HU Xiaoming 胡小明

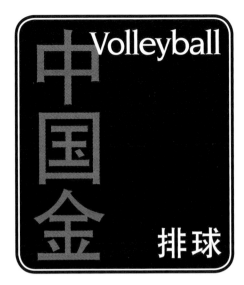

VOLLEYBALL—LIKE ITS COUSIN, basketball—was introduced in China just years after being created in Massachusetts. The reason is simple: both were the inspiration of physical education instructors at the Young Men's Christian Association (YMCA), an international organization that had become established in a number of major Chinese cities.

William G. Morgan, the director of physical education at the YMCA in Holyoke, Massachusetts, invented volleyball (which he called "Mintonette") in 1895. His intention was to create a simple, enjoyable indoor winter game to supplement what was otherwise an austere round of gymnastics-based physical conditioning exercises that were the lot of physical education students during the cold New England winter. Volleyball spread quickly because it featured clear and intuitively appealing goals.

Players hit the ball back and forth across the court net to keep the ball from touching the ground. It first spread through the United States, arrived in Asia in 1900, and reached China in 1905. Only later, in 1917, did it get to Europe, where it grew in popularity throughout the 1920s, particularly in France.

The Chinese volleyball team participated in the Far Eastern Championship Games in the 1920s and 1930s and was one of the strongest teams in Asia. The Soviets, too, became interested in volleyball, and the Soviets and their client states were to become, with Japan, major competitive players.

During World War II the number of players on a side decreased from sixteen or nineteen to six. After the war Europeans and Americans dominated international volleyball. Later Japanese women's volleyball created the "Japanese legend" under the coaching of Hirofumi Daimatsu, who was referred to as the "demon coach" for his strict discipline and the unrelenting conditioning drills that he put his players through. Although Japanese female volleyball players were physically small, they won gold medals in the 1962 World Women's Volleyball Championship and the 1964 Olympic Games with their flexibility, indomitable spirit, and special style. They dominated world women's volleyball for more than ten years.

Volleyball's Global Appeal

With the establishment of its governing body, the Fédération Internationale de Volleyball (FIVB), in 1947, volleyball became an organized international sport. The first World Men's Volleyball Championship was staged in 1947, and the first World Women's Volleyball Championship in 1952, but it wasn't until 1964 that volleyball became an official

Beach Volleyball Takes Hold

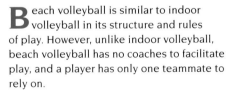

Beach volleyball is similar to indoor volleyball in its structure and rules of play. However, unlike indoor volleyball, beach volleyball has no coaches to facilitate play, and a player has only one teammate to rely on.

Beach volleyball—an Olympic sport since 1994—began during the 1920s on the beaches of southern California and Europe. By the 1950s and 1960s tournaments were held in the United States, Brazil, Canada, and France, and in other parts of Europe. During the 1960s President John F. Kennedy attended the first official beach volleyball event at Sorrento Beach in Los Angeles. During the 1990s the Federation Internationale de Volleyball (FIVB), with 214 national federations, began to govern international beach volleyball and volleyball. The FIVB World Tour, formerly known as the "World Championship Series," is the official international tour. The World Tour grew quickly since it began in 1992, and the groundwork for this growth was laid in the sands of sunny southern California.

■ KRISTINE DRAKICH

A member of China's men's volleyball team attempts to get the ball past two defenders.

Olympic event in the Eighteenth Olympic Games at Tokyo.

Volleyball, soccer, and basketball are the top three ball games in the world. As the only net sport of the three, volleyball is thought to have more of a sense of cooperation and even serenity, compared with intense rivalry of soccer and basketball. By 1997 the FIVB had become the biggest single sport organization, with members from more than 200 countries and regions, and the number of volleyball participants exceeding 150 million. Volleyball has become a popular sport with more than 800 million regular spectators, second only to soccer. (The color of the ball has changed from the original white to a vivid combination of blue, yellow, and white, perhaps giving those spectators a better view of the action.)

Today women's volleyball teams throughout the world embrace a variety of techniques and playing styles. Asian women's volleyball, represented by the Chinese and Japanese teams, is best known for its speed. Teams work around advantages their opponents might have in height and strength and defeat them with quick and flexible attacks. European women's volleyball, represented by the Russian team, generally adopts a traditional system of offense, noted for its high tosses and high spikes. Because the players are tall and physically strong, strong attacks are the easiest way to gain points. Women's volleyball in the Americas, represented by the Brazilian team, adopts an overall tactic combining Asian and European characteristics, with an emphasis on strong attacks assisted by their quickness. The combination of, and confrontation between, different volleyball techniques makes the competitions exciting for spectators.

Men's volleyball games may be less nuanced but the strength of men players and the fast pace of the game also appeal to spectators. In men's volleyball the European and U.S. teams enjoy absolute supremacy.

Volleyball in China

In 1950 the Chinese team participated in a six-player-based international game for the first time. The team adapted the "quick spike" tactic from the former nine-player game to the new six-player game and invented a set of quick-attack cloak tactics centered on these quick spikes. The Chinese tactic of quick offense created a new style in world volleyball, mainly relying on strong-attack and individual-attack tactics. During the 1956 Paris Volleyball World Championship, the Chinese men's volleyball team created a furor with its quick spikes, which were dubbed "acrobatic tactics." Later, as volleyball rules changed, the Chinese men's volleyball team created a technique of blocking that resembled the action of "putting on a cap" and a technique of spiking called the "open spike." The team's new tactics played

an important role in promoting the development of world volleyball.

In 1964 Chinese Prime Minister ZHOU Enlai 周恩来 invited Japanese coach Hirofumi Daimatsu to China to train the Chinese national teams for one month, during which time the Chinese learned techniques used in Japan.

When the Third World Cup Volleyball Tournament was held in Tokyo in 1981, the Chinese women's volleyball team, with its flexible offense and strong defense, was called the "Wall of the Tian'anmen" and became the champion. This victory began an upsurge of interest in volleyball in China and ushered in a new "Chinese era" in world volleyball. Under the guidance of YUAN Weimin 袁伟民 and headed by the ace spiker LANG Ping 朗平, the Chinese women's volleyball team swept four more world titles: the 1982 World Women's Volleyball Championship, 1984 Los Angeles Olympic Games, 1985 World Cup Volleyball Tournament, and 1986 World Women's Volleyball Championship.

During the 1980s the Chinese women's volleyball team's spirit and success in winning five world titles in succession were the best example of the strong will of the Chinese people to excel and build their country. On 20 March 1981, at a preliminary match of the Asian district for the World Cup Volleyball Tournament, the Chinese men's volleyball team turned the tables on its opponent, beating the South Korean team 3–2, and qualified for the World Cup Volleyball Tournament matches. On hearing the good news, students of Beijing University became so excited

that they marched to the Gate of the Heavenly Peace, during which they shouted the slogan, "Let's unite and develop China!" The victories in volleyball games helped push forward China's opening up to the world and inspired the Chinese to conduct their reforms with more confidence.

During the late 1980s and into the 1990s, the Chinese men's and women's volleyball teams suffered one setback after another and even lost their dominant positions in the Asian Games. In 1996 the professional league system was introduced into volleyball games in China, which turned out to be helpful in reversing the downward trend. The Chinese women's volleyball team finished second in the 1996 Atlanta Olympic Games and first in the 2003 World Cup Volleyball Tournament, then won the gold medal in the 2004 Athens Olympic Games with a win over its strong Russian opponent.

The Chinese men's volleyball team experienced similar success, reclaiming the gold medal in the 1997 Asian Volleyball Championship. Both the Chinese men's and women's volleyball teams won the Asian Games in 1998.

Volleyball Resurgence

The history of the Chinese women's volleyball team in the twentieth century and the success of the current team have once again aroused the Chinese people's enthusiasm for the sport. In international competitions, there is the exciting prospect of Lang Ping, the head coach of the U.S. women's volleyball team, and CHEN Zhonghe 陈忠和, the head coach of the Chinese women's

排球

volleyball team who was Lang Ping's assistant coach when Lang coached the Chinese women's team, meeting at the Olympics and at other volleyball competitions. The Chinese also hope for another period of success by the men's volleyball team.

Playing for China— Coaching for the U.S.A.

The legendary coach Yuan Weimin joined the Chinese national volleyball team as a primary setter in 1962. After his retirement as a player, he became head coach of the Chinese national women's volleyball team. Under his coaching, the Chinese women's volleyball team won gold medals at the World Cup in 1981, the World Championship in 1982, and the Olympic Games in 1984. Later he became the minister of the State Physical Culture and Sports Commission and the chairman of the Asian Volleyball Confederation. Yuan Weimin's tactics of using full offense and full defense and combining height and speed, swiftness and flexibility became the trend in volleyball at that time.

"Iron Hammer" 铁榔头 Lang Ping was the best representative of Yuan Weimin's tactics. In her performance on the court, the element of height in the tactic of combining height and speed was fully demonstrated. Before Lang Ping joined the Chinese women's volleyball team, the team had boasted the fastest and most comprehensive offensive system in the world. The only element lacking was the ability to gain points in counterattacks and deadlocks. With her ability to make strong attacks during deadlocks or counterattacks and her steady performance in critical situations, Lang Ping was the most effective strong-attack breaker for the Chinese women's volleyball team. The ability of Lang Ping and her teammates to hold and defend represented the first "full-offense and full-defense" strategy in the history of women's volleyball.

After her retirement in 1985, Lang Ping became a student at the Beijing Normal University. In 1987 she moved to the United States, where she continued her studies at New Mexico State University and received her master's degree in sports management. She coached the Chinese women's volleyball team and the Italian women's volleyball team after her graduation. She became the head coach of the U.S. women's volleyball team in 2005.

■ ZHANG LING 张玲

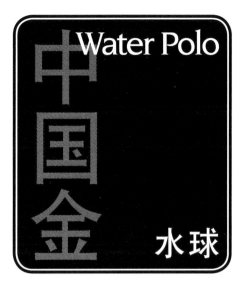

Water Polo 中国金 水球

WATER POLO IS ONE OF THE WORLD'S more diversely conceived sports. It is thought to have originated in lakes and rivers of England in the mid-1800s as an adaptation of rugby. The London Swimming Association designed a set of water polo rules for indoor swimming pools in 1870. The early rubber balls used for the game came from India and were named *pulu*—the Indian word for ball. So the sport came to be known as "water polo."

The Scots added goalposts to the game in 1877 and replaced the rubber ball with a soccer ball. They also transformed it into more of a competitive sport by establishing additional rules, which mandated that the ball stay on the surface and that the players could not be tackled unless they had the ball. The Scottish version of the game became popular in England and Europe in the late 1800s. Modern water polo is played with teams of seven players, using a water polo ball made of waterproof nylon.

Water polo is now popular around the world—in Europe (particularly in Hungary, Greece, Italy, Russia, and the former Yugoslavia), the United States, Canada, and Australia—and in recent Olympic Games China has been a significant presence.

Water polo was the first team sport added to the Olympic program, in 1900, and women's water polo made its first showing in 2000. The Fédération Internationals de Natation Amateur (FINA) was founded in 1908; it has been the international governing body for the sport since that time.

Colonial Development

After the first Opium War (1840–1842), Hong Kong became a colony of England. The English brought competitive swimming and water polo to their new colony, but until 1930, only English residents could participate in events. Nonetheless, in 1924, local Chinese built several swimming pools, allowing them to play water polo, and by 1928 the sport had spread to the mainland of China.

In 1929 the Hong Kong and Macao Aquatic Games were held in Guangzhou, the entry city to mainland China and the Pearl River Delta. Before the games the Singapore water

China's men's water polo team.

奥运体育

polo team had visited Hong Kong and Guangzhou, providing examples of "pass," "shot," and "move" techniques. The Singapore team was the first foreign water polo team to visit China. In 1930 the Zhongshan University and Yuexiu District water polo teams were founded. They later competed with water polo teams from Hong Kong.

In 1931 the Guangzhou Water Polo Championships were held. This event was the first formal water polo championship held in mainland China. After the championships elite athletes were chosen to form the new Guangzhou water polo team. Between 1932 and 1937, water polo boomed in Guangzhou; dozens of water polo teams were formed, and tournaments were held frequently. But as the Japanese troops invaded China in 1937, war put an end to this and other recreational activities.

After World War II, water polo started up again, first in Guangzhou, and then in other big cities, such as Beijing, Tianjin, and Shanghai. By 1959, ten years after the People's Republic of China (PRC) was founded, the First National Games were held in Beijing and nine teams participated in the water polo events. From then on water polo became a formal sports event in China. Due to the great famine in the early 1960s, local governments were unable to support the training of water polo teams; competitions and training stopped between 1961 and 1962.

Since 1973 water polo has begun to develop again in China. The national team swept the gold medals at the Eighth, Ninth, and Tenth Asian Games.

TABLE 1 ■ Olympic Games Water Polo Medal Winners—Men, 1988–2004				
CITY	YEAR	GOLD	SILVER	BRONZE
Athens	2004	Hungary	Serbia-Montenegro	Russia
Sydney	2000	Hungary	Russia	Yugoslavia
Atlanta	1996	Spain	Croatia	Italy
Barcelona	1992	Italy	Spain	USSR
Seoul	1988	SFR Yugoslavia	United States	USSR

TABLE 2 ■ FINA Water Polo World League Medal Winners—Men, 2002–2007				
CITY	YEAR	GOLD	SILVER	BRONZE
Berlin	2007	Serbia	Hungary	Australia
Athens	2006	Serbia-Montenegro	Spain	Greece
Belgrade, Serbia	2005	Serbia-Montenegro	Hungary	Germany
Long Beach	2004	Hungary	Serbia-Montenegro	Greece
New York	2003	Hungary	Italy	United States
Patras, Greece	2002	Russia	Spain	Hungary

However, in the 1980s the development of the game in China slowed down due to the expense of maintaining water polo teams. Many provincial teams were disbanded. China then fell behind other Asian countries. It was not until 2000 that women's water polo started to develop, and the national team was formed in the hope that China would win a medal in the 2008 Olympic Games in Beijing. Since then, the women's team has played in the 2006 and 2006 World Championships.

Twelve men's teams and eight women's teams qualified for the Beijing Olympics, with China the representative of the Asian continent. Based on past performances in the Olympic Games and the FINA Water Polo World League (see tables 1–4), Hungary and Serbia were among the favorites in men's water polo, while Italy and the United States were considered favorites in women's competition.

■ Fan Wei 樊维 and Lu Zhouxiang 吕洲翔

TABLE 3 ■ Olympic Games Water Polo Medal Winners—Women, 2000–2004				
CITY	YEAR	GOLD	SILVER	BRONZE
Athens	2004	Italy	Greece	United States
Sydney	2000	Australia	United States	Russia

TABLE 4 ■ FINA Water Polo World League Medal Winners—Women, 2004–2007				
CITY	YEAR	GOLD	SILVER	BRONZE
Montreal	2007	United States	Australia	Greece
Athens	2006	United States	Italy	Russia
Kirishi, Russia	2005	Greece	Russia	Australia
Long Beach	2004	United States	Hungary	Italy

The World of Sports

体 育 大 世 界

T he Olympics are larger than life, but the values and aspirations we celebrate every four years (and in between at the Winter Games) are part of our daily lives, too. Sports reflect our ideas about achievement, community, competition, fairness, and equality. The popularity of different sports and the way they have spread around the world helps us to understand different cultures and see how nations have influenced one another. Martial arts are not only practiced in Asia but they have developed into sophisticated forms there and then spread around the world. Women have made enormous strides in sport since the founder of the modern Games said, "Women have but one task, that of crowning the winner with garlands," but in every country this development has taken a different shape. This section of *China Gold* explains some of the unique aspects of sports in the Middle or Central Kingdom 中国, which include not only the picturesque practices of tai chi but also "disco dancing" (popular with the elderly), the growing popularity of extreme sports, and even luxury Western sports like golf.

Tai Chi in the Park: Is It a Sport?

中国

这是什么体育项目

FOREIGN VISITORS TO THE BEIJING Olympics, and visitors to China at any time who wake up early in the morning and go out to explore, will see people in China's city parks engaging in unfamiliar physical activities. They might ask themselves, "Is that a sport?" The answer is, "Maybe yes, maybe no." Some of these activities—such as Chinese folk dance, *yangge* 秧歌, and shuttlecock kicking, *ti jian zi* 踢毽—are traditional, while others such as disco dancing are modern; all have special Chinese characteristics. Some include a degree of competition—a feature of all Western sports—and all require skill, though not necessarily strength.

Since the 1990s Chinese people have begun to pay more attention to the health and fitness of their bodies. To meet people's demands for sports and exercise at the grassroots level, the Chinese government in 1995 established the National Fitness Program (NFP) 全民健身计划, which aims to

promote mass sports activities on an extensive scale, improve the people's health, and spur the socialist modernization of China.

The government has established fitness programs, built fitness paths in neighborhoods, and conducted fitness tests and surveys nationwide. As a result fitness exercising has boomed in Chinese cities. The most popular and lively spaces to exercise are city parks in the morning.

Parks Are Popular

Chinese parks are mostly located in the inner city, where the transportation system makes travel convenient. Entrance tickets to parks are cheap; some are even free. Chinese people believe the air in the early morning is freshest in parks. The relatively larger spaces and natural environments that parks offer are attractive factors to exercisers. The sports and exercise activities in parks are diverse and substantially

based on people's own preferences and requirements. People can exercise alone or play games with partners or join in group exercises. *Qigong*, tai chi, disco dancing, *yangge*, and shuttlecock kicking are the main forms of exercise available to urban Chinese in parks.

Qigong 气功 is a unique Chinese individual exercise. Through their efforts practitioners build up their health and prevent illness by combining disciplines of the mind, the body, and the body's vital force (*qi*). There are currently more than 3,300 different styles and schools of *qigong*. The practice relies on the traditional Chinese belief that the body has something that might be described as an "energy field" generated and maintained by the natural respiration of the body, known as *qi*, which means "breath" 息 or "gas" 气 in Chinese. The energy produced by breathing keeps us alive. *Gong* signifies work applied to a discipline or the resultant level of technique. *Qigong* is then "breath work" or the art of manag-

---

The World of Asian Dance

Styles of dance vary from culture to culture. Around the globe, identifiable characteristics may be associated with individual cultures. Traditional Asian dance, for example, has remained closely linked with worship, and generally has adhered to ancient forms and legends in its choreography, costumes, and musical accompaniment. Characteristics of Asian dance movement include a fluid body stance, with a flexible use of the spine. The hips, rib cage, head, and shoulders shift from side to side, while

the legs glide in a low level over the ground. The overall movement quality is multi-focused, with a bound (or controlled) flow and a light use of weight. The arms, fingers, hands, and eyes perform subtle and expressive movements, while stylized facial expressions are utilized. In most Asian dance forms, one finds a distinction between more vigorous and athletic dancing for males, and more confined and subtle dancing for females.

■ HELEN MYERS

ing one's breathing in order to achieve and maintain good health, and (especially in the martial arts) to enhance the energy mobilization and stamina of the body in coordination with the physical process of respiration. *Qigong* is mostly taught for health maintenance purposes, but there are also some who teach it as a therapeutic intervention. Various forms of traditional *qigong* are also widely taught in conjunction with Chinese martial arts.

Since the sixteenth century Chinese people have performed tai chi to keep their bodies in good condition and to prevent or heal diseases. Tai chi 太极 is also known as tai chi chuan 太极拳, a Chinese form of exercise derived from Daoism 道教, one of China's oldest belief systems. The practice of tai chi chuan is beneficial to health and it is also a subtle, sophisticated, and scientific method of self-defense. Since this system of exercise is suitable for people of all ages and requires little or no special equipment, it has gained an enthusiastic reception nationwide. Tai chi's training forms are well known as the slow motion routines that groups of people practice together every morning in parks in Chinese cities.

The movements of both *qigong* and tai chi are slow and floating in a continuous way. The main goal of both is to keep the body in peace and harmony.

Compared with these traditional exercises, disco dancing, being more vigorous, exciting, and simple, emerged in the 1980s as a new fitness activity. Unlike *qigong* and tai chi, it features music and requires no special skill. Disco resembles aerobic dance or

A man practices tai chi in the morning on the grounds of the Temple of Heaven in Beijing.

jazz using hip-swiveling and shoulder-rolling movements, with hand-clapping and cross steps included. Because disco dancing originated in the West, it is also perceived as having a modern rhythm, an alternative to traditional consciousness.

Starting as a craze among intellectuals, it became popular among workers and peasants, especially people age sixty and older. "Old people's disco" 老年迪斯科 is said to be one of the "three hots" 三大热潮 or biggest crazes in China along with tai chi and *qigong*. It was reported that in Shanghai over 100,000 people participate in disco dancing, and in almost every Beijing park in the early morning hours people gathering around cassette players, sometimes wearing heavy coats during the cold winter months.

The Chinese folk dance *yangge* 秧歌 also is popular in Chinese cities. In the past people danced *yangge* when celebrating festivals, triumphs, or marriages. *Yangge* involves dancing slowly in a circle to the accompaniment of a large drum and cymbals. Typically, most dancers are women, and the drummers are men. Women dance in pastel-colored gauze dresses and wave matching silk scarves or fans. Today, *yangge* is more a physical exercise than an art performance. It can help people to exercise their arms, legs, and waists. It is also a form of entertainment. In contrast to disco, it also stresses Chinese traditional culture and national identity.

Dating back as far as the Han dynasty (206 BCE–220 CE), shuttlecock kicking, *ti jian zi*, 踢毽子 remains a popular folk sport. It can be seen as a precursor of the modern Western sport of footbag, and is related to the southeast Asian *takraw*. Whether played as a solitary sport or between two people, shuttlecock kicking builds concentration and strength. The constant movement of the sport makes it an excellent aerobic workout.

To combine Chinese traditional sports with modern elements, some new forms of exercise and sports have been created. For example, *taiji* dancing combines the rules of taiji with dance. It not only meets the goals of exercise but also brings aesthetic perceptions to those practicing it.

On the Move

With the development of cities, Chinese people's participation in sports and exercise has merged with new spaces, forms, content, and concepts. Chinese people have begun to regard sports as a way to be entertained and to make their lives richer and more varied. Although elite sports are still tightly controlled by the state, sports at the grassroots level have become individual and social activities and new elements in Chinese urban life.

■ XIONG HUAN 熊欢

An unusual sport: throwing weighted rings and catching them around one's neck.

New Sports in China

新兴体育项目在中国

AS CHINA OPENS TO THE OUTSIDE world, sports enthusiasts across the country are revving up and teeing off. Auto racing and golf, among other sporting activities, are becoming very popular in China.

The emergence of these new sports—and the proliferation of professional sports events and luxury sports venues—is the consequence of a growing middle class and newly wealthy urban populations. Furthermore, the Chinese national sports policy, which is turning its attention from political to commercial outcomes, has only helped to spur the boom of Western luxury sports in China.

Auto Racing Roars into China

With the rapid increase in the ownership of private cars in China, auto racing is no longer considered an elite sport enjoyed only by Westerners. The Macao Grand Prix Races (MGPR), held in November in the streets of Macau, is the pioneer of China's auto racing sport. It is known for being the only street circuit racing event in which both car and motorcycle races are held; every year the event attracts more than 300 among racing drivers and cycle riders.

MGPR was originally conceived in 1954 as a treasure hunt around the streets of the city, but shortly thereafter it was suggested that the hunt's track could host an amateur racing event for local motor enthusiasts. The race continued as an amateur event until 1966, when Belgian driver Mauro Bianchi entered the race with a car by Renault Sport, mostly to promote Renault's image in Hong Kong; this move by Bianchi led to more and more professional teams entering the Macao Grand Prix. Then, in 1967 a motorcycle race was introduced. In 1983 it was decided by the organizers that since Formula Atlantic (single-seat formula cars with engines not exceeding 1600 cc in capacity) was becoming obsolete, the race would be held as a Formula Three (lightweight tube-frame chassis powered by 500 cc motorcycle engines) event.

Today, MGPR consists of the Macau Motorcycle Grand Prix, the World Touring Car Championship Guia Race, and the Macau F3 Grand Prix. The winner of the Macau Formula 3 Grand Prix is awarded the FIA Intercontinental Formula 3 Cup. In addition there are the Porsche Carrera Cup Asia race, the Formula Renault 2000 race, the Macau Cup. and the Scooter race in Macau.

MGPR is not only a sporting event, but also a tourist attraction for Macao.

China's Emerging Elite

Golfing now starts young among China's new upper class. In 2006, the *International Herald Tribune* (26 September 2006) reported on affluent Chinese parents who give their five-year-old children daily golf lessons during summer vacation at a Shanghai golf complex . The individual, two-hour lessons with a Scottish golf pro carry a $200 price tag. During the school year, weekend practice sessions at the local driving range will have to suffice. Other newly popular sports for children of the elite include horseback riding, ice skating, skiing, and polo.

Upper-class Chinese adults are finding that luxury cars are becoming the item of choice.

According to the *Wall Street Journal* (12 April 2007), Jaguars, Mercedes, Bentleys, and Cadillacs are showing up among China's new elite—with owner clubs springing up as well. With luxury-car sales doubling between 2004 and 2007, it's not surprising that Rolls-Royce has opened a showroom in China—though, interestingly, the location is Chengdu, a city where incomes are far lower than in Beijing or Shanghai. And Ferrari has a showroom in Dalian, another city not known for its affluence. While only about .038 percent (about half a million) of China's population has sufficient disposable income to pay from $200,000 to $700,000 for luxury cars, that group is increasing by an astounding 20 percent annually.

Rock-climbing walls are a popular new activity in China.

The development of sports tourism is one of the tourist policies of the Macao Special Administrative Region government.

In June 2004 Shanghai completed the construction of a state-of-the-art racing circuit. However, Shanghai lacks the experience of hosting an international racing event. Macao has hosted MGPR for fifty-four years, which is almost as long as the history of Formula One races. Macao is willing to share its organizational experience and provide technical support and personnel training to assist Shanghai in hosting its Formula One Grand Prix. There is another reason why the MGPR has attracted special attention: Guangdong Province, Beijing, and Shanghai were given the green light by the central government to pilot individual travel to Hong Kong and Macao beginning in August 2003, which was expected to substantially increase the number of spectators to the MGPR. (Prior to August 2003, travelers from mainland China to Hong Kong and Macau could not travel on an individual basis; they could only travel on business visas or in group tours.)

The Federation of Automobile Sports of the People's Republic of China (FASC) is a newly organized sports organization responsible for the development of automobile sport under the leadership of China's National General Administration Bureau of Sports. The rapid development of China's auto industry and the rise of people's living standards certainly have pushed China's auto sports to a higher level of development. Now, FASC is determined to guide the development of China's auto and auto-related industries as contributors to the Chinese economy. It will also contribute to enriching the after-work life of the people. Through years of hard work, FASC has established a perfect publicity work system. FASC has promised that it will upgrade the status of auto sports continuously, as well as make it a popular entertainment for the general public.

Golf Takes Hold

Golf in China has come a long way since the country's last emperor, PU Yi 溥仪, took lessons from his English tutor in the 1920s. In Beijing today, being a member of the right golf club is becoming the same status symbol for the Communist elite as it is for capitalists in the West. Although golf is still an elite sport in China, there are now more than two hundred officially registered courses throughout the country, with one thousand more under construction. In China golf means more than watching Tiger Woods on the course or acting as a spokesperson for Accenture or Rolex.

Golf also means profit. Major East Coast and interior cities now feel they must have a course to cater to foreign investors and tourists. Whereas golf was a forbidden pastime in the 1950s and 1960s, it is now a virtual requirement for any Chinese town hoping to assert its economic viability to have a course.

As a golfing destination, China offers arguably some of the best golf facilities anywhere in the world. Everything about a Chinese golfing experience is first class. The accommodations are superb, the food is gourmet, and the shopping, sightseeing, and culture makes a golf tour to China an unforgettable adventure.

Major Golf Tournaments

The BMW Asian Open is a men's professional tournament. The tournament began in 2002 and was played in Taiwan for its first two years before moving to mainland China. It is cosanctioned by the Asian Tour and the European Tour and is part of the European Tour's drive to expand into Asia in general and China in particular.

The HSBC (Hong Kong Shanghai Bank of China) Champions is a men's professional seventy-two-hole tournament played annually since November 2005, in Shanghai.

The TCL (one of China's largest consumer electronics enterprises) Classic is a men's professional tournament played annually in Sanya on Hainan. The tournament was first played in 2002 and sanctioned by the Asian Tour. The tournament was not held in 2003 or 2004 but was reintroduced in 2005 with cosanctioning by the European Tour, consistent with the latter's expansion into China,

The Volvo China Open is a men's tournament that is cosanctioned by the European Tour and the Asian Tour. The event was first played in 1995 and has been part of the European Tour's schedule since 2003.

■ XIONG HUAN 熊欢

A young golfer practices at a driving range.

Extreme Sports Come To China

极限运动在中国

THE ASIAN X GAMES TOOK PLACE in Shanghai in 2007 and the 2008 Olympic Games launches BMX racing as an official medal sport, joining "extreme" events such as mountain biking and canoe and kayak slalom. The inclusion of BMX, much like the inclusion of snowboarding at the 1998 Winter Olympics, is a way for the International Olympic Committee to appeal to a younger generation, and in addition to medal events the IOC has made action- and extreme-sports demonstrations part of the Games. This exposure will no doubt increase the visibility of extreme sports in China, but no one knows whether this will lead to active participation—or simply to more interest in extreme sports products and events.

The Making of "Extreme" Sports

Taking risks with ones life in sport competition is nothing new in the human experience. Gladiator competitions in ancient Rome and jousts in medieval Europe are two examples of sports that fit the modern definition of extreme.

In the 1990s, some U.S. corporations grouped a number of marginalized, youth-dominated sports, such as skateboarding, BMX (bicycle motocross) riding, and BASE (building, antenna, span, Earth) jumping, under a new label: extreme sports. Over the past decade, extreme sports have experienced rapid growth in many Western countries. In 2003, for example, five of the top ten most popular sports in the United States were extreme sports, with inline skating ranked first, skateboarding second, snowboarding fourth, and wakeboarding ninth. Extreme sports have also grown exponentially in some Asian countries, particularly Japan and Korea, but only since the late 1990s and early 2000s have extreme sports gained appeal among the rapidly growing Chinese middle class and in particular Chinese middle-class youth. Today young Chinese males and females participate in snowboarding, skateboarding, BMX, surfing, rock climbing, and various other extreme sports. However, although the number of extreme sport aficionados is growing in China, the growth has been considerably slower than in many other countries. In terms of injury rates, most

The world's largest skateboarding ramp, which helped launch Californian skateboarder Danny Way over the Great Wall of China in July 2005.

PART THREE THE WORLD OF SPORTS

Base-jumping off
of the Jin Mao
tower in Shanghai.

extreme sports are no more dangerous than the majority of organized sports, yet the "risky" and "daredevil" images associated with these sports discourage many Chinese people from participation.

Extreme Sports Get Government Support

The Chinese government has begun to support the development of extreme sports. In October 2005, the world's largest skate park opened in Shanghai. Three times bigger than the largest skateboard park in the United States and rumored to have cost more than US$8 million—paid by the government—the park is set to host a number of national and international extreme sport events and encourage more Chinese youths to take up skateboarding, BMX, and inline skating.

China is also increasingly hosting large international extreme sports events, for example, the Shanghai Showdown Gravity Games, Nanshan Snowboarding Open, the 720 China Surf Open, and the 2007 Asian X Games.

The Manufacturing Connection

Since the mid-1980s, Chinese manufacturing firms have been commissioned by foreign companies to produce extreme-sports–related clothing and equipment. Only recently, however, have these foreign companies recognized the potential of the Chinese youth market. In 2003, for example, action-sports giant Quiksilver entered a joint venture with Chinese-owned and -operated apparel manufacturer Glorious Sun Enterprises with the goal of opening retail stores in Shanghai, Beijing, and Hong Kong and tapping into the rapidly growing Chinese market. "We are very excited about this initiative," said Quiksilver CEO Bob McKnight.

Burton Snowboards also recognizes the potential of China. In 2005 Burton Snowboards signed a three-year deal to sponsor the National Snowboard Team of China, which consists of six young men and six young women, selected solely on their athletic (rather than snowboarding) abilities. According to Bryan Johnston, vice president of global marketing for Burton Snowboards, "snowboarding's expansion into China presents a huge opportunity in the sport's overall growth . . .

and we're extremely pleased to have the chance to work with the National Snowboard Team of China."

Many U.S.-based companies are also investing heavily in major events and spectacles to help raise the profile of extreme sports and, by association, their companies, among Chinese youth. For example, professional California skateboarder Danny Way grabbed headlines around the world when he, with the financial support of his key sponsors Quiksilver and DC shoes, constructed the largest skateboarding structure ever built (36.58 meters tall, with a gap distance of 27.43 meters) and performed a 360-degree rotation while jumping over the Great Wall of China on his skateboard. Interestingly, the Chinese government approved this media stunt; a number of government officials, including an official from the Ministry of Culture, attended the event. However, although Way's spectacular stunt was well received by the Chinese people, the research firm Label Networks suggests that it did not encourage more youths to take up the sport. Rather, the stunt had the opposite effect; it was perceived locally as "an oddball 'American' thing."

A Tentative Approach to Extreme Sports

Indeed, despite the support of the China Extreme Sports Association and the aggressive marketing by Chinese and Western—particularly U.S.—companies, many Chinese youth and their parents are tentative about participating in these sports. Although the X Games are on the rise in Beijing, they are developing slowly. Chinese parents worry about their children getting involved in dangerous sports. And top-quality coaching and equipment are too expensive for the average person to afford. The *Shanghai Star* reports that many Chinese youth are "under heavy

Wakeboarding in China.

pressure to study" and that some consider extreme sports "a waste of time."

Drawing on two studies on Chinese youth culture, Label Networks notes that few parents want their only child to participate in extreme pursuits and that they still prefer basketball, table tennis, and martial arts. Indeed, these studies identify Jackie Chan 成龙 as the "real 'extreme' hero in China." Although extreme sports have spawned a new culture among youth in China, participation tends to be based on the consumption of apparel, footwear, and events, inspired by U.S. and Japanese action sports heroes rather than on active participation.

■ HOLLY THORPE

Danny Way Jumpstarts Skateboarding in China

Danny Way's skateboarding feats on the Great Wall in 2005 dazzled the world. Just before the event, Way explained his motives: "Skateboarding has yet to realize its full potential, and by bringing this event to the people of China and the rest of the world, I hope to contribute to the future of skateboarding and bring my sport the global attention it deserves."

The event was sponsored by Quiksilver, the company that owns DC Shoes—which makes skateboarding shoes that are endorsed by Way. Bob McKnight, Quiksilver's CEO, understandingly had a more entrepreneurial take on the jump: "Quiksilver continues to grow around the world, and China is an important region for our brand. Danny is the perfect athlete to bring this feat of skating excellence to this nation, and his jump will serve as a bridge to a country which has discovered its passion for skateboarding. It also represents an enormous opportunity to bring our boardriding lifestyle to the youth of China and the tremendous excitement surrounding this sport."

SPORTS MEDICINE HAS BENEFITED Chinese athletes for more than five decades and contributed to China's achievements in national, regional, and international events. The Chinese Association of Sports Medicine and the newly formed Chinese Association of Clinical Sports Medicine have played major roles in clinical and sports science research and education, general public health, and athletic training and performance in China.

In 2006, the Twenty-ninth FIMS International Conference of Sports Medicine was held in Beijing, with representatives from the World Health Organization and the International Olympic Committee in attendance. The use of traditional Chinese medicine in the treatment of sports injuries is of considerable interest to sports therapists, who are today making use of a much wider variety of methods to help athletes in their training, recovery from illness, and even in psychological preparation for competition.

Development of Sports Medicine Education and Research

In 1953 the Central Institute of Physical Education, now Beijing Sports University, offered courses in anatomy and physiology for the first time in China; later other courses, such as hygiene, sports medical intendance, and exercise therapy were developed. Five years later, the National Research Institute of Sports Science was established by the Ministry of Sports. This institute includes sports medicine, exercise physiology, and biochemistry research departments. In the same year, a sports hospital affiliated with Chengdu Institute of Physical Education, in Chengdu, a major city in Sichuan Province in southwestern China, was set up under the leadership of Marshal HE Long 贺龙 who was the Minister of Sport at that time. It was the first sports hospital in China and has become well known for its treatment of sports trauma by traditional Chinese medicine, such as the application of Chinese herbs, traditional osteopathy, and acupuncture.

This sports hospital, known since 1984 as Chengdu Sports Trauma Institute of National Sports Council, has cooperated with national sports teams and has provided Chinese Olympic athletes with services in both research and clinical treatment. Physicians apply traditional Chinese and modern Western medicine in their practice and have been successful in the treatment of acute and chronic sports traumas, especially in fractures and soft tissue and joint injuries.

In 1959, with the support of the Chinese National Sports Council, Beijing government, and Beijing Medical University, Professor QU Mianyu 曲绵域 established the Research Institute of Sports Medicine (now the Research

Chinese Sports Medicine

QIAN Jinhua, the general-secretary of the Chinese Association of Sports Medicine explains how the practice of traditional Chinese medicine (TCM) affects the physical conditioning and treatment of athletes in China.

Athlete selection, bodily function evaluation, training, and preventing and controlling injury and sickness are all important components of the Chinese sports medicine system. In the last few years we have incorporated a good deal of theory, experience, and methodology from overseas, but we still use many elements of TCM. For instance, we treat chronic and acute soft-tissue damage with TCM massage as well as acupuncture and moxibustion [the burning of herbs on or near the skin to stimulate healing]. Doctors with Western medical training have become more popular with athletes for other types of problems, however. For instance, athletes are tired of using traditional Chinese herbal remedies; they prefer Western prescriptions.

Institute of Sports Medicine at Beijing University) in the Third Affiliated Clinical Hospital of Beijing Medical University. It was the first institute to combine scientific research and clinical treatment of sports medicine in China and has become a top-ranking institute for teaching, research, and clinical treatment by experts in sports traumatology, sports nutrition, sports medical intendance, and sports rehabilitation.

This institute also has been appointed by the National Sports Council and the Chinese Olympic Committee as a medical treatment center for Chinese Olympic athletes. It has contributed to the general health and performance of many Chinese sports stars and Olympic champions.

Since the 1960s most major physical education institutes and physical education department within universities have offered sports medicine courses. In 1981 the sports medicine programs at several medical universities and physical education institutes were upgraded to offer bachelor's, master's, and doctoral degrees in sports medicine. In recent years the major in sports medicine has been developed or strengthened at other sports institutes and universities. Most of the sports medicine centers have their own clinics or are affiliated with the universities or hospitals. Chinese doctors and physicians now work in sports medicine all over the world.

In 1986 the Chinese National Sports Council set up the National Research Institute of Sports Medicine, including the China Doping Control Center and Sports Nutrition Center. The China Doping Control Center is the only authorized center for doping control in China. It is in charge of doping control in international and national sports games and the testing of the medicine, food, and nutritional products used by athletes. It is the only lab in Asia that has passed the examination of the World Anti-Doping Agency continually for nineteen years.

Chinese Association of Sports Medicine

The Chinese Association of Sports Medicine has contributed greatly to the popularization and application of sports medicine in China. In 1978 the association joined the International Federation of Sports Medicine (FIMS). In 2006 the Chinese Association of Clinical Sports Medicine was founded as a part of the Chinese Medical Association and approved by the Chinese Association of Science and Technology.

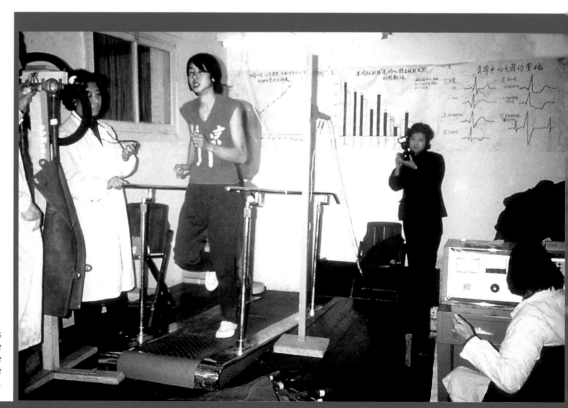

An athlete is assessed at the China Institute of Sport Science in Beijing.

The international status of the Chinese Association of Sports Medicine has been greatly elevated in the past twenty years. Since it became a member of FIMS, Professor Qu Mianyu was elected as a vice president of FIMS in 1986 and served until 1994. In 1990 the association became a founding member of the Asian Federation of Sports Medicine (AFSM), and Professor Qu was its first chairman.

Sports Medicine Associations and Publications

In China many branches of the Chinese Association of Sports Medicine are located in provinces and cities. These branches connect scholars with sports medicine therapists and provide a way for them to share their studies and experiences of teaching, research, and clinical practice. Since 1980 the National Conference of Sports Medicine has been held annually. In addition, each branch of the Chinese Association of Sports Medicine, such as sports traumatology and exercise therapy, hold conferences twice or three times a year. The *Chinese Journal of Sports Medicine* (CJSM) was first published in 1982 and is now one of China's core science journals.

In 1985 the first Beijing International Conference of Sports Medicine was held. Twenty-one years later, in 2006, the Twenty-ninth FIMS International Conference of Sports Medicine was held in Beijing. It was the first FIMS

Acupuncture

Acupuncture is an ancient treatment technique still routinely used in traditional Chinese medicine and also in Western medicine. Techniques for making bamboo needles and for casting bronze needles developed during the Shang dynasty (1766–1045 BCE). During the Song dynasty (960–1267 CE), the Jurchen Jin dynasty (1126–1234 CE), and the Yuan dynasty (1267–1368 CE), acupuncture developed widely in China. However, during the Qing dynasty (1644–1912) the practice was banned from general use by decree because it was perceived as unsuitable for application to the emperor. Although banned, acupuncture continued to flourish in local use. Although acupuncture had been popular among the Chinese-American community for over one hundred years, non-Chinese Americans became more aware of acupuncture after President Richard Nixon's 1972 visit to China.

In China acupuncture is used to treat diseases in nearly every branch of medicine, whether it is cardiology or dentistry, infectious diseases, or obstetrics. Responding to research, acupuncture techniques have embraced such new technologies as laser and electrical stimulation. In Chinese hospitals that provide acupuncture services, the acupuncture section is always called the department of acupuncture and moxibustion (moxibustion is the burning of medicinal substances, usually herbs, on the acupoints for therapeutic effect). Although the predominant treatment in the department is acupuncture, moxibustion plays an important role. Even as Western medicine becomes more common in China in the twenty-first century, acupuncture continues to be used, especially in hospitals that rely on traditional medicine and also those that combine traditional and Western approaches.

■ BAO-XING CHEN AND GARÉ LECOMPTE

congress held in China and brought sixteen hundred representatives from all over the world to Beijing during the preparations for the Olympic Games. Representatives of FIMS, the World Health Organization, International Olympic Committee, Chinese Department of Health, China's General Administration of Sport, and the Organizing Committee of the 2008 Beijing Olympic Games attended.

Many training courses in sports medicine are held in China. These courses focus on the theory and practice of sports traumatology, sports nutrition, sports medical intendance, and exercise therapy. The course in the traditional Chinese medical treatment of sports injury—which has attracted sports therapists from all over the world—is especially popular.

■ GUO HONG 郭红

RICHARD POUND, PRESIDENT OF
the World Anti-Doping Agency (WADA),
points out that every sport has had
its share of cheating, and there's little
doubt every country has its share of
doping in sports. China is no exception. Because the issue of doping—in
U.S. baseball and the Tour de France
as well as at the Olympic Games—has
drawn much attention in recent years,
the International Olympic Committee (IOC) and China have undertaken
unprecedented measures to ensure a
doping-free Olympics.

How It All Started

China retook its seat on the International Olympic Committee (IOC) in
1979 after a twenty-one year absence
because of the dispute over the "two
Chinas" issue, and in the country's first
appearance, it won fifteen gold medals. This impressive return performance
in Los Angeles in 1984 did not arouse
much suspicion about doping, in part

due to the absence of the USSR, which
was boycotting the games. However,
with the Seoul Olympics in 1988, Chinese athletes began to be implicated in
a string of drug scandals, culminating
at the 1994 Asian Games, where eleven
Chinese athletes returned positive
results from doping control. And at the
World Swimming Championships in
Australia in 1998, a Chinese swimmer
was caught at the Sydney airport with
a growth hormone in her luggage, and
four swimmers tested positive at the
event in Perth.

China's remarkable progress within a
short time inevitably aroused suspicions of a systematic doping scheme
backed by the government, reminis-
cent of doping scandals in the former
East Germany and the Soviet Union.
Compared with winning merely five
gold medals at the 1988 Seoul Olympics, China won thirty-two gold medals

and grabbed the second position in the
gold medal count a mere sixteen years
later, at the 2004 Athens Olympics,
claiming its position as an emerging
sports superpower. In this relatively
brief period, China tasted the sweet-
ness of victory but also the bitterness
of doping scandals. In fact suspicions
of doping have lingered around every
unexpected success that Chinese athletes have achieved, from the world-
record-setting female distance runners
coached by MA Junren 马俊仁 in the
early 1990s to the stunning performances of Chinese female swimmers at
the World Swimming Championships
in 1994.

The Risks of Reform

To understand the history of drug
abuse in Chinese sports, it is worth-
while to understand that China's
return to the Olympic family coin-

Performance Enhancement in Ancient Times

The record of performance-enhancing
drugs dates back to 400 BCE in Greece,
when achievements in sports were first
found to increase social status, political
power, and economic well-being. Although
the crown of olive leaves was the only "official prize" for an Olympic victory, records
indicate that Olympic winners could gain
great wealth from lucrative prizes awarded
by their city-state. In addition to money,
winners might receive homes, food, tax
breaks, and even exemption from duty in
the armed services. Because the stakes
were high, athletes were open to any means
that gave them the edge over opponents,

such as ingesting mushroom extracts, plant
seeds, or any concoction thought to enhance performance.

During the Roman period chariot races and
gladiator competitions filled the stands with
spectators. Knowing that a victory could be
their ticket to social and economic prosperity, competitors fed their horses potent
mixtures of herbs and other plants to make
them run faster. They also fed themselves
herbal substances that acted as doping
agents to make for a more intense and
bloody battle, one that would satisfy the
adoring crowds.

■ LIBBY ALBERS

Participants at a session of a 1984 conference on sports medicine and doping issues in Beijing.

cided with China's embarking on an unprecedented open-door economic reform, which brought about profound changes in every aspect of social life in China and also transformed the role of sports. Sporting success was identified as an instrument that could help create a new national image as part of the country's rejuvenation. Winning gold medals at international competitions, particularly the Olympic Games, was considered a way to achieve national glory. The overwhelming priority given to Olympic sports gave rise to a win-at-all-cost mentality at different levels of elite sports. At the same time, the meaning of sports success for individual athletes also changed dramatically.

In the early 1980s, a world championship brought an athlete only political prestige and higher social status, whereas twenty years later an Olympic championship meant the creation of a millionaire overnight. Prize money poured in not only from government rewards but also from the private sectors, in the form of commercial endorsements, for example. Driven by the win-at-all-cost mentality and tempted by overwhelming financial rewards,

some coaches and athletes turned to performance-enhancing drugs or other methods to gain an edge over their opponents. And so it was that doping seeped into China during the mid-1980s.

From Zero Tolerance to Doping Scandals

Undoubtedly, China could not afford to have its reputation tarnished by the doping crisis, and certainly the crisis was at odds with the country's ambition as it bid for the Olympics in 1993 and 2001. China responded by seriously addressing the situation. The first doping control tests were carried out in 1990. A series of anti-doping regulations was formulated to curb drug abuse in sports. Remarkable progress was made from the mid-1990s when China began bilateral cooperation with some leading countries in anti-doping, such as Norway, Australia, Sweden, and Canada.

A full-fledged national anti-doping program was established by the end of the 1990s. Great attention was also paid to the quality of testing, with China's National Doping Control Quality System

receiving international certification in 2004. The annual total of tests soared from fewer than two hundred in 1990 to more than nine thousand in 2006, with more than half conducted as out-of-competition tests, the most effective means of detection. A groundbreaking government decree, Regulations on Anti-Doping, promulgated by the State Council, came into effect 1 March 2004. Despite their significance not being fully appreciated outside China, the regulations provided a foundation for government authorities to make concerted efforts to combat doping in sports.

At the same time, China took part in international anti-doping affairs, representing Asia on the foundation board of WADA since its establishment in 1999. China was among the fifty-one governments that signed the Copenhagen Declaration to recognize and implement the World Anti-Doping Code at the Second World Conference on Doping in Sport in 2003. In October 2006, China became the first Asian country to ratify the United Nations Educational, Scientific and Cultural Organization (UNESCO) International Convention against Doping in Sport.

Anti-doping Challenges

Eliminating doping from sports is a long-term battle around the world. What are the complexities of the battle and the key challenges for China? First, the motivation for drug abuse is becoming more sophisticated and diversified, and doping is not restricted to elite athletes competing for gold medals at international competitions.

Olympic Anti-doping Rules Get Stronger

In April 2008, the International Olympic Committee (IOC) announced on its website (www.olympics.com) the implementation of tougher anti-doping rules "as a clear demonstration of the IOC's commitment to ensuring athletes play fair in Beijing."

The new rules include:

■ The provision that all athletes participating in the Olympic Games in Beijing will be subject to doping controls at any time or place, with no advance notice.

■ The fact that athletes who miss a test on two separate occasions during the Games or on one occasion during Games plus two in the 18 months prior, will be considered to have committed an anti-doping rule violation.

■ Possession of any substance from the list of prohibited substances would constitute a violation (previously only a selection from the prohibited list would have applied).

Doping appears to be seeping into sports for young student-athletes, compelling the sports authority to introduce doping control at national youth sports events. In recent years reports of positive results from doping tests conducted on high school students at the national university entrance examinations and at the Provincial Junior Games have increased. The world was shocked when officials of the Chinese Olympic Committee Anti-Doping Commission (COCADC) raided a training camp of the Anshan city sports school in northeastern China in August 2006, and seized in the headmaster's room prohibited drugs, including erythropoietin (EPO), testosterone, and hypodermic needles. The youngest doped athlete was only fifteen and the oldest eighteen, and they were preparing for their Provincial Youth Games.

To link such an incident to China's preparation for the 2008 Olympics would show a lack of knowledge of the Chinese sports system. China has a variety of domestic comprehensive sports events, such as the National Games, the National Urban Games, and the Provincial Games. For many coaches and sports administrators at the provincial and city levels, the performances of their athletes at the local Provincial Games are not directly related to the national Olympic program but rather more often serve as stepping-stones in their own careers. How many gold medals a city wins at these local sports events and how many young athletes are scouted by professional teams determine the promotion of some team officials and coaches. Furthermore, the athlete population at these amateur sports schools is huge and technically outside the registered testing pool controlled by the national program.

Second, in Chinese cultural tradition the notion of food and medicine is nuanced. Sometimes medicine is food and food is medicine. Even an ordinary Chinese housewife will add some Chinese medicinal herbs when stewing meat or making a soup. The extensive use of traditional Chinese herbs in food preparation and the complexity of their ingredients put Chinese athletes at high risk of drug abuse and make doping prevention and education more sophisticated.

Third, a national anti-doping organization (NADO) independent from sports and government has been identified as a key strategy to effectively fight doping in sports. With the 2008 Olympic Games on the horizon and the increasing international attention, China is under close scrutiny both in terms of its ability to control its athletes through the national program in the lead-up to the games and its handling of doping control during the games. No doubt more resources and expertise need to be dedicated to this effort, and an independent Chinese NADO would be a strong indicator of the country's commitment to doping-free sports. Other key issues faced by Chinese sports include the alignment of domestic policy with the World Anti-Doping Code and the control of the manufacturing and trafficking of illegal substances.

Some people may ask how China views doping in relation to its sports. A comment from a senior government sports official, quoted on the Chinese Olympic Committee Anti-Doping Commission website, may be the best answer: "China won 32 gold metals at the Athens Olympics. Evidence of doping-free performance was like a 33rd gold medal for the Chinese team, and without it, the other 32 gold medals would be meaningless."

■ CUI YING 崔颖

Women in Sports: Holding Up Half the Sky

IN CHINESE SPORTS, NOT ONLY IS the phoenix (the symbol of women) rising, but it is also waggin' the dragon (the symbol of men). The ascension of Chinese women in sports has aroused world interest and acclaim. After the Chinese Communist Party won national power and established the People's Republic of China (PRC) in 1949, the Communists promised that a new China would embrace gender equality. Since then, "Women hold up half the sky" 妇女撑起半边天 has been more than just a slogan made popular by Chairman MAO Zedong 毛泽东. Chinese women's sports have been promoted, and Chinese women have made outstanding achievements on the international sports stage.

Women in Elite Sport

The first Chinese female athlete to break a world record and leap into world sports history was ZHENG Fengrong 郑凤荣. Zheng, at the age of twenty, scored a high jump of 1.77 meters, beating the previous mark of 1.76 meters. The new record, set in 1957, was the first women's world record for the People's Republic of China. The jump made Zheng the first Asian athlete to break a world track and field record since 1936. Dubbed "a spring swallow" who awakened Chinese sports, Zheng sent a message to the world that China was no longer the "sick man of the East" 东亚病夫.

The first Chinese women's sports team to catch the attention of the world was the volleyball team, which in 1981 defeated Japan and won the World Cup. In the next five years, the team won five world champion titles. Team members were regarded as national heroines. The spirit of the women's volleyball team inspired millions of Chinese people in the 1980s, and the team's success brought women's sports to prominence in the world.

The number of Chinese women participants in Olympic Games and the

TABLE 1 ■ Comparison of Chinese Olympians by Gender				
	1992	1996	2000	2004
Women	132	200	188	269
Men	118	110	93	138

■ Percentage of women competitors

	52.8	64.5	66.9	66.09

TABLE 2 ■ Comparison of Chinese Olympic Gold Medalists by Gender					
	1988	1992	1996	2000	2004
Women	2	12	9	16.5	19.5
Men	3	4	7	11.5	12.5

number of medals they have won are evidence of the extraordinary performance of Chinese women in sports. In every Olympics since 1998, Chinese female athletes have outnumbered their male counterparts and have played a major role in raising China's standing in the gold medal tally (see tables 1 and 2).

Why the Phoenix Rose

The outstanding performances of Chinese sportswomen have many people

Women and Sport in Ancient China

Through most of China's recorded history, racket games were popular among women. A Ming-dynasty (1368–1644) scroll painting, *Grove of Violets*, depicts elegantly attired ladies playing *chuiwan*, a game combining elements of modern billiards and golf. According to the *Wanjing* (1282), the players took turns striking a wooden ball and sending it into holes marked with colored flags. The ethos of the game stressed fairness and harmony among the players.

If Marco Polo (1254–1324) can be believed, the Mongol dynasty produced a royal heroine comparable to the Greek girl Atalanta, who raced against and defeated a number of suitors. Princess Aiyaruk was said to have owned more than ten thousand horses, winning one hundred at a time as she outwrestled a long line of doomed suitors.

■ ALLEN GUTTMANN

The Chinese women's soccer team celebrates a championship.

wondering why the phoenix can fly higher than the dragon. To answer this question, we must put women's sports in the context of the change of political objectives, gender relationships, sports ideologies, and the management system in China.

When the People's Republic of China was newly established, it needed to develop its economy and strengthen its national defense. Therefore, sports policy sought to train strong citizens to reconstruct the country. It required of its women not only immense patriotic enthusiasm, scientific knowledge, and work skill, but also healthy bodies. The government believed that only when women had healthy bodies would they

be able to participate in economic, cultural, and military work—and produce and nurture a healthy new generation. Chinese women since then have been encouraged to participate in sports nationally and locally.

With the introduction of an open-door policy and the reinstatement of Chinese membership by the International Olympic Committee (IOC) in 1979, Chinese female athletes had the chance to enter the world sports arena. The Chinese Sports Ministry emphasized that all professional teams should recruit and train women athletes. China emphasized development of female elite athletes as part of its determination to raise the whole

standard of Chinese elite sports, and in the belief that women's involvement in elite sports would be evidence of gender equality in the new China. Sports would be instrumental in showing the advantages of socialist gender policy. Millions of young girls were carefully selected, tested, and graded for athletic potential, and the best were put through a disciplined, military-type training that included conditions of hardship and injury so the athletes would develop toughness of spirit and body, skill, training, and competition. The so-called sports spirit emphasized Chinese women's traditional qualities, such as endurance and obedience.

But although China's female elite athletes were achieving satisfactory results on the world's stage and making crucial contributions to China's advances in world sports, they were also suffering from suppression of their self-expression, self-fulfillment, and self-realization. This suppression caused contradictions in Chinese women's sports: concern and cruelty, hardship and enjoyment, conformity and individuality, obedience and defiance.

Sports at the Grassroots Level

The emphasis on the political function of women's sports on the international stage created an imbalance between elite sports and mass sports: although female athletes were successful on the international stage, women's physical activity at the grassroots level remained at a low level.

However, just as the Chinese economy has acquired new characteristics as it has become more market oriented, so too has Chinese women's participation in sports, which now combines nationalism, commercialism, and individualism. Today, women's sports participation at the grassroots level is booming, as evidenced by the increase in the number of gym sports, park sports, community sports, voluntary sports organizations, and fitness clubs. The concept of sports as a way of life has gradually been replacing the concept of sports as a political tool. "Sports for all" 全民健身 is a new value, one that gives women more access to and meaning in sports.

Stars of Half of the Sky

YANG Wenyi 杨文意, one of the Five Golden Flowers in China's swimming pantheon, was born in Shanghai on 11 January 1972. She began training as a swimmer at the age of six and joined the Shanghai municipal team in 1984. Two years later, she became a member of the national team. Yang Wenyi was the first Asian swimmer to break a world record when she set a new mark in the women's 50-meter freestyle in a national event. She broke the world record again in the 1992 Olympic Games.

The 1984 Olympics—China vs. CSSR.

XIE Jun 谢军 is a female chess player who made history when she dethroned Maya Chiburdanidze of the former Soviet Union at the 1991 world chess championships, breaking a longtime Soviet dominance in world chess. She also challenged Russian great Anatoly Karpov in a six-game series, the first time in the game's history that a woman's world champion challenged her male counterpart. Xie Jun was widely known for her optimism and vivid attacking style. Her success did much to popularize international chess in China and throughout Asia. She is now an official of the Beijing Sports Commission working with chess players and athletes in other sports.

FU Mingxia 伏明霞 became China's youngest world champion at age thirteen when she won the 1991 World Swimming Championships. The next year she became China's youngest-ever Olympic champion, winning the gold medal for the 10-meter platform event. She won titles in the next two Olympic Games and became a star in the world of international diving.

The "Golden Lilies"

As women's participation in sports has expanded, it's been necessary to change our notions about female beauty. As the extract below illustrates—from Mary Isabella Bryson's Child Life in China *(1890)—bound feet were once a sign of wealth and considered highly attractive in China.*

But the most important part of a young girl's dress in china is her shoes. Such tiny shoes they are, of coloured silk or satin, most tastefully embroidered, with brightly painted heels, just peeping beneath the neat pantalette; the feet are supposed to merit the poetical name bestowed upon them of "golden lilies." . . .

Three inches is the correct length of the fashionable shoes in which Chinese Ladies toddle and limp, supporting themselves on a child's shoulder, or by means of a strong staff. Some very wealthy ladies are the possessors of feet which are almost useless, and, as they can hardly walk from one room to another in their spacious mansions, they are not unfrequently carried, especially about their gardens, on the backs of their large-footed attendants. Women whose feet are not quite so small, though still tightly bound, manage to walk occasionally, with great difficulty, a distance of several miles. "Their movements are as the waving [of] the willows," says a Chinese poet in reference to these tiny feet; but to English eyes the gait appears to be by no means elegant, and bears a strong resemblance to what would be obtained by walking on our heels.

GAO Ming 高敏, known as the "Diving Queen," was born in the city of Zigong in southwest China's Sichuan Province. She won eight gold medals in major events such as the Olympic Games (1988, 1992), World Swimming Championships (1986), and the World Cup (1987, 1989). She won more than seventy titles in her career. She was also chosen as the World's Best Diver of the Year by the U.S. magazine *Swimming World* from 1987 to 1989.

China had achieved little in women's middle- and long-distance running until the 1993 World Championships in Stuttgart, Germany, where WANG Junxia 王军霞 won the 10K-meter gold medal and broke the world record. One month later, she broke the world record in the same event in China's eighth National Games. In 1994 she beat a strong field and received the Jesse Owens International Trophy Award, presented to the world's best amateur athlete, in New York. In 1996 at the Olympics in Atlanta, Georgia, she capped her career with a 5K-meter gold medal and a 10K-meter silver medal. Wang Junxia is regarded as the best runner in China's sports history, famously called the "Oriental Divine Deer" 东方神鹿.

Wang Junxia was born into a peasant family in northeast China's Jilin Province in 1973. As a child she was weak and pale and her family had little to do with sports. It was unimaginable that this running champion would one day become famous for her tenacious spirit and inflexible will, which played a big part in her athletic achievements.

CHEN Lu 陈露 was China's first star in figure skating. She was born in Changchun in 1976, the daughter of an ice hockey coach and a table tennis player. As a young skater in the early 1990s, Chen demonstrated both athletic ability and artistic potential, out-jumping many of her contemporaries and the world's top figure skaters. She made an impact in 1995 at the World Figure Skating Championships in Birmingham, England, where she won the women's singles title to become China's first world champion in figure skating. She was one of the most decorated skaters of the decade, winning two Olympic medals, four World medals, and nine national titles.

DENG Yaping 邓亚萍 was a table tennis legend. She was born in 1973 in Zhengzhou, Hannan province, where Chinese culture originated. At the age of four, she began to play table tenning under the guidance of her father. At eight she won the national amateur championship. In 1988 she became a member of the National Training Team. Deng Xaping was not only the first Olympic table tennis paddler to defend her title in two straight Olympics, but she was also the only winner of four Olympic gold medals in the table tennis competition in the history of the Olympic Games. Apart from these four Olympic gold medals, she also won six gold medals in Table Tennis World Championships between 1989 and 1997. In total, she has won some eighteen world championships and Olympic medals.

■ XIONG HUAN 熊欢

PART FOUR

Welcoming the World

奥运在中国

Olympic Games often transform their host cities, and Beijing has indeed undergone a dramatic and perhaps long-lasting "makeover." Its Olympic Green, the central area for the Olympic contests, now boasts a massive National Stadium. Known as the "Bird's Nest," this architectural wonder seats 120,000 people. After the Games, the Green will serve as a cultural and commercial center with conference facilities, shopping, and sporting events. Western Beijing—once a belt of pollution-spewing steel plants—is now the location of Olympic shooting ranges, indoor cycling, and a basketball stadium. Construction, tourism, and changes to the city's infrastructure, among other factors, have been estimated to bring an additional $13.2 billion and 1.82 million jobs to Beijing. But the Olympics are certain to have more than an economic impact on the city—and on China itself. Part Four of *China Gold* looks at how Beijing and other Chinese cities have prepared for the Olympics. It considers as well the impact the Games will have on a nation that welcomes to its shores 300,000 tourists from overseas—and some 20,000 foreign journalists—while the whole world watches.

Where the Action Is

中国金比赛场地

COMPANY'S COMING—LOTS OF company—and China has made the dust fly: renovating or building thirty-six gymnasiums and stadiums and fifty-nine training centers as China prepared to host the 2008 Olympics—not only in Beijing but in Tianjin, Shanghai, Hong Kong, Qingdao, and Qinhuangdao.

New venues include the Beijing National Stadium, Beijing National Indoor Stadium, Beijing National Aquatics Center, Olympic Green Convention Center, Olympic Green, and Beijing Wukesong Culture and Sports Center. Some will be owned and governed by the State General Administration of Sports, for use after the Olympics as facilities for future national sports teams and events, while US$2.1 billion (17.4 billion Renminbi [RMB]) in corporate bids and tenders are expected to fund almost 85 percent of the construction, with investment from corporations that will have ownership rights after the Olympics.

Sports Venues in Beijing

The concepts of both centralization and decentralization—"one center plus three areas"—were used in the general distribution of the sports venues in Beijing. The "one center" is the Olympic Green, and the "three areas" are the University Area, the Western Community Area, and the North Scenic Spot Area. Five other venues, including the Workers' Stadium, will be renovated or expanded to facilitate cultural and sports activities for neighboring residents after hosting training and contests of the Olympics.

Olympic Green

The Beijing Olympic Green 北京奥林匹克公园 is the central area for the Olympic contests, along with the National Stadium, the National Sports Venue, and the National Aquatics Center, as well as the Conference Center, which will serve as a temporary fencing hall. After the Olympics the Conference Center will serve as a conference and exhibition site, and the Olympic Green will become a public activity center for sports contests, conferences, exhibitions, entertainment, shopping, and cultural and commercial activities.

National Stadium

The National Stadium 国家体育场—designed by Herzog & De Meuron Architekten, ARUP, and China Architecture Design & Research Group and known as the "Bird's Nest"—lies east of the north end of the central axis of Beijing inside the Beijing Olympic Green. With a seating capacity of 100,000, including 20,000 temporary seats, the stadium will be the main venue for the Olympics, where the opening and closing ceremonies, as well as track and field and men's soccer finals, will be held. The stadium will become a center for sports and other entertainment as well as the host stadium for Beijing Guo'an Soccer Club.

National Aquatics Center

Located inside the Olympic Green, the National Aquatics Center 国家游泳中心, known as H_2O^3 or the "water cube," faces the National Stadium at the north part of Beijing's central axis. Together they exemplify many of the historical and cultural features of Beijing. The National Aquatics Center is the venue for swimming, diving, synchronized swimming, and water polo events, with a seating capacity of seventeen thousand.

National Indoor Stadium

With a seating capacity of eighteen thousand, the National Indoor Stadium 国家体育馆 is composed of a main hall, a nearby warmup gym, and other outdoor facilities. It will host the artistic gymnastics, trampoline, and handball events. The stadium's design was inspired by a traditional Chinese folding fan.

Olympic Forest Park

With a total area of about 680 hectares, the Olympic Forest Park 奥林匹克森林公园 is separated into southern and northern districts by Beijing's North

The uniquely designed Beijing National Stadium, known as the "Bird's Nest," hosts the track and field events at the 2008 Olympics.

Fifth Ring Road. Covering an area of about 300 hectares, the northern district not only boasts natural ecological landscapes but also serves as a water treatment system. The northern section is equipped with temporary facilities for the Olympics, including hockey and archery fields, tennis courts, and the International District of the Olympic Village. The northern and southern districts are linked by China's first "ecological corridor," a bridge astride Beijing's North Fifth Ring Road provding passage for both wildlife and people.

Olympic Sports Center

The Olympic Sports Center 奥体中心 was the main venue for the Asian Games held in Beijing in 1990, and lies in the southern part of Beijing Olympic Green. Olympic soccer, handball, and the running, equestrian, and swimming events of the modern pentathlon, as well as water polo, will be staged at the main sports stadium and in the Ying Tung Natatorium (once the largest indoor swimming facility in Asia) of the Olympic Sports Center.

University Area

Some events of the Olympics will be held in the gymnasiums of five universities:

■ Peking University Gymnasium 北京大学体育馆 is the venue for table tennis. Equipped with equipped with six thousand permanent seats and two thousand temporary seats, the facility will be adapted for use as a comprehensive gymnasium for the university after the Games.

■ China Agricultural University Gymnasium 中国农业大学体育馆, seating eight thousand, hosts the wrestling events.

■ Beijing Science and Technology University Gymnasium 北京科技大学体育馆 is the scene of the judo and tae kwon do events.

■ Beijing Institute of Technology Gymnasium 北京理工大学体育馆 is the venue for volleyball.

■ Beihang University Gymnasium 北京航空航天大学体育馆 is the venue for weightlifting events.

Hong Kong's Head Start

By early 1938, after the Japanese blockaded Shanghai and other Chinese ports, half of China's foreign trade was diverted through Hong Kong. Banks such as the Bank of China and the Communications Bank moved to Hong Kong, making the colony the exchange-banking center for all of China. The massive influx of refugees from China exacerbated the colony's already crowded housing conditions and strained its resources, but Chinese entrepreneurs also brought capital—even entire factories, some of which produced military equipment for the Chinese war effort. This helped build an industrial base that would greatly assist Hong Kong's economic recovery after the war.

In early 1946, Hong Kong's population was around one million. Trade had returned to almost 60 percent of its prewar level. During the same year, Hong Kong got its own airline, Cathay Pacific, a predominantly British corporation. The economy recovered so quickly that the government enjoyed a budget surplus for the 1947–48 financial year. Hong Kong's economy also benefited greatly from the Chinese civil war between the Nationalists and the Communists, as its industry, which was already reasonably well developed, was given a boost by Chinese entrepreneurs escaping the war. The colonial government later estimated that the infusion of capital and business experience from Shanghai gave the colony a head start of at least a decade over the rest of East Asia.

Hong Kong's colonial history also accounts for its leadership in another area of commerce—horse racing. Founded in 1884, the Hong Kong Jockey Club has long been a world leader in promoting racing and betting. Hong Kong's reputation as an equestrian sporting center was a major factor in the decision to locate the 2008 Olympic equestrian events here.

■ JOHN CARROLL

Other Beijing Venues

The Capital Gymnasium 首都体育馆 is in Beijing's Haidian District, in the midst of hotels and parks. The gym accommodates eighteen thousand spectators and will be used for volleyball events.

Western Beijing once was one of the main pollution sources in Beijing. However, after steel plants and other large companies responsible for most of the pollution moved out of Beijing, the area was converted into a number of venues for the Olympics.

■ Beijing Shooting Range Hall 北京射击场 is the scene of eleven shooting events of the Olympics, including rifle, pistol, and running target events and all the shooting events of the Paralympic Games. The trap events take place in the Clay Target Field inside Beijing Shooting Range.

■ Laoshan Velodrome 老山自行车馆 is the cycling venue.

■ Wukesong Indoor Stadium 北京五棵松体育中心, part of the Wukesong Culture and Sports Center, hosts the basketball events.

■ Fengtai Softball Field 丰台体育中心垒球场 is the venue for softball events.

The North Scenic Spot Area includes such venues as the Olympic Aquatic Park by the Chaobai River in Shunyi, Beijing Country Equestrian Park, and the Xiaotangshan Softball Field in Changping. They will be used mainly for rowing events, canoe/kayak, canoe/kayak slalom, equestrian, and softball events and will become an important district for tourism and leisure vacation in north Beijing.

Other venues within Beijing include Workers' Stadium 北京工人体育场, which can accommodate the Olympic soccer matches; Chaoyang Park 朝阳公园沙滩排球场, the scene of beach volleyball; and the Thirteen Ming Tombs Reservoir 十三陵水库, the triathalon venue.

Venues outside Beijing

In addition to the many sites for Olympic events in and around Beijing, other cities in China will host events ranging from water sports to soccer.

Qingdao International Sailing Center

On the southern coastline of the Shandong Peninsula sits a beautiful port city, Qingdao City (pop. 7.2 million) of Shandong Province. In the northern part of the city lies Laoshan Mountain, which was said to be a mountain of God in the past. The Qingdao International Sailing Center 青岛奥林匹克帆船中心 is located on the old site of the Qingdao Beihai Shipyard by Fushan Bay on the eastern coast of the city. It will host all of the water sports held at sea during the games.

Shanghai Stadium

As the biggest city in China, Shanghai (17.8 million) serves not only as a center of economics, finance, and cultural education in eastern China but also as the most important hub for marine and air transportation in China. Located at the junction of Metro Line 1 and Inner Ring Road in southwest Shanghai, the Shanghai Stadium 上海体育场 was the main venue for the eighth National Games in 1997. It consists of the main stadium, which has a seating capacity of eighty thousand, the indoor stadium, capable of holding up to ten thousand people, and the Shanghai Aquatic Stadium. It will host some of the soccer competitions.

Tianjin Olympic Center Stadium

Covering a land area of 34.5 hectares, the Tianjin Olympic Center Stadium 天津奥林匹克中心体育场 lies in the Olympic Center of southwest Tianjin. It was designed by Axs Sawto Inc. (Japan), with a grandstand capable of holding sixty thousand spectators. With close proximity to Beijing and a similar climate, Tianjin (pop. 10.3 million) served as a training base for the Olympic teams of several other nations, including Norway.

Qinghuangdao Olympic Stadium

As a summer resort on the coast of the Bohai Sea, Qinghuangdao City (2.6 million) is the scene for some of the soccer preliminaries of the Olympics. The Olympic Center Stadium 秦皇岛市奥体中心体育场 is a six-story stadium that holds thirty-five thousand spectators. The stadium, with the blue sky as its background in the daytime, resembles a white sail rising on the sea. With the light of the floodlights at night, it resembles a large shining seashell resting by the sea—the characteristics of seaside architecture are fully represented. In addition, the sports center has an indoor stadium with a seating capacity of 5,425 as well as a comprehensive gymnasium and two outdoor soccer training fields.

Shenyang Olympic Stadium

Once the capital of the Qing dynasty 清 (1644–1912), Shenyang (pop. 5.3 million) is now the capital of Liaoning Province and a popular soccer city in northeast China. Mukden Palace, the former imperial palace of the early Qing Dynasty (now a UNESCO UNESCO World Heritage Site) is located here. The Olympic Sports Center Stadium 沈阳奥林匹克体育中心, in Wulih 五里河 district, will be one of the soccer preliminary venues in the Olympics.

Hong Kong Sports Institute

The Olympics steeplechase and dressage events' main competition venues take place in Hong Kong (pop. 7 million) at the Hong Kong Sports Institute 香港奥运马术比赛场. In addition the cross-country events will be held in the Beas River Country Club of the Hong Kong Jockey Club and the adjacent Hong Kong Golf Club.

■ TAN HUA 谭华

The colorful, eye-catching Beijing National Aquatics Centre, nicknamed the "Water Cube," hosts the Olympic water sport events.

Setting the Stage

中国金筹备奥运

ON 13 JULY 2001, A NATION OF 1.3 billion people heaved a collective sigh of relief as the International Olympic Committee (IOC), meeting in Moscow, announced which city would host the 2008 Olympics: Beijing, China.

After the first round of voting by the IOC, only Beijing, Toronto, Paris, and Istanbul had remained in contention; Osaka was eliminated after having received only six votes. In the second round Beijing received an absolute majority of votes—with fifty-six—and no subsequent voting was required. Although some people claimed that the bids from Paris and Toronto were technically superior, the IOC, under

Juan Antonio Samaranch, was eager to see China, the world's most populous country, host the Olympics. Although many nations praised the decision, a few groups objected, arguing that China's human rights issues made the nation unfit for the honor. To quell such objections, the city of Beijing chose the motto "New Beijing, Great Olympics" 新北京, 新奥运 to emphasize the country's move toward a new image for the new millennium.

Logo

The official logo of the games, called "Dancing Beijing" 中国印舞动的北京 features a stylized calligraphic character *jing* 京, meaning "capital." (Beijing means "northern capital." The logo was unveiled in August 2003 in a ceremony attended by 2,008 people at Qi Nian Dian 祈年殿—the Hall of Prayer for Good Harvests in Tian Tan 天坛, the Temple of Heaven in Beijing.

The logo draws on elements of Chinese culture, depicting a traditional red Chinese seal above the words *Beijing 2008* and the Olympic rings. The seal is inscribed with a stylized calligraphic rendition of the character *jing* in the form of a dancing figure. The curves are also meant to suggest the body of a wriggling Chinese dragon. The open arms of the figure symbolize the invitation of China to the world to share in its culture. Red, the dominant color of the emblem, is an important color in Chinese society, signifying good fortune.

The logo was designed to symbolize China's journey to the future, the promise of the nation, the beauty of the city, the heroism of the athletes, and China's desire to welcome the world to its capital city.

Mascots

Fuwa 福娃 were unveiled as the mascots of the games by the National

With an influx of English-speaking athletes and tourists during the Olympics, Beijing residents of all ages and professions are taking classes in English.

Society of Chinese Classic Literature Studies on 11 November 2005, at an event marking the one thousandth day before the opening of the games.

Fuwa consist of five members: Beibei, Jingjing, Huanhuan, Yingying, and Nini. The five mascots incorporate fish, giant panda, fire, Tibetan antelope, and swallow designs, respectively, and each also represents one of the five Olympic rings. When the five names are put together, they form a pun on the phrase, *Běijīng huānyíng nǐ*, 北京欢迎你, which means, "Beijing welcomes you."

Slogan and Songs

In June 2005, the Beijing Olympic Committee announced that the slogan for the 2008 Olympics would be "One World, One Dream" 同一个世界, 同一个梦想. Since 2003, there has been a competition underway for songs that would spread the Olympic spirit of *Citius*, *Altius*, *Fortius* (Swifter, Higher, Stronger), promote the theme of "Technological Olympics, Humanistic Olympics, and Green Olympics," and celebrate the culture and humanism of China.

Broadcasting

The Olympics will be broadcast worldwide by a number of television and radio networks:

■ Mainland Chinese state-owned CCTV, predominantly CCTV-5, will have the same coverage rights as the rest of its broadcast partners around the world.

■ Channel Seven in Australia will broadcast the events.

Olympic Volunteers from the Hawkeye State

In the Olympics of the early twentieth century, host cities enlisted volunteers for such simple assignments as couriers, flag-bearers, and safety marshals. After World War II, Olympics volunteers became increasingly important in a much broader variety of capacities. The preparations by the Beijing Organizing Committee of the 2008 Olympic Games (BOCOG) have elevated the celebration and deployment of volunteers to new heights.

There are an estimated 100,000 volunteer positions at the Beijing Games (70,000 at the Olympics and 30,000 at the Paralympics—with close to half a million more expected to work as "city volunteers" offering information, language, and emergency services at stations across the municipality, and a million more "social volunteers" for related tasks leading up to and during the Games). Among this vast number are about three hundred students recruited from a dozen universities and colleges in the United States, United Kingdom, and Australia to assist with media work.

The University of Iowa in Iowa City, Iowa, where I teach, is one of six U.S. schools in the program. In 2005, my longtime friend XU Jicheng—a senior sports reporter and editor for Xinhua News Agency whose additional role as a China Central TV commentator on National Basketball Association broadcasts makes him recognizable throughout the country—went to work for BOCOG's Media Operations Department.

Upon learning that Big Xu—as everyone calls him—would be running the Main Press Centre for the Games, I half-jokingly asked him if I could volunteer as his assistant. He replied with a request that I recruit students whose native language was English to assist the Olympic News Service (ONS) with competition coverage.

The ONS supplies detailed information to the international media on every Olympic and Paralympic event, with English as the first language (followed by French and Chinese). Big Xu asked me to deliver sixty to one hundred students! I said twenty or so was more realistic.

The result: twenty-four students from our university in the U.S. heartland—after prolonged preparations in journalism, Olympics and sports studies, and Chinese language, history, and culture—are spending the summer of 2008 in Beijing making their contributions to the Olympic movement. Eleven will cover tennis for the ONS; five will cover wrestling (an especially appropriate assignment given an Iowa tradition that has produced a string of Olympics champions in this sport); six will work in the International Broadcasting Centre; and two will work in the Main Press Centre.

These young people know they are in for the experience of a lifetime. Meanwhile, I'll be in the best seat in the house—my own house in Iowa, watching TV.

■ Judy Polumbaum

■ CBC and Radio-Canada and its properties, along with TSN and RDS in Canada, will broadcast across Canada.

■ NBC Universal, with NBC and its cable properties in the United States, will handle the U.S. broadcast.

One of the oldest pastimes in China, kite-flying, takes wing with the new logo of the Olympics.

■ In the United Kingdom the BBC will carry the Olympics.

China will also stream all events over the Internet.

Tickets

The Beijing Olympic Organizing Committee announced in August 2006 that it would sell more than 7 million tickets for the Olympics. The chief of the committee said she hoped that all people in China will have a chance to attend the games. The committee therefore set the admission prices very low to encourage the Chinese to become involved in the Olympics. For the opening ceremony, ticket prices range from 200 Renminbi (RMB) (US$25) to 5,000 RMB (US$625). For the individual sports events, the price range is from 30 RMB (US$3.75) to 800 RMB (US$100), determined by the degree of popularity of the sport in China. In addition to the public, tickets were set aside for sponsors, officials, and members of the IOC.

Public Transportation

In preparation for the games Beijing's subway system has undergone expansions to more than double its size. The system had been composed of four lines and sixty-four stations. An additional seven lines and more than eighty stations have been constructed, including a direct link to Beijing Capital International Airport.

Firing the Imagination: The Olympic Torch

On 26 April 2007, the Beijing Organizing Committee for the Games of the XXIX Olympiad (BOCOG), in the presence of the International Olympic Committee, unveiled the Lenovo-designed Beijing 2008 Olympic torch, called the "Cloud of Promise" 祥云. Since its inception in 1936, the Olympic torch has come to represent the history and culture of the host country and city. Lenovo's approach for the Beijing 2008 Olympic torch incorporates a sleek and modern design with historical Chinese symbolism.

The torch was carried by torchbearers around the world in the Olympic torch relay that precedes the start of the Beijing 2008 Olympic Games. The torch, fashioned from a polished aluminum-magnesium alloy, measures 720 millimeters by 50 millimeters by 40 millimeters and weighs 1,000 grams. The 2008 Olympic torch was also designed to evoke the traditional Chinese concept of the five elements that make up the universe: metal (gold), wood, water, fire, and earth, with primary coloring of deep red and bright silver, and an embossed pattern of clouds, which represents the ever-developing Chinese culture. "Inspired by the shape of a traditional Chinese scroll, the imagery of the 'Cloud of Promise' represents the traditions of China, while the shape, texture and technology evoke the Olympic spirit," said Yao Yingjia, executive director of the Lenovo Innovation Design Center in Beijing.

The Torch Relay

After being lit in Olympia, Greece, the torch relay (called the "Journey of Harmony" 和谐之旅) traveled to the Panathinaiko Stadium in Athens and then to Beijing, arriving on 31 March. The torch traveled to twenty countries around the world, including the United Kingdom, France, United States, Australia, India, and Japan, creating no small amount of controversy in Europe and the United States. The torch relay includes visits to cities on the Silk Road, symbolizing ancient links between China and the rest of the world, with an attempt to carry the flame to the top of Mount Everest, as well as to Taiwan, Hong Kong, Macau, and 113 cities in China, arriving at its final destination in Beijing for the opening of the 2008 Olympic Games.

■ XIONG XIAOZHENG 熊晓正

Sponsorship of the Beijing Olympics

ALTHOUGH THERE HAVE BEEN sponsors as long as there have been modern Olympic Games—the U.S. company Eastman Kodak was a sponsor the first of the modern Olympic Games in 1896—it has only been in the last twenty-four years that companies have been able to pay for the privilege of calling themselves the "official (retailer, outfitter, beverage, car, camera) of the Olympics." Coincidentally, 2008 is also be the twenty-fourth year since China returned to the games after more than thirty years away. More importantly, it is the first time that China has hosted the game, another milestone in the seemingly endless list of firsts for China as its global influence grows.

China as an International Host of Sporting Events

China has hosted several large-scale sporting events recently, including the Shanghai Showdown (China's first Gravity Games, an extreme-sports competition), the Nanshan Open (a snowboarding event), and the 720 China Surf Open. The Asian X Games, which have previously been held in Thailand, Malaysia, and South Korea, were held for the first time in the People's Republic of China in May 2008, attracting more than two hundred of the world's top extreme-sports athletes.

The Korean automaker Kia Motors was just one of the sponsors of the 2007 X Games, which were also backed by ESPN, ESPN STAR Sports, and the Chinese Extreme Sports Association. Kia Motors, a secondary sponsor of the Asian X Games since 2005, renewed its support with a three-year primary sponsorship both to build the event in China and to gain product exposure. According to Kia Motors, in 2005 alone, exposure from the Asian X Games was worth approximately US$12 million.

With these successes under its belt, and given the enormity of the Chinese market, the Beijing Organizing Committee for the Games of the XXIX Olympiad (BOCOG) had little trouble lining up sponsors and partners to help finance and coordinate the Games.

The Beijing 2008 sponsorship program consists of three tiers of support: partners (who pay approximately $40 million), sponsors (who pay approximately $20–30 million), and suppliers (who offer goods and services). Johnson & Johnson, one of the Beijing Olympics' U.S. sponsors, was eager to take advantage of the billions of viewers who, in the words Brian Perkins, the company's vice president of corporate affairs, will be "looking at Beijing and China with amazement." Herbert Heier, CEO of the German sportswear manufacturer Adidas, whose sponsorship is reportedly between $80 and $100 million in cash and services, sounded a similar note: "The Beijing 2008 Olympic Games will once again be a worldwide visible proof of our dedication to athletes, products, innovation and leadership. At the same time, the Beijing 2008 Olympic Games provides us with a unique platform to build the Adidas brand image and business in China, as well as the whole of Asia," he said in 2005, when the sponsorship was announced.

The Bank of China (BOC), the most internationalized of China's commercial banks and the second-largest bank in China, is another institution benefiting from the first Olympics being held in China. In July 2004, it became the sole banking partner of the Beijing Olympics. As such, it is the exclusive provider of both commercial and investment bank services and products. It is also a large player in the BOCOG licensure and ticketing programs, partnering with Visa, the premier credit card company, to improve and upgrade the financial infrastructure necessary for ticketing, automatic teller machines (ATMs), and other point-of-sale services. Multinational partnerships such as this also provide Chinese companies with an opportunity to learn and benefit from the experience of long-time Olympic sponsors like Visa, which has been a global Olympic sponsor for more than twenty years.

Chinese manufacturers such as Haier, which produces home appliances, televisions, mobile phones, and theater systems, are also major sponsors of the 2008 Olympics. As a sponsor, Haier will provide funds, home appliances, and other services to the Beijing 2008 Olympic Games, the Beijing 2008 Paralympic Games, BOCOG, and the Chinese Olympic Committee. Haier is based in Qingdao, the sister-city host of the Olympics, where sailing events will be held. Chances are good that

most viewers of the Olympics won't see the home appliances Haier is providing, but the benefits of sponsorship extend from simply being able to promote itself as an official sponsor to leapfrogging its efforts at global brand recognition. When the sponsorship was announced, BOCOG Executive Vice-President and Secretary-General WANG Wei 王微 said. "Sponsoring the world's greatest sporting event also provides Haier with an unparalleled platform to build up its prestige on a global basis."

Other Chinese companies that are sponsors and partners of the Beijing Games—hoping that 2008 will catapult them into foreign markets—include the computer manufacturer Lenovo, the SINOPEC energy company, Air China, Tsingtao Brewery Company, and more.

International brands such as Coca-Cola are competing fiercely to get exposure during the Games.

Challenges for Foreign Sponsors and Partners

With the games in Beijing, foreign companies are finding that they must also weigh the advantages of the publicity and attention that sponsorship brings against potential backlash from protestors, activists, and politicians who are using the games as an opportunity to sound off against the Chinese government.

It should be pointed out these are not the first games to meet opposition. The so-called Nazi Olympics of 1936 are often mentioned but there are many examples, including the 1976 boycott of the Montreal Games by the Organization of African Unity (OAU) based on the sporting links many countries had at that time with South Africa, where apartheid (racial segregation) remained entrenched. The Moscow Games of 1980 and Los Angeles Games are other noteworthy examples, and indeed, any country that has hosted the Olympics in the past twenty-four years has had its detractors, ready to protest the host country and ready to call for boycotts of the sponsor companies.

Longtime Olympic sponsors such as Coca-Cola, Eastman Kodak, and General Electric, with their widespread influence, have often been the targets of such activism. The difference today is that with so much media, Internet, and global connectivity, the Beijing Olympics may be the first games for which grassroots activism could have as large an impact on the image of the games as the athletic competition itself.

Critics of Beijing protested before the awarding of the 2008 Games to China,

Sport Politics

Sports have the ability to act as a metaphorical background or a pressure relief valve for both nations and individuals. On a number of occasions the sporting arena in general and the Olympic Games in particular have provided a stage where the two superpowers could compete in a sporting environment in front of the eyes of the world. In a number of instances politics has adversely affected the proceedings. Indeed, one can argue that without politics a broad interest in international sports would not exist today. The use of the Olympic Games as a tool in boycott politics during the 1970s and 1980s was possible only because of the influence of the mass media on global society during the latter half of the twentieth century.

The Olympic Games during the Cold War provide examples of this inherent tension within the developing sporting exchange.

The Moscow Olympic Games of 1980 and the Los Angeles Olympic Games of 1984 were tarnished by boycotts related to ongoing fractious superpower relations. Yet, in 1976 in Montreal the Olympic Games were boycotted by the Organization of African Unity in protest of South Africa's apartheid regime. Although the 1976 boycott was clearly political, perhaps the best examples of Cold War tensions in sports were the boycotts of the early 1980s. At both Moscow and Los Angeles the Olympic Games acted as a showcase for the political ideologies of Communism and capitalism, respectively. Too often in the history of the Olympic Games opportunities to learn about people in other countries and to develop a sense of social responsibility have been undermined by the subordination of sports and recreation to political and commercial goals.

■ JONATHAN M. THOMAS

anyone anywhere—true or not—can impact your brands everywhere . . . That [fact] will be increasingly important between now and August 2008 when three billion people tune in to television and the Internet to watch the Olympic Games in Beijing. There, center stage will be not only the athletes, but corporations as well." According to Future 500, companies need to approach the games with a measured amount of support for both the activist causes and their Chinese hosts. One issue that has been problematic for the Beijing games has been the genocide in the Darfur region of Sudan and China's continued investment there.

When confronted by activists about another issue of concern—labor conditions in China—Adidas said that the company would pressure its suppliers in China, with whom the company has direct influence, but that it would not attempt to pressure the Chinese government. That approach—working to address poor labor conditions, human rights abuses, or other problems without directly confronting the Chinese government—may be the least risky and therefore most palatable.

Olympic sponsorship, while risking controversy based on the political climate of the times, is generally too appealing to pass up. With an audience in the billions, foreign companies increase their brand recognition and future profits in China, while Chinese companies use the Olympic platform to introduce their brands to the rest of the world.

■ SCOTT ELDRIDGE II

and continued to protest about issues including censorship and media control, unfair working conditions, China's role in Sudan, and control of religious practice in Tibet.

Despite their deep pockets and global clout, international sponsors such as Adidas, Coca-Cola, General Electric, Johnson & Johnson, and McDonalds care about their corporate image and the reputations of their brands and must take into account opposition to Beijing's hosting of the Olympics. But they also have to think beyond the Olympics, to how they are going to grow their businesses in and with China. It often seems that companies

have two choices, both with unappealing ramifications: they can acknowledge the activists and risk alienating the Beijing government, or ignore the activists and alienate the Western consumers who rally to their cause. Public relations firms and organizations such as the group Future 500, a nonprofit liaison service between corporations and stakeholders, are trying to tread the narrow middle ground. Future 500's China initiative is designed to foster constructive interaction between corporations and nongovernmental organizations and other activist groups. As Future 500 reminds companies on its website, "For industries that operate on the global stage, anything said by

The Economic Impact of the Olympics

北京奥运与经济

CLEARLY CHINA, PERHAPS THE world's hottest market, does not need a major sports event to catapult an ailing economy back into growth mode, as was the case with the 2006 FIFA World Cup in Germany. On the contrary, the Chinese government will host the Olympic Games amid rumors of an overheating economy (growth accelerated to more than 11 percent in the first quarter of 2007). China possesses the largest foreign reserves of any country in the world—the government can spend lavishly to produce ultramodern stadiums for the games and to upgrade Beijing's infrastructure.

However, officials estimate that the 2008 Olympic Games will add 0.8 percent to Beijing's annual growth rate between 2004 and 2008, adding $13.2 billion to the capital's economic output and 1.82 million jobs. Tourism, infrastructure, finance and insurance, retail, and wholesale are among the economic sectors that will profit most from the games. Investments in hotels are running high because Beijing expects an additional two million tourists, 300,000 of them from overseas, to visit in 2008, spending an average of $150 (domestic tourists) and $1,050 (overseas tourists).

However, assessing the impact of a single event on the macroeconomic development of an economy is difficult, and in most cases the ex-post analysis of costs and contributions to economic development has had to be revised considerably. Some observers even argue that there is no proof of long-term economic benefits at all from large-scale sporting events.

The official budget for hosting the Olympics is a state secret too sensitive to be revealed even to the National People's Congress, formally the highest state organ in China. Some of the investments are disappearing in the labyrinthine bureaucracy of China's two-tier economy and are impossible to quantify; in any event, statistics on China's record-breaking economic development over the last twenty-odd years

The Olympics as Civic Boon

Cities the world over mount energetic and elaborately detailed plans in order to win the approval of the International Olympic Committee to host the Olympic Games. Such campaigns are underpinned by various motivations: civic and national pride and prestige, political gain, economic benefit. The quest by Los Angeles to host the Olympic Games provides an early example. A desire to promote the City of Angels as a tourist and vacation mecca, as a climatically healthful place in which to live, and as an area of great economic potential through the investment of capital for handsome dividends prompted Los Angeles to bid for the Games of 1920. Pierre de Coubertin's intent to hold the 1920 (Antwerp), 1924 (Paris), and 1928 (Amsterdam) Games in Europe stalled the Los Angeles bid. But the persistence of William M. Garland and his Los Angeles colleagues finally paid off and the city received the Games for 1932.

By the eve of the Games of the Tenth Olympiad, the United States, indeed much of the world, was in the midst of a devastating economic Depression. Despite this, the Games went on, and, it might be argued, in glorious fashion. Funding much of the festival from a $1 million state appropriation gained through a public referendum, the main events were held in the relatively new Los Angeles Memorial Coliseum. An Olympic Village was built for the first time, but only for men; the women were accommodated in the Chapman Hotel in downtown Los Angeles. Were the expectations of California's tourist and land speculators realized as a result of bringing the great world sporting spectacle to Los Angeles? One has only to gaze on the City of Los Angeles and the State of California today to arrive at the answer.

■ ROBERT BARNEY

have a remarkable history of academic doubts and ex-post corrections.

Tourism and Construction

The most obvious economic impact of the 2008 Olympics is on two major sectors—construction and tourism—but even in those sectors, quantifying the direct impact of the games is difficult because both sectors have experienced continuous growth in recent years. Reports of 10,000 hotel beds added in Beijing appear impressive, but then, China is considered to be a hot spot for hotel investment anyway, having become a must-see destination. More important, the lack of qualified service personnel is said to remain unresolved in spite of efforts by the municipal and central governments. Undoubtedly the campaigns to introduce international standards in behavior and communication and to widen the spread of English among taxi drivers, restaurant staff, shop owners, and so on will have lasting effects on the development of Beijing's service sector if the campaigns result in a sustained and sustainable improvement in human capital.

The boom in the construction sector has been a double-edged sword for China's long-term economic modernization. Overall investments in 2002–06 reached a level that caused concern among economic analysts and policy makers alike, but the central government's attempts to rein in growth through economic measures such as hikes in interest rates and political measures such as pressure on local

The new headquarters of Chinese Central Television, the chief broadcaster of the Beijing Olympics, under construction.

and regional leaders has had only limited success.

A Positive Influence or a Negative One?

Although the modernization of Beijing's infrastructure and municipal buildings is definitely an asset to the people living and working in China's capital, the contributions to gross domestic product are, as mentioned above, hard to estimate because no one can know how much money would have been invested in Beijing without its successful bid for the Olympics. Then too, the benefits accruing from the Olympics are at least partly countered by the potential harm that may be caused by a real estate and investment bubble—for example, residents of Beijing have found that affordable apartments are harder to come by in the run-up to the Olympics.

Most investors agree that the Chinese government has done everything in its power to prevent a financial crisis during the run-up to the Olympics. One of the most striking features of China's financial markets is the dominance of the state as a central actor who owns most of the shares of most of the companies, controls nearly all of the brokerages, governs the exchanges, and limits the market entrance of foreign firms. However, although from a social perspective the prevention of a financial crisis is one of the most important tasks of any government, in the case of China, efforts to prevent such a crisis may mean the delay of desperately needed reforms for the sake of public appearance.

Sports Media in China

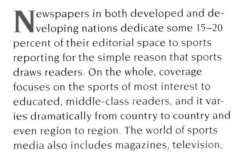

Newspapers in both developed and developing nations dedicate some 15–20 percent of their editorial space to sports reporting for the simple reason that sports draws readers. On the whole, coverage focuses on the sports of most interest to educated, middle-class readers, and it varies dramatically from country to country and even region to region. The world of sports media also includes magazines, television, radio, and the Internet.

Sports coverage in China, naturally, focuses on the country's most popular sports, and ranges from national and international competitions to information about various national fitness program. *China Sports Daily*, the first leading sports newspaper, is an official publication of the General Administration of Sport. Other more specialized newspapers have appeared, as well, including *Sports in the South* and *Football*, and there are more than one hundred sports magazines in China—not yet rivaling the U.S. or some European countries, but still a large number with considerable popular influence.

Almost every radio station in China broadcasts sports programs, ranging from news and competitive events to fitness exercises, but televised sports programs are broadcast mainly by CCTV-5—the most important and popular sports channel—as well as by regional and international satellite sports channels. Many sports fans now also go to the Internet to read sports news, watch matches, and play electronic sports.

Media at the Games

In the 2001 bidding procedures for the 2008 Games, Beijing assured the International Olympic Committee "that there will be no restrictions on media reporting and movement of journalists up to and including the Olympic Games." The Beijing Organizing Committee for the Games of the XXIX Olympiad (BOCOG) established a media operations department four years before the start of the Games to serve the foreign journalists covering the events and the more than thirty foreign television networks broadcasting the Games around the world.

The presence of so many foreign media representatives—estimated at over 20,000—may well have an effect on Chinese media professionals and the companies focusing on sports, as Chinese reporters have a unique opportunity to interact with and learn from their Western colleagues.

■ QIU XIAOHUI

Transparency and Accountability

The lack of transparency and accountability within China's socialist market economy hinders analysis of the economic impact of the Beijing Olympics. When a Beijing newspaper quoted a government document that cited an increase of about $700 million on the original estimates of $1.34 billion for the cost of the games, the newspaper was censored. Pressure from the National People's Congress on the Chinese leadership to disclose to it the budget for the games led to nothing. In official statements, the Chinese government reiterates its position that total expenditures remain close to those of the 2004 Olympic Games in

Athens ($1.4 billion planned, $2.2 billion spent).

Calling for improved transparency and accountability, though, was hardly an act of defiance by the Congress. The Chinese leadership under HU Jintao 胡锦涛 sacked a number of high-ranking Communist Party officials, among them the mayor of Shanghai and the vice secretary of the Beijing Chinese Communist Party, who headed construction work for the Olympics, referring to their embezzlement of public funds and to massive corruption.

Publicly acknowledging party officials' corrupt behavior in the last few years serves several political purposes: it is an attempt to stem the illegal transfer of state assets into private bank accounts, and it also addresses one of the most urgent grievances in the everyday lives of the people of China.

Questions Remain

During the preparations for to the Olympics, the whole world has seen Beijing's remarkable economic success. Whether the investments in Beijing's infrastructure would have occurred without the games and whether these stimuli truly add .8 percent to Beijing's growth rate are of secondary significance. Obviously China does not need the Olympics to add dynamism to its incredible socioeconomic transformation. The more urgent question is the impact of hosting the games on China's emerging socialist market economy. Raising public awareness, introducing measures to improve the sustainability of the economic boom, battling corruption, and improving the working conditions of foreign journalists all may contribute to an increase in transparency and accountability in China's policies—and if transparency and accountability increase, then the economic impact of the games will be tremendous.

■ Jörn-Carsten Gottwald

PART FIVE

The Olympic Ideal and the Three Themes of the Beijing Olympic Games

奥林匹克理想与 北京奥运三大理念

In the 112-year history of the modern Olympics, the Games have been criticized and even boycotted for different reason, but our enduring love of sports and abiding desire to see countries come together in peace tends to trump political disagreements. The 2008 Games are unique in Olympic history because they are being held in a country poised to rise to new prominence on the global stage. The Olympics are a creation of Western civilization, but as China resumes a bigger international role, these Games—only the third to take place in Asia—give it a chance to integrate some of the Olympic ideals into its perspective on global leadership and also an opportunity to influence an event that has unique meaning for many people around the world.

The Olympic Ideal

中国金 奥林匹克理想

IN THE AFTERMATH OF VIOLENCE in Tibet in spring of 2008 and at the Olympic torch relay in England and France, rising nationalistic feelings in China drew media attention, and Chinese people around the world complained about the bias and anti-Chinese racism of the Western press. Ironically, it is just this sort of international tension and nationalism that the Olympics were instituted to allay.

Pierre de Coubertin created the modern Olympic Games as more than simply a spectacle or a romanticized imitation of the glories of ancient Greece. He was an educator with a global vision, acting at a time when the world was suffering from upheavals and conflicts—and when more conflicts loomed. He saw peaceful competition as something that would give the world's young people maturity and confidence, and thus the ability to respond to the social, political, and economic challenges of the early twentieth century. Coubertin and his supporters were also aware that friendly international contacts would reduce prejudice, increase trust, and diminish the dangers of excessive nationalism. The Olympic Charter—the rules and regulations of the Olympic Games and the International Olympic Committee—puts it this way: "The goal of the Olympic Movement is to contribute to building a peaceful and better world by educating youth through sport practiced without discrimination of any kind and in the Olympic spirit, which requires mutual understanding with a spirit of friendship, solidarity and fair play."

Pierre de Coubertin and the Birth of the Modern Olympics

Baron Pierre de Coubertin (1863–1937) of France is known as the founder of the modern Olympic Games. However, even before Coubertin, people had attempted to reestablish the ancient Olympics of Greece. However, these attempts—in Greece, France, England, and the United States—failed because they lacked the internationality that has been the elixir of today's modern Olympic Games.

Coubertin did not reintroduce the Olympic Games merely to stage an ancient sports festival but rather to offer nations of the world a chance to compete peacefully. He hoped that young people would develop a maturity that would lead to an ability to cope with social, political, and economic challenges of the early twentieth century and become responsible and democratic citizens. Coubertin and his supporters also hoped that the Olympic Games would foster "international contacts," allowing people to represent their country and get to know people of other countries and encourage a reduction of hatred, distrust, and prejudice. Nationalism and internationalism do not, in Coubertin's opinion, exclude each other. Coubertin believed that, properly understood, peaceful internationalism corrects a narrow-minded nationalism but also acknowledges the differences and characteristics of other nations, thus disassociating itself from superficial cosmopolitanism. By reintroducing the Olympic Games Coubertin planned to consolidate and extend interest in international competition. The Olympic Charter—the rules and regulations of the Olympic Games and the International Olympic Committee (IOC)—addresses this goal: "The goal of the Olympic Movement is to contribute to building a peaceful and better world by educating youth through sport practiced without discrimination of any kind and the Olympic spirit, which requires mutual understanding with a spirit of friendship, solidarity and fair-play."

The Olympic Games were reestablished and the IOC founded in 1894 at the Olympic Congress in Paris. Coubertin was the organizer of the congress and was supported foremost by Charles Herbert of England and William Milligan Sloane of the United States. Athens was chosen as the first host city for the rebirth of the Olympics Games in 1896.

■ KARL LENNARTZ AND STEPHAN WASSONG

THE IMPORTANT THING IN THE OLYMPIC GAMES IS NOT WINNING BUT TAKING PART. THE ESSENTIAL THING IN LIFE IS NOT CONQUERING BUT FIGHTING WELL.

BARON de COUBERTIN

Opening Ceremony of the 1948 Olympiad.

China is increasingly trying to weave together Western ways of thinking with Chinese values that derive from its traditional philosophies, such as Daoism, Buddhism, and Confucianism. One expression of this comes in the three themes that the Beijing Olympics Committee chose, along with the Olympic slogan, "One World, One Dream," to relate China's traditional philosophies and five-thousand-year history to the ideals of the games and to the challenges of the twenty-first century. These three themes are "technological Olympics" 科技奥运, "humanistic Olympics" 人文奥运, and "green Olympics" 绿奥运.

■ Karen Christensen

The Technological Olympics

中国金科技奥运

FROM THE ORIGINAL ANCIENT GAMES to the modern Olympics, the central focus of Olympic competition, and of competitive sports in general, has been the development of the human body in order to achieve victory over an opponent. Originally, however, many sports were designed for religious and ritual purposes and to foster harmony between body and soul—and even balance between man and nature.

Yet a technological approach to sport has been present at least as far back as the 1890s, when Baron de Coubertin, who revived the Olympic Games in 1896, said, "Exercise science has devised several means for strengthening professional performance. It views the body as a complex performance machine comprised of many parts. Each part is independent and interchangeable."

Feelings about the role of technology in sports are often mixed. On the one hand, athletes' application of new sports technology makes competition more exciting and enjoyable, but on the other, some worry that such an approach encourages athletes to ignore the nature of the human body.

A high-tech Olympics has several goals. First, it aims to demonstrate the advanced technology and innovation of the new China, which made possible a clean, beautiful, safe, and convenient Olympic environment. Second, it seeks to integrate advanced Chinese and foreign technology. Third, it hopes to stimulate further development of high technology and to increase the use of such technology in everyday life.

The technology used in competition, however, represents only a small part of the application of technology at the 2008 Olympic Games. Most of the technology goes into serving the needs of the Olympic spectators. Olympic security, transportation, communication, the construction of venues and other assisting facilities, the management of the games, even the way people think about the games are all affected by the use of modern technology. This has been true from the time that Berlin broadcast live Olympic programs on worldwide television in 1936 and has only become more true with each technological advance in communications, engineering, and so forth. The spread of the Internet has made the games even more available to the public; in 2004, nearly everyone had firsthand, instant access to event results.

Technological Innovation and the Olympics

Innovation improves performance, opportunity, and interest. The fastskin swim suits which ignited controversy at the 2000 Olympic Games in Sydney, Australia, significantly reduce drag in the water and thus the swimmer's time. Sprinters now wear Lycra bodysuits to cut down on wind resistance.

Composite skis transformed skiing into a popular recreational activity and allowed for innovative designs which led, decades later, to shape skis that allow previously blue skiers to quest black diamond trails. In the 1980s, by moving the center of gravity of the javelin forward, those athletes with precise technique were able to achieve victories that went previously to physically stronger athletes.

The International Olympic Committee is dedicated to protecting the integrity of its games by assuring that victories go to athletes and not engineers. The IOC allows each sport to write its own rules for technology policy but requires that new innovations be available to all the athletes to make sure no one athlete has an unfair advantage. The individual sports are thus charged with determining which innovations will be permitted on the field of play during sanctioned competition. After the 1960s the policy of ignoring technological innovation as many organizations did (cycling and golf are notable exceptions) created crises for many sports governing bodies.

■ J. NADINE GELBERG:

New municipal facilities for dealing with an influx of tourists and athletes have been constructed with water use and environmental impact in mind.

The main stadium for the Beijing Olympics, the "Bird's Nest" 鸟巢, is a good example of technology in the service of the Olympics. It is a steel web that can hold 100,000 people. The outside looks like a nest formed of branches. Its gray steel grid is like a transparent outer membrane, surrounding a red bowl-shaped stadium. The entire building is free of supportive pillars; the bleachers form a bowl without any obstructions, creating a unique theaterlike feel and a huge field of vision.

Another special feature of the Bird's Nest is the designed-in "bulges" that contain 20,000 seats' worth of additional spectator facilities. This bit of architectural ingenuity saved money and spared Beijing from further excavation and building. GUAN Zhaoye 关肇邺, the president of the Appraising Committee and a China Engineering Institute scholar, remarked that the Bird's Nest had not one bit of wasted material or space. The shape is a product of its function; its form and its structure are unified.

High-tech media broadcasting is also crucial to a successful Olympics, and China has been making rapid advances in this area. In the overall strategy of the Beijing Games, digital technology will play an important role in Olympic entertainment. The 2008 Beijing Olympic Games will be the first in the history of the games to use high-definition broadcasting. Mobile phone transmission in color will be among a series of advanced-technology services provided during these games.

In sum, the technology that supports the games, whether physically, as in the actual infrastructure and transportation systems, or electronically, for communications and media systems, represents perhaps an even more important portion of a "technological Olympics" than the technological advances that help the athletes themselves.

■ JIN YUANPU 金元浦

人文奥运

The Humanistic Olympics

中国金人文奥运

TAKING INTO ACCOUNT THE ROLE OF the Olympic Games as a unique vehicle of cultural diffusion, China has designated the 2008 Games as the "humanistic" or "people's Olympics." While the concept known as "humanism" is Western, Chinese culture has a concept that closely parallels it, "humanistic" 人文 meaning "affairs in the human world." This term first appeared in the Shang 殷 and Zhou 周 dynasties, approximately 3,000 years ago. In the

Tang 唐 dynasty (618–907), the Chinese used the term to mean "harmony between man and nature." As the notion evolved, some Chinese began to theorize that man was at the center of the universe and therefore should be given a place of utmost importance.

In the West, the term "humanistic" first appeared as the Latin word *humanitas* in the works of the Roman philosopher Cicero (106–43 BCE). Cicero advocated the ancient Greek style of education, which Cicero admired for developing human character and promoting students' "pure nature." He found a certain correspondence between the Latin word *humanitas* and the Greek *paideia*, "education." Historically, humanism refers to the Renaissance ideology that placed humanity at the center of

the universe, respected human interests and needs, and recognized the human potential for creativity and development.

Today, humanity is reevaluating the classical concept of humanism. As our environment worsens day by day, we begin to question if humans should be seen as the center of the universe. The relationship between mankind and nature is shifting: people must learn to live in harmony with nature.

On the one hand, this humanistic Olympics has the burden of spreading knowledge of the ancient Greek Olympics to the Chinese population; on the other, it also gives the people of China the opportunity to share traditional and modern Chinese culture with the world: "The world gives China sixteen

A Beijing power plant chimney gets painted blue with fluffy clouds to give it a more harmonious look against the sky.

days; we will give the world five thousand years." (世界给我16天, 我还世界5000年)

In the realm of sports alone, China has much to share with the world. Among China's traditional and folk sports are ancient gymnastics, *qi gong* (气功), Chinese martial arts, wrestling, dragon-boat racing (龙舟赛), mountain climbing, and various ball sports. Many modern Western sports, such as football, are similar to ancient Chinese games. In addition, China's fifty-six ethnic minority groups have their own folk games and athletic competitions.

A humanistic Olympics is a positive answer to the expectations of modern Olympic Games. A humanistic Olympics seeks to promote the physical, mental, and ethical development of humans and a harmonious relationship between humans and their living environment. It also encourages cultural exchange between China and the world. A humanistic Olympics is an Olympics for all humanity, giving not only the 1.3 billion Chinese but

The World as One Family

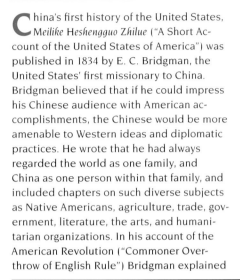

China's first history of the United States, *Meilike Heshengguo Zhilue* ("A Short Account of the United States of America") was published in 1834 by E. C. Bridgman, the United States' first missionary to China. Bridgman believed that if he could impress his Chinese audience with American accomplishments, the Chinese would be more amenable to Western ideas and diplomatic practices. He wrote that he had always regarded the world as one family, and China as one person within that family, and included chapters on such diverse subjects as Native Americans, agriculture, trade, government, literature, the arts, and humanitarian organizations. In his account of the American Revolution ("Commoner Overthrow of English Rule") Bridgman explained

how the colonies in North America grew, prospered, and greatly expanded their trade and commerce. In describing how the King of England began to impose unfair taxes upon the people, Bridgman noted that one of the taxes was levied on one of China's important exports—tea, which was brought to the colonies aboard British vessels. Bridgman knew that his description of the rectitude of George Washington, who refused to make himself king, would remind his Chinese readers of Yao and Shun, two legendary sage-kings of ancient China who sought the most meritorious of their subjects to succeed them instead of creating a ruling dynasty.

■ MICHAEL LAZICH

also all the populations of the world the opportunity to participate in its endeavors and carry on its spirit. The traditional Chinese notions of "peace, harmony, love, and balance" (和平, 和谐, 友爱, 平衡) supplement the Olympics' ideals of *citius, altius, fortius,* or "faster, higher, stronger."

■ JIN YUANPU 金元浦

绿奥运
绿世界

CHINA FACES SERIOUS POLLUTION
problems, but its position as host of
the 2008 Olympics has provided a
strong impetus for ecological reform
while simultaneously creating opportunities for critics who say that the
country is not doing enough, or doing
it fast enough.

One of the major obstacles to China's
winning the competition to host the
2008 Olympic Games was widespread
fear among observers that people attending the games would suffer from
the severe air pollution in China's capital (not, incidentally, a criticism unique
to China; the same anxiety had been
expressed about the previous host city,
Athens, and others as well).

But for China, declaring that the Beijing
Olympic Games would be green was
more than a public relations move.
It was widely known to address one
of the most serious problems China

faces: trying to secure environmentally friendly, sustainable growth for
the years to come. Whereas the 2000
games in Sydney, Australia, and the
2004 games in Athens, Greece, failed
to deliver on their promises to stage
green Olympics, the Chinese government has been making substantial
progress in improving China's dismal
ecological record.

The State of the Environment in China

Reports about China's environment
have become increasingly alarming.
All but four of the world's most air-
polluted cities are in China, and 75
percent of the surface water in China's
cities is not fit for drinking. China's polluted water contributes to certain cancers; the nation has the world's highest
rate of liver cancer.

Since the mid-1990s, Chinese leaders
have increasingly addressed the health
hazards resulting from air pollution,
inadequate drinking water, desertifica-
tion, and erosion. However, even where
resources meet the political will to
fight pollution, the implementation of
environmental policies is often ham-
pered by local interests that put short-
term economic growth and income
creation above long-term ecological
objectives. Environmental protection
and careful and efficient use of natural resources rank high among China's
policy goals, but are clearly second to
the overall goal of high-speed economic growth.

Conceiving a Green Olympics

Originally, the environmental organization Greenpeace drafted the concept of
a green Olympics for the 2000 Olympic
Summer Games in Sydney. The International Olympic Committee subsequently mandated that all summer
Olympic Games be green Olympics. In
2005, the United Nations Environment
Programme and the Beijing Organizing Committee for the Olympic Games
agreed to try to make the summer
Olympics of 2008 environmentally
friendly. The Beijing Organizing Committee promised to make environmental protection a priority, not only in the
designing and construction of Olympic venues, but also through affores-
tation campaigns, beautification of
urban and rural areas, increased public
awareness, and promotion of green
consumption.

Implementing the Concept

From the athletes' perspective, tackling
air pollution in the Chinese capital was
one of the prime challenges. The image
of runners in the marathon competing
in clouds of smog has become a consistent nightmare of athletes, journalists, and bureaucrats alike. To prevent
this nightmare from becoming a reality,
the government sought to improve
the energy structure to reduce carbon
soot, eliminate 15,000 taxis and 3,000
buses and replace them with 4,000
buses powered by natural gas, close
major coke ovens, put desulphurization
technology in place at coal-burning
power plants, and control the pollution

Energy-efficient buses are now part of the Beijing transportation system, in an effort to make the city and the Games more "green."

of flying dust. However, implementing these measures takes time. Beijing still exceeds the limits set by the World Health Organization for air pollution in spite of the extension of public transport, the introduction of ecological standards for cars, and the introduction of low- and zero-emission buses for use at the Olympic Village and the Media Village.

Adequate sewage treatment is another daunting challenge. The need to recycle water has become more urgent because of successive years of drought in Beijing. Therefore, any improvement in sewage treatment is a welcome relief, even if the first steps are concentrating on the inner districts of the capital. And, in contrast to its disappointing

record in implementing environmental policies before 2005, the government met its goal of treating 90 percent of Beijing's water in 2006 and recycling half of the water by 2007.

Beijing authorities have also promised to put into place a real-time pollution monitoring system in rivers and lakes. If this system leads to faster and more transparent reaction to serious spillages of poisonous liquids into the capital's waterways, then changes made for the Beijing 2008 Olympics will have produced a lasting improvement.

Long-term Improvement

When representatives of the International Olympic Committee visited Bei-

jing in the 1990s, the local government resorted to the use of artificial color to "green" the yellow grass along the roads and squares to improve the city's environmental credentials. On the eve of the Olympics, at least some of the environmental goals have indeed been met. A city as huge as Beijing cannot be turned into an ecological showcase overnight, but authorities have managed to implement policies that do more than just apply short-term makeup, and their efforts indicate that China is likely to play an active role in international efforts to deal with global environmental problems in the years ahead.

■ Jörn-Carsten Gottwald

After the Games: China Gold

中国金 奥运会以后 中国金

THE BOOK YOU ARE HOLDING IS, of course, about gold medals, world records, and stunning physical achievement. It has told the stories of great athletes, great leaders, and great moments in sport. It has shown the sweat, the tears, the challenges, and the glory involved not only in hosting the 2008 Olympic Games, but in aspiring to win Olympic gold. The competitions draw the world's largest audience—bringing people to their knees in prayer or stomping their feet in exaltation in front of television sets around the globe. But as mentioned in the Foreword, it is also about something closer to alchemy—the relationship of humanity and nature that accentuates the importance of transformation in both.

The notion of transformation has informed some of the West's greatest writers and philosophers (Shakespeare, Sir Isaac Newton, Carl Jung) and has been developed within Daoism as well. Chinese alchemists followed a tradition known as the Way of the Golden Elixir (*jindan* 金丹 *zhi dao* 之道). Gold (*jin*) represents the state of constancy and immutability that contrasts with the change and transience characteristic of the physical world. *Dan*, or "elixir," evolves from the root meaning of the word "essence," and pertains also to the true nature of an entity, its most basic and meaningful elements or qualities Like the term *China gold*, these concepts are aspirational and, as such, fit with the ideals of the Olympic Games.

As we look beyond the Olympics of 2008, we can be certain that the values of the Olympic Movement and the themes of the Beijing Games will have educated us. As China, the United States, and the other nations of the world face the challenges of the twenty-first century, we can bring to those challenges the Olympic ideals and the understanding of one another's perspectives that the Olympics foster. The alchemist aims to develop the knowledge and techniques that can bring nature and society into harmony—and into full flower. At its most idealistic, this transformation is what the Olympics are all about.

■ KAREN CHRISTENSEN

For current Olympics and China information, author and editor blogs, modern sports photographs, and historical documents and photographs, visit **www.chinagold2008.com**

Further Reading

Barmé, Geremie. *The Forbidden City*. London: Profile Books, 2008.

Booth, Douglas, and Holly Thorpe, eds. *Berkshire Encyclopedia of Extreme Sports*. Great Barrington, MA: Berkshire Publishing Group, 2007.

Brownell, Susan. *Beijing Games: What the Olympics Mean to China*. Lanham, MD: Rowman & Littlefield Publishers, 2008.

Fan Hong, ed. *Sport, Nationalism, and Orientalism: The Asian Games*. London: Routledge, 2006.

Fan Hong, and J. A. Mangan. *Sport in Asian Society—Past and Present*. London: Frank Cass, 2003.

Guanxi: The China Letter. Special issue: How China Will Change the Olympics. (July 2006).

Guanxi: The China Letter. Special issue: Olympic Update. (July/August 2007).

Guttmann, Allen. *The Olympics: A History of the Modern Games*. Champaign, IL: University of Illinois Press, 2002.

Guttmann, Allen. *Sports: The First Five Millennia*. Amherst, MA: University of Massachusetts Press, 2004.

Hessler, Peter. *Oracle Bones: A Journey between China's Past and Present*. New York: Harper Collins, 2006.

Jin Yuanpu. *Culture Guide of the Olympics for College Students*. Beijing: Higher Education Press, 2006.

Li, Lillian M., Alison J. Dray-Novey, and Halli Kong. *Beijing: From Imperial Capital to Olympic City*. Basingstoke, UK: Palgrave, 2007.

Luo Shiming. *The Olympics Come to China*. Beijing: Tsinghua University Press, 2005.

Pound, Richard. *Inside Dope: How Drugs Are the Biggest Threat to Sports, Why You Should Care, and What Can Be Done about Them*. Mississauga, Ontario: John Wiley & Sons Canada, 2006.

Sang Ye. *China Candid: The People of the People's Republic*. Berkeley, CA: University of California Press, 2007.

Wasserstrom, Jeffrey. *China's Brave New World—and Other Tales for Global Times*. Berkeley, CA: University of California Press, 2007.

123

About the Editors

 **FAN Hong** 凡红 is a professor and director of the Irish Institute of Chinese Studies at University College Cork. She was born in Sichuan and trained as a swimmer in Beijing before pursuing an academic career in the UK. Fan's recent publications include *Sport, Nationalism and Orientalism: The Asian Games* (2006).

 **Duncan Mackay** is an award-winning British sports journalist. He studied Chinese history and politics at university and has covered every Olympics since Barcelona 1992. He now writes for the *Observer* and is publisher and editor of www.insidethegames.com, a website devoted to the Olympic Games. He carried the Olympic torch in London in April 2008.

 **Karen Christensen** worked with hundreds of sports experts as coeditor of the *Berkshire Encyclopedia of World Sport* and senior editor of the *International Encyclopedia of Women and Sports*. She is CEO of Berkshire Publishing Group and publisher of *Guanxi: The China Letter*.

About the Authors

CAO Shouhe 曹守和 is a professor of sports history at Hangzhou Normal University, China. His recent publications include *Modern Chinese Sports History*.

CHANG Sheng 常生 is a professor of sport sociology at Nantong University, China, who specializes in athletics in China.

Bjoern Conrad wrote his Master's thesis on the political and economic implications of the Beijing Olympics and is currently studying at Harvard's Kennedy School of Government.

CUI Ying 崔颖 coordinates worldwide out-of-competition testing programs for international federations at the World Anti-Doping Agency (WADA) in Montreal, Canada.

Scott Eldridge II is a journalist who has written for *Guanxi: The China Letter* and was a reporter in Washington, D.C., covering U.S.-China international trade policy and economics.

FAN Wei 樊维 is the director of swimming teaching and research at Chengdu Sports University, China.

Jörn-Carsten Gottwald is a lecturer at the College of Business of Law and the Irish Institute of Chinese Studies at University College Cork.

GUO Hong 郭红 is a professor at South China Normal University. Her research areas are sports medicine and sports physiology.

HU Xiaoming 胡小明 is a professor at Huanan Normal University, China. His research interests focus on sports history and sports anthropology.

JIN Yuanpu 金元浦 is a professor of literature at Renmin University of China. He is executive director of the Research Centre of Humanistic Olympic Games in Beijing.

LUO Shiming 罗时铭 is a professor of sports history at Soochow University, China, and author of the *History of Olympics in China*.

LU Zhouxiang 吕洲翔 is a lecturer in the College of Sports at South West University of Science and Technology, China.

REN Hai 任海 is a professor at Beijing Sport University. He is known for his work in Olympic studies with special reference to China.

TAN Hua 谭华 is a professor in sports history and sociology at South China Normal University in Guangzhou. His publications include the *History of Sport of the People's Republic of China* (1999).

Holly Thorpe is a lecturer at the University of Waikato, New Zealand, and coeditor (with Douglas Booth) of the *Berkshire Encyclopedia of Extreme Sport*.

XIONG Huan 熊欢 is a lecturer at the Irish Institute of Chinese Studies, University College of Cork in Ireland. She has written widely on women and sports.

XIONG Xiaozheng 熊晓 is a professor at Beijing Sports University. His publications include *Chinese Ancient Sport* and *Readings of 2008 Beijing Olympic Games*.

ZHANG Ling 张玲 is a physical education instructor at Guangdong University of Foreign Studies.

125

Index

129

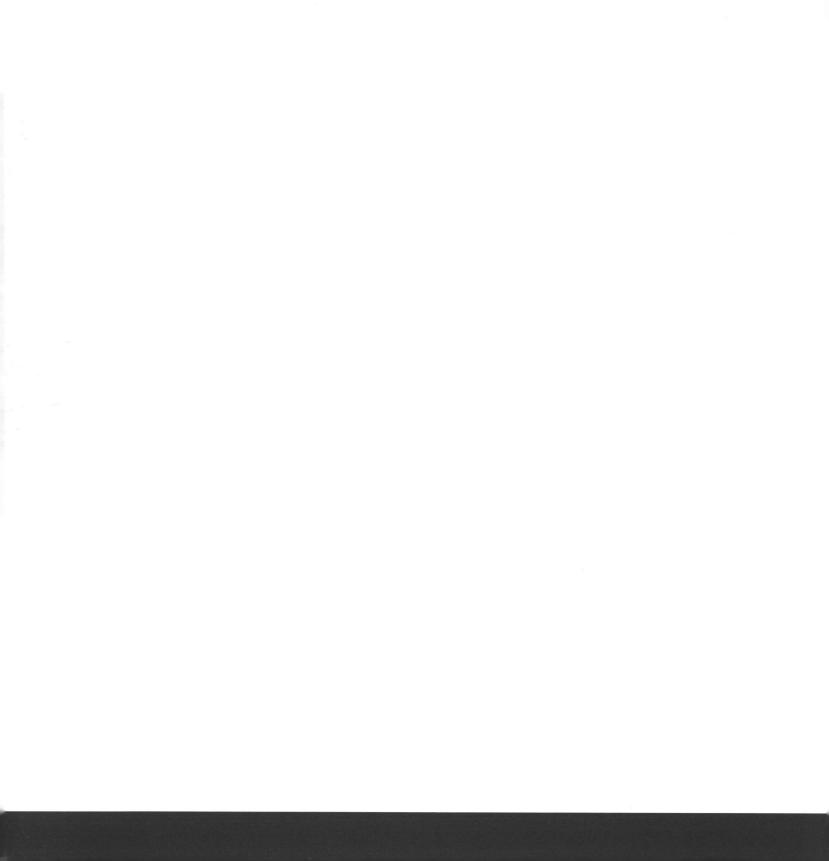

Photo Credits

Berkshire Publishing Group

Cover (from left):image 2, 3, 6; page 2, 33, 37, 39, 50, 52, 79, 80, 94

Jan Berris

Page 4

China Foto Press

Cover photos (from left): image 1, 4, 5; page 5, 11, 14, 17, 32, 34, 35, 41, 42, 43, 44, 48, 49, 62, 65, 69, 83, 102, 104, 110, 117, 118, 121

Corbis

Title page

Garage Industries

Page 84

Getty Images

Frontispiece, page 1, 7, 10, 12, 20, 22, 24, 26, 30, 54, 55, 56, 72, 75, 77, 82, 97, 99, 101, 107, 113, 115

Howard Knuttgen

Page 88, 91

istock.com

Page 85, 86

China Gold 中国金

China's Quest for Global Power and Olympic Glory

路漫漫：从辉煌奥运到世界强国

For information on quantity purchases, please contact:

Special Sales
Berkshire Publishing Group
122 Castle Street
Great Barrington, MA 01230
U.S.A.
cservice@berkshirepublishing.com
TEL +1 413 528 0206
FAX +1 413 528 5241

Available through all major distributors worldwide.

www.chinagold2008.com

Berkshire publishes a variety of books, encyclopedias, and educational and professional publications on Chinese culture and business, including *Guanxi: The China Letter.* Visit **www.guanxionline.com** for full details and trial subscriptions.

FROM THE GOOD EARTH

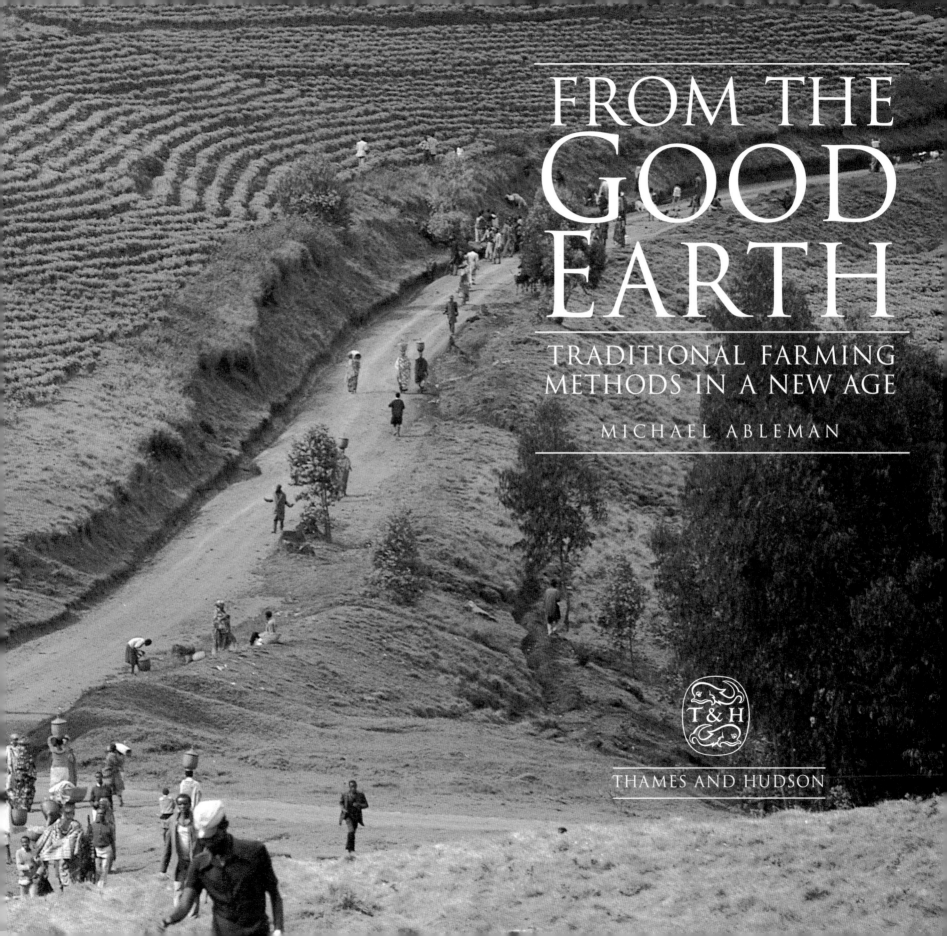

FROM THE GOOD EARTH

TRADITIONAL FARMING METHODS IN A NEW AGE

MICHAEL ABLEMAN

THAMES AND HUDSON

Wes Jackson would like to thank
J. Stan Rowe for his insight about going inside a cell.

page 1: Basket of compost. China
pages 2–3: On the way to market. Ijenda, Burundi
page 6: Aaron Ableman. Autumn, Fairview Gardens Farm

CONTENTS

To my son, Aaron, who grew up with the making of this book

FOREWORD

Imagine that we humans could make ourselves small enough to enter some average-sized cell and, once there, continue to miniaturize to the point that we needed binoculars in order to examine various parts off in the distance. The parts with dynamic processes we would undoubtedly call living, and we would inevitably designate some things—crystals, some membranes—as dead. If we used this living vs. dead taxonomy, it would only be because we had lost our ability to see the larger perspective during the shrinkage. Lacking our former more comprehensive mind, we would think that some things count more than others.

Now imagine that a proportionally large creature were to arrive in our solar system and, after some shopping, pick the Earth to visit. Imagine such a creature able to shrink to our size but, unlike us losing our perspective, the visitor keeps the larger perspective in mind. He or she or it would soon discover that a most amazing species has changed the face of the Earth in some dramatic ways to grow food and fiber. Our visitor, at first glance, might think that humans are basically artists bent on dressing the earth with their own designs.

Now imagine that to our visitor the Earth is a sort of field site, an object of study for something like a doctoral dissertation. Maybe it is a long-term study in which the investigator visits our planet every two hundred years or so beginning ten thousand years ago. On this, the fiftieth visit, this student of the Earth would realize that the population of one particular species, self named *Homo sapiens,* is rapidly increasing in number and that as it does, it pollutes and destroys more and more of the parts of the planet necessary for the maintenance of what it calls life.

Many humans in thousands of places over the globe *have* been truly artful. But, as our visitor would realize, there is cause for alarm. During the two hundred years between the last and the present visit, many deposits of energy-rich carbon have been discovered in pools and seams and employed to power the agricultural enterprise.

From the outside perspective, when the traditional cultures relied exclusively on contemporary sun power, agriculture, culture, and nature were so intimately united they were difficult to distinguish. This phenomenon was art, yes. It was culture, yes. But it was the body and the mind at one with the materials of the creation. There was no separation. Food was not just fuel then, either, and the tools necessary to capture sunlight and provide diet—air, water, soil—if they were dead, they were dead in the same way as a crystal or membrane is dead in the cell. This is no mere detail. Such a designation as nonliving invites a prejudice. Since air and water and soil are just dead stuff lying around we act as though we can pollute or destroy them at will.

All of this points to the importance of this book. Michael Ableman is one of those artists mentioned here. His tool is not the brush. Like good farmers everywhere, he has several tools, such as the pitchfork, the hoe, the rake, the shovel, pruning shears. Like almost all good agricultural artists, he is interested in the creations of others who have worked with the same tools. So intense has that interest been that he has traveled around the globe to see what other artists have done and are doing. He took his camera on this pilgrimage, and lucky for us that he did, since he knows how to make a picture.

Whether in China, Peru, Africa, or Sicily, or among the Hopi of the American Southwest, the artists featured here have emphasized wisdom over cleverness. They experiment, but experimentation is subordinate to tradition. The true artist honors a balance of emotion and technique, people and land, individual and community, plant and animal. Michael Ableman's photos capture the beauty of that balance.

Since the 1930s, industrialized agriculture has been increasingly promoted by the industrial mind. But now, a small but growing minority realizes that these high-energy subsidies from the geologic past destroy information of both the cultural and biological varieties. This approach not only hot-wires landscapes, it rooster-tails the finite supply of nutrients from our agricultural lands into the supermarkets, into the kitchen sinks, onto the chopping boards, onto the table, and into the human gut, and, once there, more or less heads only one way, downstream and into the sewers and graveyards.

Maybe our problem is that we are unable to keep the perspective of that outside observer, for we fail to absorb what we know: that all nutrients must cycle, that we shouldn't introduce chemicals into the environment without regarding them as guilty until proven innocent, that fossil fuels are finite, that nuclear power requires the repealing of Murphy's Law to be safe, that agriculture—not agribusiness—is the source of culture, that the parts are important to the whole. We have to ask: is the deterioration of the environment an outward mirror of an inner condition? Probably so.

Though the realities of industrial agriculture are represented here, this book is no "ain't it awful" checklist. It is primarily about an agriculture with a human face and the new pioneers bent on the most important work for the next century—a massive salvage operation to save the vulnerable but necessary pieces of nature or culture and to keep the good and artful examples—put there by people who are at one with the earth—before us.

The point of art, after all, is to connect. A sound agriculture is done and will be done by artists who have realized with Dante that "who paints a figure, if he cannot be it, cannot draw it."

Wes Jackson

STARTING

INTRODUCTION

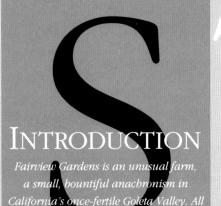

Fairview Gardens is an unusual farm, a small, bountiful anachronism in California's once-fertile Goleta Valley. All around, where orchards and fields thrived, the deep, rich topsoil has been graded, compacted, paved over, and built on.

It has been a great joy for me to watch my young son on his foraging adventures around our farm, tomato seeds splattered across his clothes, black soil covering his knees, and a piece of fruit in each hand. He was grazing before he could walk, crawling across the orchard floor in determined pursuit of a fallen peach, or in the fields, digging his way to a tender carrot with little concern for the rich topsoil that accompanied this treat. Earthworms and snails were his first playmates, the fields and orchards his first classroom. I have observed as his knowledge of the farm and the bounty it provides has helped to build a strong body and a spirit to match.

I think of children on other farms, only hours from here, whose homes are separated from their factory-like fields—miles of single-crop monotony where posted signs warn "Keep Out." I think of those who have never even seen a farm, whose experience of food and the earth comes in a package.

I remember my own childhood and the trips "downstate" with my grandfather in his old Cadillac. Everyone in southern Delaware knew Granddad, so we stopped continually to chat with old friends. But the main focus of these trips was food: we were modern-day hunter-gatherers, collecting crabs from the Indian River inlet and carrying bushel baskets of tomatoes and peaches down the creaky steps at Mr. Dewey's fruit stand.

My grandfather lived through the lean times of the depression, so nothing gave him greater pleasure than to watch his family eat. Rather than sit, he stood at the

POINTS

head of the table with a watchful eye, always ready to fill an empty plate. Nanna piled the steaming corn on the cob so high that it blocked my view of my family sitting across the table.

The corn at my parents' house was another story. It frequently came disguised in cream sauce, often from a frozen package.

It took me many years to realize that the journey of our food from the field to the plate was a series of assaults: on the land and the people who produce the food; on our bodies, as we consume unquantified amounts of chemical poisons on foods disguised by dazzling colors, perfect shapes, or fancy packages; and on an environment withering under the miracle of postwar techno-chemical agriculture.

That the tainted food on our plates has consequences beyond our own personal health is a connection few can or dare to make. Our separation from our food sources—the fact that farms are "out there," out of view—has blinded us to the effects agriculture is having on the earth.

In fact, modern agriculture might be the root cause of the greatest environmental damage to this planet. Many foods that we take for granted are produced in ways that seriously affect our world. How brutally ironic that the common potato, strawberry, loaf of bread, or hamburger can be directly linked to the destruction of the rain forests; nitrate pollution of groundwater; the poisoning of our land, water, and wildlife through the use of pesticides; and, perhaps most urgent of all, the rapid depletion of the earth's placenta, the thin layer of topsoil upon which all life depends.

The way we secure our food is essential to our health as individuals, the bonds that hold together our families and communities, whether rural or urban, and the future of our life-supporting environment—locally, nationally, and globally.

Once I began to make the connection between my health, the health of the earth, and my food choices, I knew that I had to participate consciously in the process of growing food.

———————

Fairview Gardens is an unusual farm. Situated in the once-fertile Goleta Valley of southern California, it is a horticultural paradise producing some seventy-five to a hundred varieties of

In the peach orchard, Fairview Gardens Farm. Less than two minutes away are six gas stations, eight banks, and twenty fast-food restaurants.

fruits and vegetables. It is surrounded by suburbia, hemmed in by places where the valley's deep, rich topsoil has been graded, compacted, paved over, and built on.

But Fairview Gardens has been spared, blessed for the last twenty years with people who have protected it as a valuable community resource. The farm grew from the vision of a remarkable couple, Roger and Cornelia Chapman. Committed to growing food without chemicals and in a way that regenerates the land, they purchased the Fairview property in 1974.

It was a shambles when they took over. On one three-acre field that now yields literally tons of fresh vegetables, the topsoil had been scraped off and sold. The rest of the land had been neglected for so long that most of it had been taken over by an impervious layer of weeds.

The Chapmans hired Chris Thompson, a local farmer, who began the slow, painstaking process of rebuilding the soil. By the time I arrived in early 1981 with my wife and baby son, Chris had established a beautiful foundation. Later that year, when Chris decided to move on, the Chapmans asked me to take over the farm. We entered into a successful partnership that continues to this day.

Living and working on a farm in the midst of suburban housing tracts and busy roads has not always been easy. Many times, while I've stood in the orchard pruning or in the fields harvesting, fumes of hamburgers and french fries have wafted up from the nearby burger joint,

Southern California's overlapping seasons provide an embarrassment of riches at Fairview Gardens Farm: sitting amid carrots and cauliflower, my son, Aaron (left), and his friend Tobias share apricots and strawberries while the summer's plum crop ripens behind them.

shaking my illusion of rural quietude, reminding me that less than two minutes away are six gas stations, eight banks, and twenty fast-food restaurants. A few times, while cultivating strawberries in a field that borders the road, I've been assaulted by the screams of "Dirtfarmer!" from high-school kids speeding past in shiny new cars.

Over the years the headlines in the local Santa Barbara papers have chronicled our struggle: "Progress Hangs Concrete Shroud On Goleta Farm" (Nov. 1985), "Compost Pile May Land Farmer In Jail," and "Nuisance In Nose Of The Beholder" (both Aug. 1990)—the sweet, rich smell of my compost pile offended the urban sensitivities of a neighbor who had recently moved into one of the new tract houses abutting the farm. Recently there were the "Rooster Riots," as the local media followed the story of our roosters and three neighbors who wished to silence them.

We have weathered all the controversies, and for the people we feed in this community— some five hundred families—our commitment to the land and the fresh food we produce has been an anchor of sanity in fast-changing, fast-paced southern California, where orchards and farms disappear daily.

In this temperate climate we can fill our fruit stand with a cornucopia of fresh fruits and vegetables, eggs from our hens, and honey from our bees. The sign overhead reads "We grow what we sell," a reminder that much of what is on display was picked fresh that day.

Roadside produce stand. Fairview Gardens Farm

Many people who taste our food for the first time instantly become nostalgic for days gone by, memories triggered by a vividness that only taste and smell can stimulate. To a suburban population that has forgotten its agrarian roots, one bite of our sweet corn or a tree-ripened peach is like a trip into the past, a ticket to a time when they too knew the earth, its feel, its smell, and the taste of real food from the fields.

––––––––––––––

Aaron Ableman, one year old.

My life as a farmer has always been interrupted by a photographer's wanderlust. In 1984 I left the farm to travel in the Himalaya Mountains in Nepal. But on the way there, during a stopover in Hong Kong, a friend encouraged me to take a short side trip into mainland China. This detour provided an experience that would alter the course of my life.

I had been in China for only a few days when my curiosity forced me to ignore the restrictions that kept most foreign tourists out of the countryside. I walked for several hours away from the city of Chengdu, the capital of Szechwan province, eventually up a trail to the edge of a small settlement.

I stood balancing on a narrow pathway separating the fields. All around, as far as I could see, was a network of intensive raised beds, every inch meticulously planted with a diversity of vegetables, surrounded by an elaborate network of waterways and paths. Four thousand years of Chinese agriculture seemed to merge in this moment. I stood in awe of a system so sound that the same fields could be farmed over and over for forty centuries without any apparent depletion of soil or loss of fertility.

I found myself photographing like crazy. I had so often struggled to reconcile my farmer's hand and photographer's eye. Now in China the two aspects inside me came together.

Over the next six years I traveled to many countries seeking out the remote, often-neglected traditional farmers. I wanted to understand how my own approach to food and farming—as a natural bond between community and a generous earth—had been lived out for thousands of years, how and why our society has destroyed that bond, and how we can redeem it.

I later returned to China to study the oldest agricultural tradition in the world. In Africa I visited ancient Kenyan farming cultures, and in the mountains of Burundi I saw a remarkable interconnection between farmer and farm. In the fields of Sicily, where rocks seem to out-number crops, I stayed with farmers who still maintain the traditions that once fed much of Europe. In the Andes I witnessed a culture's incredible adaptation to a vertical terrain, and I was repeatedly drawn back to the land of the Hopi, to a people who have survived in a harsh desert ecology solely through their deeper understanding and connection to the earth and its spiritual forces.

Exploring food sources also took me to the landscapes of modern industrial farms where earth-crunching machinery and deadly chemical sprays at times suggested scenes from a war-ravaged nightmare. This was the provocative contrast.

Peach and plum trees cast late-
afternoon shadows across the rows
of beans, basil, carrots, chard,
and kale.

But my wanderings did not stop there. This alone would have only offered a vision of what we have lost.

I wanted to discover some examples of hope. I began recording those who have quietly been working to restore the earth garden—to bring back purity, nourishment, taste, and beauty to our food. Here on these farms and gardens of the future a growing number of visionaries have combined ancient wisdom, new and often unorthodox science, and a lively sense of aesthetics to create living farms that produce living food. From the fields and orchards of organic farms, to urban ghettos where food gardens have been built on abandoned lots, to communities where developmentally disabled people are nurtured through working with the land, small steps are being taken—small, but powerful, steps.

I traveled over 100,000 miles and across five continents. Through my travels came the realization that a common thread connects all these stewards of the earth. Titus, the Hopi farmer singing to his corn on a remote desert mesa in Arizona; a community of some sixty people in the steep mountains of Peru, working together to plant a field of potatoes for those who cannot work; Dick Harter, an organic rice grower in Chico, California, who cares as much about the number of birds on his farm as the number of grains of rice; and Alta Felton, an eighty-year-old woman whose cotton, black-eyed peas, and yams grow below the railroad tracks in South Philadelphia—all represent a small but far-reaching movement: they all reclaim and renew the earth one spadeful at a time, one bucket of compost at a time, one handful of seeds at a time.

———————

My son, now eleven years old, comes home from school and disappears into the green folds of our farm. Depending on the time of year I always know where to look for him. In May or June he's certain to be stuffing himself with strawberries or swinging from the branches of the mulberry tree. In July, if I crouch down low, I can scan the orchard floor and spot him under a peach tree or seeking out the first apricots. In August he leaves a trail of corn husks not difficult to follow. In October piles of discarded guava skins give him away, and in November the bloodlike stains of pomegranate juice on his face tell me exactly where he's been.

The first fruit of each season has always been his. Somehow he always knows, out of hundreds of trees, where to find the first ripe plum or sweet orange and which of the thousands of plants have the earliest red berries.

For him the starting point has always been food; the dominant food of each season has marked many of his life passages. He was weaned on fresh fruit from our trees, first walked at the peak of navel orange season, and started school with the last of the year's avocados sliced onto his sandwich.

"Food," he recently told me, "is the most important thing in life, besides you and Mom."

Colquepata, Peru. In the end, I traveled more than 100,000 miles to satisfy my curiosity about food and farming.

INTO THE

CHAPTER ONE

On steep slopes above the Valle Sagrado, Peruvian farmers grow beans and barley on terraces that fed their Inca ancestors.

I arrived in Colquepata riding on top of seven thousand bottles of beer destined for the Amazon jungle. I had come to this remote pueblo high in the Peruvian Andes to learn about a culture that had survived for more than sixty generations on land so steep that farmers there have been known to fall out of their fields.

Careening down a narrow, rutted dirt road, every few miles the truck would become mired in knee-deep mud, and we would leap over the sides to the driver's call of "*Pico! Pala! Pico! Pala!*" for the picks and shovels to help to dig it out. Then we were off again, bouncing and sliding, the top-heavy truck swaying out over sheer vertical canyons; it was a full day into the four-day journey before I could bring myself to look at anything but the road.

As the truck forged deep into the mountains, glimpses of life began to draw me in. A dense mist filled a canyon, concealing all but the most distant views. As the sun burned through, the vertical face of a mountain came clear, broken into hundreds of mysterious shapes of brown and green: terraced fields of potatoes, barley, and beans.

Made by hand and expertly engineered by eye, some terraces were no larger than a suburban front lawn yet contained more than thirty varieties of potatoes. In fact, some terraces, as I later learned, had been in continuous use since the time of the Incas, whose short, hundred-year reign had created a range of tools and techniques that allowed people to flourish in a difficult environment. I imagined the many hands and ancient footplows that had made their indelible mark on that steep hillside—a land worked for centuries—yet I could see virtually no erosion.

PAST

Upper left:
Near Pagan in the north of Burma, farmers repeat a timeless procession to harvest. Five thousand Buddhist temples consecrate this ancient landscape, many still in use after nearly one thousand years. The fields are older still.

Lower left:
Cradled by green pastures in the hills of Burundi in central Africa, cropland and homes have maintained a balance with nature for centuries.

Right:
An abandoned fattoria *in a landscape of wheat recalls a time when Sicily was the breadbasket of Europe.*

The day after my arrival I climbed up a steep mountain trail that wound high above the village. Up at almost 15,000 feet were a hundred people working together. On one side of an open valley the men were creating a perfectly patterned field later to be sown with potatoes. They worked with the indigenous *chaquitakla*, a footplow that looks like a curved wooden spade with a metal blade, designed for turning sod in preparation for planting. Working in teams, two men with footplows sliced into the earth at a right angle to each other and pulled back, lifting a chunk of sod; a third person, usually an older man or a child, would turn it over. Twenty or more teams moved across the field with a speed, efficiency, and quality of work that no tractor could equal—even if one existed that could negotiate these slopes.

Women and children collected wild herbs while large pots steamed with quinoa soup and potatoes. By the time the men persuaded me to join in the plowing there had been several toasts to Pachamama (Earth Mother). Maybe it was the altitude or the pure cane alcohol, but the unfamiliar tool felt awkward in my hands, and the vigorous pace of my teammates was difficult to match. What as an observer had appeared an effortless dance turned out to be some of the most strenuous work I had ever done. Even so, stopping often to eat and drink, surrounded by joking and talking, by evening I felt like I'd been at an all-day party, not plowing a ten-acre field by hand.

In southern Yunnan, China, food grows everywhere—on every hill, in every valley. The village of Shanzui is virtually invisible, its earthen walls blending into the surrounding earthen landscape.

25

The chaquitakla, *or footplow,
has its roots in Inca Andean
agriculture. It is uniquely
appropriate to the culture, for it is
almost always used by teams
and groups.*

*Above the pueblo of Colquepata,
at fifteen thousand feet in the
Peruvian Andes, a community
prepares a field for potatoes
that will feed single and
widowed women.*

Left:
Fields of potatoes, barley, and
beans engulf the tiny pueblo of
Huasac, east of Cuzco, Peru.

Below:
Returning home from the
fields above the pueblo of
Colquepata, Peru.

Tired, well fed, and a little drunk, we wandered happily back toward the pueblo on horseback and foot, with llamas, sheep, children, pots, and tools in tow.

For me, the day's work, the ingenious tools, and the men, women, and children working as a community represented a legacy of the Incas that was far more profound than the much-visited ruins of Machu Picchu. More than a glimpse into the past, this was an experience of the living—of a magnificent and enduring adaptation to a vertical terrain.

———

One week after my arrival I was speeding down a two-lane blacktop to Zhangzhou, Fujian province, where government officials had promised to provide the appropriate permits and assistance to enter the Chinese countryside. A brief glimpse of Chinese agriculture a year and a half earlier had prompted me to return prepared to stay for three months, eager to see more.

At a fenced-in compound, a throng of government agents ushered me past limousines with curtained windows into a large room where some forty officials and their personal stenographers were waiting. To my surprise I was to be the guest of honor at a banquet with the provincial governor, to be followed by a tour of an orange plantation. But as my letters of introduction circulated around the room the hospitality came to a tense halt.

"They cut down all the trees to make fields," a Chinese farmer remembered. "According to Chinese wisdom: leave this tree alone—it is just like God. To worship it is to let the field grow better." In the early 1950s, Mao Tse-tung imposed his Grow More Grain program. The rural population was instructed to plant rice everywhere, and the result was widespread deforestation. Changing political influences can create massive environmental degradation, but among traditional farmers one finds a remarkable understanding of care for the land.

The Chinese are feeding a billion people—twenty-two percent of the world's population—on only seven percent of the earth's arable land. Over an agricultural history that spans seven thousand years, they have developed practices of intensive organic farming so sound that fields cultivated during the Han dynasty are still fertile after twenty centuries of continuous use.

Right:
Several crops may share the same field: one ready for harvest, one developing below, and one newly seeded. In some cases ten crops can be harvested from one bed in a year. Outside Chengdu, China, clay pots with removable lids protect the new transplants beneath: first the lids will be removed, as will, eventually, the whole pot.

"There is a problem," the interpreter solemnly informed me. "You want to take pictures and write a book to show the world!"

I had turned out not to be the wealthy American businessman they had expected, eager to negotiate an agricultural enterprise of some sort. I would have thought my dirty sneakers and backpack made that clear.

With official permission withheld, I accepted an offer from a Chinese friend to be secretly guided to villages in southern Yunnan province, some thousand miles away. We would travel

Working among the onions, cabbage, and ripening rapeseed. Near Anning, Yunnan province, China

33

Left:
Eroded landscape. Yunnan, China

Right:
Population pressures, loss of prime lands to development, and external market demands are forcing many indigenous farmers to work marginal lands and use methods that are contrary to their local knowledge. The result is, too often, dramatic soil erosion. A hillside in Peru bears the scars.

with another Chinese friend to Kunming, the capital, and from there into the countryside.

The road out of Kunming was desolate, the soil the color of brick, and construction gangs worked the roadsides most of the way. Several hours into the trip, dense yellow smoke from a steel plant filled the bus with a burning stench. When the air cleared I lifted the shirt I'd used to breathe through and was rewarded with a wondrous sight. As far as I could see was a vast, patterned expanse of cropland, an agricultural quilt woven over thousands of years of Chinese history.

We were surrounded by mustard, wheat, beans, and green vegetables. As I got off, the passengers remaining on the bus looked on with disbelief. I later learned I was only the second foreigner ever to come to this part of Anning county.

Tea—along with coffee and sugar—is among a range of commodities that have changed the face of many developing countries. Often planted on the best land and requiring heavy chemical use, these crops are raised for foreign markets, having little food value for the native peoples who grow and harvest them. Western Burundi

*Right:
On the outskirts of Chengdu, China, a farmer bunches bok choy for the next day's market. Privatization and market incentives have provided an income to many suburban Chinese farmers that far exceeds that of some professionals.*

Left:
A father and three sons harvest
oats near Moray, Peru.

Below:
Near the city of Xiamen, China, a
family transplants cabbage.
Children grow up in the fields in a
natural apprenticeship, their skills
and knowledge absorbed
through observation.

*In Asia and Africa ninety percent
of the farmland is worked with
draft animals. In a small field
near Xiamen, China, a boy plows
down rice stubble.*

Our host was a quiet farmer named Jiang. Over the course of my visit we shared thoughts
about growing and the earth. Philosophical discussion was often difficult as my friends
struggled to interpret the local dialect. But in the fields, farmer to farmer, Jiang and I could
often understand each other without too many words. I began to get an intuitive sense of
how well adapted this farming was as I came to see the complex techniques that had evolved
over centuries of trial and error.

Here was an integrated system far more sophisticated than my own and much of what I
had seen in the West. On permanent raised garden beds, ten harvests of different crops could
occur in one year. All required only minimal space, water, and external inputs, yet produced
sustained high yields. Soil fertility was maintained year after year through composting and
through rotating food crops with "green manure" crops (grown specifically to be turned
under, adding natural nitrogen and organic matter to the soil). Some beds were surrounded

In the Valle Sagrado near Urubamba, Peru, a farmer prepares a field for planting. The boy rides along for extra weight.

by waterways supporting other nitrogen-fixing plants—food for ducks and geese and food for the soil. All resources and waste materials were carefully managed, with everything used, reused, and then used again.

Refined craft and a commitment to sustaining their soils had been passed down through generations. While the broader Chinese environment has been devastated by political and economic pressures, the "simple peasants" in their fields retain a knowledge that has enabled

Returning from the fields.
Ijenda, Burundi

them to bring forth food on the same land year after year, century after century—an accomplishment unheard-of in the West.

On the last night we sat in Jiang's small home with our hands over a coal brazier taking turns washing our feet, a Chinese bedtime custom. My thoughts wandered to the complexities of my life at home.

"Are you aware of nuclear weapons?" I asked. "Nuclear weapons are none of our business," he answered. "They cannot kill the pests. All we can think about is to grow better crops and the next bowl of rice."

———————————

Only a day's drive from urban Los Angeles, a Hopi woman stood on the edge of a cliff winnowing beans. Her basket moved in a rolling motion, sending the beans into the air in a wave, catching and tossing them in the stillness. I observed as she coaxed the wind out of

"You can't carry a tractor over your neighbor's fields," a local farmer explained. The patchwork of small plots so common to China makes tractors impractical. Two of China's greatest resources are still hands and animals.

the dry heat of the day, talking to it and encouraging it like an old friend, until a light breeze grew strong enough to blow away the chaff.

On that particular morning, I had driven to pick up an old farmer at his daughter's house. Bacon and eggs sizzled on the stove, a television blurted the news, and a group of kids waited for the bus that would take them to school. I had come to drive my friend to his field. This outing was not to work—his body was no longer able—but only to look and talk.

We drove to the top of a rock outcropping that rose from his land. From here we could see the whole of his field and beyond, into millions of acres of open desert. There was nothing more sacred, nothing more important in this man's life than his field of corn. I could see it the moment we arrived from the way he touched his plants and looked down and beyond the rows.

Later in the day he sat in the hot Arizona sun silently examining the few ears of corn we had harvested. One by one he picked them up, turning them over and over in his hand. There were white, blue, red, and yellow—representing, I was told, the four human races and the four directions.

A Hopi woman winnows beans in Arizona. Halfway around the world, in northern Thailand, a Karen tribesman echoes her rhythm.

Many times, while out walking on these desert mesas among sage and tumbleweeds, I would discover a lush field growing in the dry, cracked earth. Nothing else around, no pipes delivering water, no houses, no roads—only intense dry heat, and then, suddenly, rows of carefully tended corn sometimes interplanted with beans and melons.

As a farmer, it went beyond my practical understanding of how things grow. Ultimately, I discovered that there was more than farming technique that made this possible.

I remember with a laugh how I explained to my friend that when I need water to irrigate I just open a valve.

"We always pray for rain, smoke for rain," he said. "We dance kachina dance and smoke in the kiva."

"Then the rain comes?" I asked.

"Sometimes. For long time when we pray for rain we got rain, but now only wind. All change. When the whites come here there is no more. We had a good time for long time, but not now."

Background:
In the high desert of Arizona, the green corn of the Hopi appears like a mirage. Skill and spiritual tenacity sustain a people who must coax their food from a sandy soil and call the rain to irrigate their fields.

Above:
"Sometimes I come to the field in the evening and stay all night because the porcupines were eating my corn. I'd sing all the way up and down the rows. My dad said this corn is like children and you have to sing to them and then they will be happy."
Hopiland, Arizona

Below:
Hand over hand, in a rhythmic dance of hoe and seed, an African woman plants her peas.

Right:
Made from the grasses, soil, and wood of their surroundings, the round, thatched homes of the rugo *complex burst forth from the landscape like mushrooms. Concentric circles of terraced cropland envelop these compounds, where family, livestock, and plants participate in a continuous, inter-dependent cycle.*

The road to Ijenda climbed high above the capital city of Bujumbura. We wound our way through thousands of workers, descending on foot from the hills to work in the dark city below.

I had come to Burundi as a farmer, to look with a farmer's eyes, so I passed quickly through the dusty streets and tin shantytowns that housed a growing population of rural refugees. I wanted to see some remnants of traditional Africa, where farming still sustained the people and their land.

Higher up in the mountains, bananas and manioc gave way to maize and peas, and women walked with baskets and hoes balanced on their heads. Here life was contained within the traditional *rugo*. The first time I saw a *rugo* I was amazed. This cluster of round thatched homes looked as if it had been seeded and had grown right out of the landscape. Each one was surrounded with concentric circles of terraced cropland planted with grains and vegetables, hedged with grasses for feed and to control erosion.

East Africans were pastoralists long before they were farmers. Cattle still represent wealth, their worth more reliable than money in an unstable local economy. Cattle provide the milk and meat that can mean survival in years when crops fail and markets change.

According to United Nations estimates, Africa may see its population double over the next twenty years. Increased population puts pressure on overtaxed pastures as traditional systems of range management give way to overgrazing. These young Samburu herdsmen watch their cattle on an eroding landscape, land that may become useless within their lifetimes.

Each *rugo* provided for several generations of a family, their animals, and their food; there was even a separate hut for compost.

Over the weeks of spring planting, as I watched the women tend their fields, barefoot and consumed in the rhythmic dance of hoe and seed, I observed true integration—a way of life a child learns riding on its mother's back as she works, a closed circle where homes are ringed with crops and humans and animals feed each other and the earth.

_____

A Peruvian herder moves his menagerie down from its high-country pasture. Diversity insures survival—the cows, sheep, and goats provide a variety of products, from milk and meat to wool.

53

Half of our world neighbors are supported by subsistence farming and live quietly off the land. We seldom hear much about them unless there is a major famine, civil war, or natural disaster.

They are silent, for the rhythm of their lives requires little from the outside. Yet the communities they live in and the way in which they have sustained themselves has much to offer our modern world where we no longer understand the most basic skills of feeding ourselves and the land.

It is not out of nostalgia or blind romance that we must listen to these cultures. There is nothing romantic about their day-to-day lives. The experience of Chinese farmers working in harmony with their families and the land does not dispel the horrors of Tiananmen Square; in the Peruvian village where I stayed, a family committed suicide by drinking the Western-made pesticides that were supposed to bring them a better harvest. Tribal conflicts beset farmers in Burundi, and widespread alcoholism and a long history of imposed change and control from outsiders have left few Hopi who continue the traditions of their elders. Everywhere, the

Taking his turn at the well, a Chinese farmer fills his buckets and moves to the field. More than fifteen people share the well and, balanced on narrow pathways, water onions in a beautiful, rainlike shower.

Millet, a staple food crop in parts of Africa and Asia, is an important source of nourishment, high in protein and able to survive on poor soils with little rainfall.

A diversity of pumpkin, bean, and squash seeds displayed in a European marketplace. Through the care of individuals, many traditional heirloom varieties are preserved and disseminated. With genetic erosion threatening our future food supply, farmers and local seed dealers may be the guardians of our most important resource.

Kiwicha, a type of amaranth, remains one of Peru's most revered food crops. Many such indigenous foods contain an entire cultural history passed down through their seeds. In the Andes ancient farmers experimented with thousands of varieties to adapt to their mountainous ecology and provide insurance against the failure of an individual species. The Irish potato famine is one example of how millions starved when a single crop variety was destroyed by disease.

Inca legends say quinoa was the remains of a heavenly banquet. It has endured for more practical reasons: this grain is as nutritious as milk, with a protein content of nineteen percent, compared with seven percent for rice and thirteen percent for wheat. Before it can be eaten, quinoa requires several labor-intensive steps; here the multicolored grains are stripped from their stalks.

In many parts of Asia, human
waste is recognized as a treasure,
which it is, when properly
processed. In some Chinese cities
signs outside toilets are posted to
encourage passersby to stop and
make a deposit; contractors pay
for the right to haul this resource
off to local farms. When synthetic
fertilizers were introduced

in 1960, yields increased
dramatically, but now farmers
blame chemical use for land
that was "getting harder, more
difficult to work." Farmers also
complained that rice was "harder
and not as good to eat," saying
"if you use only family fertilizer,
it is better to taste."

pressures of new cash economies and competition for scarce resources create poverty where before there may have been enough. But beneath the hardships are examples of enduring qualities and techniques, threads that connect all true earth dwellers whether they are Peruvian potato farmers or Chinese rice growers.

First, they work with their land. They are always on it, walking it, touching it. There is a farmer's saying that "the best fertilizer is the farmer's footsteps on the field." I remember my Hopi friend describing the way he visits his fields at night, walking up and down the rows, singing to his corn.

In traditional agricultural communities, there is a careful balance of hands to acres, an appropriate scale that allows for intimacy with the land, the crops, and the animals. In the fields of modern American farms one person may be responsible for the management of thousands of acres, a fleeting glimpse from a pickup truck offering too little information to aid in careful stewardship and management.

Traditional farmers take all, but no more, than a generous earth can give. They use and tend every inch and often draw forth far greater yields on their land than modern farmers do on theirs. They understand the subtleties of rotation, of sensitive fertilization, and the appropriate use of hoe and plow.

His basket loaded with compost, a boy makes his way to fields just outside his home in Burundi. Kitchen and animal waste is recycled, swept daily into a compost pit that lies at the low end of each family compound.

They give back to the earth all they can—everything they have—in some cases, literally the shirts off their backs. I've seen Chinese peasants who will patch a piece of clothing till it can't hold another patch and then throw it into the compost. Human waste is recognized as a treasure, which it can be when properly treated. They nurture their scanty resources as a community, not just because community is pleasant in itself but for mutual survival. It's a very practical matter.

In traditional farming societies, food raising is a family affair. The knowledge is passed on, a sense of the wisdom of the earth. In Sicily I've seen four generations all working together harvesting or preparing a field. And with the passing down of knowledge is also the passing down of seeds—seeds that contain a whole cultural history within their germ, representing

A Sicilian man harvests and stores hay for the winter.

local adaptation, disease and pest resistance, nutrition, and taste. The diversity of native food varieties has provided a key to the survival of those cultures, especially in areas where the climate and growing conditions are harsh.

And, finally, traditional food growers take absolute responsibility for their own food—for virtually every mouthful they and their children eat. They don't leave that responsibility to supermarkets, chemical companies, the EPA, or the FDA.

Like the Peruvian potato that can survive and produce tubers at altitudes where we find it difficult to breathe or the Hopi corn that can push its way through ten inches of soil to bear fruit in the harsh desert landscape, traditional societies have also had to adapt to changes around them: economic, political, social, and environmental. That many of the practices of these cultures have survived under such pressures, some over millennia, is testimony to the power of shared traditional values, values that provide a cultural identity that allows them to persist.

An old Chinese woman scours the road for pieces of manure. Even the jacket she wears, patches on patches, will eventually go into the compost.

If there is one thing the tenacity of these cultures has to offer us, it might be the example of a true and integrated ecological sensitivity, one that is manifested in the careful management of local resources and a fair exchange with the natural world around them. It is this ecological sensitivity, not intellectually derived but born out of the need to survive, that must become a part of our culture. Without it every attempt at environmental conservation or restoration will ultimately fail.

Day's end. Caltavuturo, Sicily

Left:
To protect themselves from malaria mosquitoes and hostile neighbors, the Keiyo and Marakwet tribes of Kenya live on escarpments high above the remote Kerio Valley, where they farm. This woman walks as much as three hours to her fields each day.

Below:
The angle of the short-handled Peruvian lampa, *or hoe, (used for hilling up potatoes and beans) mirrors the angle of the land— terrain so steep that farmers have been known to fall out of their fields.*

Left:
*An African woman gleans small and damaged ears left behind from the main harvest.
Ijenda, Burundi*

Right:
Nothing wasted, mustard weeded from a barley field near Chincheros, Peru, is carried home to feed the donkeys.

Above:
"Since we are born, we have been surviving because of the land. The hoe is our instrument of survival," a Burundi farmer (right) said. "The hoe is the most important

thing here and all over the world. There is nothing better than a hoe." In Sicily (left) farming goes on in much the same way it has for centuries.

Above:
"We come from the earth and are returned to it," a Burundi farmer told me. "Where we are buried becomes fertile land for future generations."

Right:
"It would be easier for me to go to the stars, to the moon, or to the heavens than to visit Beijing." This man's son will grow up to work these fields. Yunnan, China

FIRE ON THE

Vulnerable perfection. During this century scientists and plant breeders revolutionized agriculture. Hybrid seeds, mechanization, and heavy chemical use allowed large amounts of food to be raised in huge single-crop fields. The dramatic harvests had hidden costs. Crops bred for high yield require pesticides and synthetic fertilizers to substitute for natural resistance and soil vitality. A monocropped environment, lacking natural checks and balances, is an invitation to pests and disease.

Way, way in the distance, where a field with no apparent end meets the sky, a fire is raging. Even from here you can see a red glow beneath the shifting plume of black smoke and the heat waves shimmering in the hot air like a mirage.

They're burning off the rice fields or the remains of some other crop—maybe wheat or corn. What else could be burning out there? Not a house; the fire is too big, covers too much sky. It's impossible to be sure from this distance.

You begin driving, navigating northward on a network of roads that intersect at right angles, holding giant tracts of land together in a quilt. There are paved roads with names like J3 and J5, and others, smooth dirt tracks, the interstices of this agricultural matrix. They go right through vineyards of table and wine grapes, groves of almonds and walnuts and citrus, orchards of peaches and prunes and figs, and great fields of green beans and corn, barley and wheat and oats, tomatoes and eggplants and peppers.

You assume these are farms, but this is not what you see when you close your eyes and think "farm." Farms are in the country, and this is definitely not the country. There is no welcoming farmhouse on this lonesome landscape; no natural brook glides by; no barn or silo relieves the infinite flatness of the fields; no native tree casts a solitary line of shade; no cattle browse peacefully in a pasture. Where are the people who work this land? Where are their families? Where has everyone gone? Only the cars and trucks that occasionally speed along the two-lane roads that frame these anonymous fields suggest human life.

But all this food is here. Fields and fields of it, thousands of miles of it, millions of acres of it. They call this the Central Valley. Actually, it is two valleys—the Sacramento and the San

HORIZON

Above:
Swords into plowshares. The technology of two world wars found a peacetime role on the nation's farms. Tank traction was applied to tractors; munitions factories and their nitrate reserves were converted to fertilizer production; and nerve gas stockpiles were used in pest control—the spirit of conquest turned toward the land.

Right:
Sprinkler irrigation evaporates in the afternoon sun. Each year a volume of water six times the annual flow of the Mississippi is removed from the world's rivers, streams, and underground aquifers. Farming absorbs seventy percent of this water, yet only twenty percent of that actually reaches crops or animals due to inefficient application and transport methods.

Lower right:
Huge pumps suck billions of gallons from the Sacramento and San Joaquin rivers, most of which travels long distances to supply farms in California's Central Valley. Overpumping the rivers draws salt water from the bay into the Sacramento delta's fresh-water habitats and nearby cropland. This, along with pollution from local agriculture, is endangering the once-rich and diverse delta ecology. Throughout the western states overdrawing of limited water creates similar problems and a dependence on unsustainable supplies.

Joaquin—stretching four hundred miles from Redding in the north to Bakersfield in the south. In these twenty thousand square miles of semiarid California desert they grow more than one-third of all the fresh vegetables, fruits, and nuts Americans eat. In 1991 this amounted to about six million tons of fresh vegetables and eleven million tons of fruits and nuts.

The sheer scale of this cropland is dumbfounding; it's like nothing you've ever seen before. You discover it's next to impossible to get your mind around such colossal quantities of food produced on such immense tracts of land. It is a little like being on a boat in the middle of the ocean; nothing is distinguishable from anything else—there are no landmarks to judge distances—and, for all its bounty, the awesome expanse leaves you feeling insignificant and lonely.

Stop for a moment. Step out of the car, and the heat is like a dead weight on your head. Everywhere you look there are flat fields of grapevines, with their perfectly formed bunches of immature fruit hidden among the leaves. A black drip hose loops from one vine to the next and the next, stretching off into infinity. It emits a single drop of water every few seconds at the

Nearly two million gallons of water per acre are required annually to produce alfalfa hay in the naturally arid valleys of California. The water travels as far as six hundred feet up from wells to green these desert circles. Some of the world's driest areas pump irrigation water from underground aquifers, in some cases, mining "fossil water," an ancient source that cannot be replenished.

To satisfy the American appetite for beef, 100,000 cattle are slaughtered every twenty-four hours. Livestock production consumes almost half the energy used in all U.S. agriculture and seventy percent of the country's grain. Cattle produce 250,000 pounds of manure per second in the U.S. alone and 60 million tons of methane worldwide, which some scientists feel is a major contributor to global warming.

Before the 1940s few if any pesticides were used on crops. Currently more than 800 million pounds are used yearly in the United States, yet the percentage of crops lost to pests has increased nearly twenty percent.

base of each vine in this row and in every other row throughout the enormous factory plantation—all in a series of precisely timed and computer-controlled drips.

Close your eyes, and that's what you hear: just the carefully timed drip, drip, drip onto ground as hard as a tennis court. But for the grapevines, there is not a living thing here: no weeds poking their heads out of the packed clay; no worms tunneling or insects buzzing; no songbirds trilling overhead or small rodents scurrying in the understory; not even one solitary vulture circling. Just grapes. And, beyond the drips, silence.

And if it's not grapes, it's tomatoes or peppers or peaches. It's all the same.

These fields and orchards were designed to produce great quantities of cheap food. And to accomplish that, we are told, there must be high-input industrial efficiency. Fields are laser-leveled as flat as tabletops. Rows are precision-spaced with food crops bred to accommodate machinery and to last on store shelves. First the earth is drilled with synthetic fertilizers developed from the same research that perfected explosives and poison gas in World War II, and then it's pumped with fumigants and doused with herbicides to inhibit soil-borne disease and retard the growth of weeds. Crops are sprayed and dusted with broad-spectrum insecticides that kill harmful insects, along with most others, in order to maintain high yields and guarantee consistency of appearance in the supermarket.

A tractor with insect-like mechanical arms that span many rows creeps along in a bean field. Sprayer jets in the tractor's arms are drenching the plants with chemicals. The man in the tractor has a lunch pail beside him. When he eats, he will have to remove his respirator and the rubberized gloves that protect his hands. He's learned not to inhale the chemicals he's spraying—the same sprays that, according to World Health Organization statistics, result in one million acute poisonings per year and, according to the Federal Drug Administration (FDA), leave traces behind on the food we eat.

In fact, many agricultural chemicals currently in use have been determined by the Environmental Protection Agency (EPA) to be potentially injurious to health. Some are classified as probable carcinogens, some attack the nervous system, and others cause birth

On the Oxnard plain in southern California, pest control specialists begin their day spraying celery with fungicides. The EPA has ranked agricultural chemicals as one of the nation's most serious health hazards, some linked to cancers, sterility, and birth defects.

defects and sterility. Even so, the EPA considers chemicals, even possible or probable carcinogens, to be acceptable within certain limits when the benefits outweigh the risks. This explains why, although pesticide residues were found on forty-eight percent of all food sampled by the FDA between 1982 and 1985, the food supply was still considered to be "safe."

The FDA monitors pesticide residues based on EPA guidelines that were derived from figures describing the "average" American's eating patterns three decades ago. In some cases that means only 7.5 ounces of a given fruit or vegetable annually. For example, the agency assumes that in a year you will eat only about one avocado, a couple dozen shelled almonds, one medium-sized zucchini, a small wedge of honeydew melon, and only about one tangerine. Eat more of those foods, as well as others on a long list, and you put your health at risk.

The process seems even more frighteningly lacking when we consider that the FDA examines only about one percent of the food supply. Its most sophisticated testing methods are currently able to detect the presence of fewer than half of the almost 654 pesticides,

Pesticide shop, Urubamba, Peru. Pesticides banned in the United States are still produced and sold to developing countries, only to return to us in a circle of poison on many of the foods we import. According to the U.S. Department of Agriculture, sixty-four percent of imported produce sampled by the FDA in 1990 showed detectable residues of pesticides, including the banned chemicals DDT, Hexachlor, dieldrin, aldrin, chlordane, and chlorobenzilate.

Two men near Urubamba, Peru, use unmarked bottles of pesticide concentrate and no masks or protective clothing. Mixing by eye and sometimes tasting for strength, they fling the concentrate onto the potatoes with a bundle of branches while the child stands close by. Based on officially reported cases alone, the World Health Organization estimates that there are one million accidental pesticide poisonings and twenty thousand deaths each year.

herbicides, and fungicides currently in use. What's more, the EPA has never studied the health effects when several chemicals have been combined on a single crop—a commonplace occurrence these days.

Even when chemicals are banned for use in this country, manufacturers continue to export them to agricultural nations in the developing countries, where little consumer or worker protection exists. Ironically, these countries, most notably Mexico, continue to export huge amounts of produce right back to the United States—more than half of our winter's supply of fruits and vegetables, according to an industry analyst for the International Trade Commission. This in part may explain why the FDA continues to find residues of DDT on carrots, onions, potatoes, spinach, and sweet potatoes, twenty years after the ban went into effect.

The situation is such that in 1991 the Circle of Poison Prevention Act was introduced in both houses of Congress. The bill would outlaw the export of pesticides that are either banned or unlicensed for use in this country. "In the blind pursuit of corporate profits," said one of the bill's sponsors, Senator Patrick Leahy of Vermont, "U.S. chemical company giants . . . dumped their poison overseas and devastated the lives of thousands of unsuspecting

77

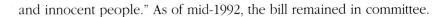

To clear the fields and to fight stem rot, over 400,000 acres of rice straw are burned in California's Sacramento Valley each year. According to research done by the University of California at Davis, the resulting smoke carries seven thousand tons of hydrocarbons, 58,000 tons of carbon monoxide, and six thousand tons of particulants. Effects on humans range from asthma and bronchial complaints to lung cancer; effects on the earth range from loss of valuable organic material to additional risk of global warming.

and innocent people." As of mid-1992, the bill remained in committee.

The ultimate irony is that, while the use of toxic pesticides increases and questions about their effect on human health persist, more and more insects become resistant, and crop loss to pests is on the rise.

Pesticides are not the only chemicals wreaking havoc with the health of the land and people. Excessive runoff from synthetic fertilizers is polluting groundwater supplies; the EPA has identified agriculture as the largest non-point source of water pollution and acknowledges groundwater pollution in thirty-eight states. Ask anyone old enough to remember and they will tell you that food grown in the age of chemical fertilizers bears no resemblance in taste to food grown before. And there is increasing documentation that, apart from the chemicals they may carry, factory-field–grown food lacks the nutrition and vitality of food produced on healthy soils.

———————

Noon, and the heat is intense. At the intersection of J5 and J7 there is a restaurant. Pick-up trucks are parked out front, while groups of men sit at tables inside and play dice as they eat. Their baseball caps bear the names of seed companies, tractor manufacturers, and chemical producers.

The waitress puts on a sad face. "The fire?" she says, "Oh yeah, I heard it was someone's house, and it's been burning all morning."

A heavyset middle-aged woman in office attire reads a newspaper at the next table and waits until the waitress is out of range before she says, "That's not anybody's house, I can tell you that. They're burning off rice stubble. Some farms do it, and some of us don't. We don't do it on our farm, the farm I work for. My boss talks to these other farmers, tells them it's not a good practice. 'So big deal,' he tells them, 'so you have some straw left after plowing. That's not so bad.' But like I say, some still do it."

She describes how helicopters douse the fields with napalm and then set them ablaze. The fires spread so fast they consume everything in sight. "Scorched earth," she says. "Like warfare. I heard that the chemical residues in the stubble eventually settle down to earth and make people sick, but our distributor didn't think so."

The American Lung Association has made a ban on crop burning one of its highest priorities in California's agricultural areas—the smoke from fires that blacken thousands of acres each year contains silica fibers and other substances that are believed to be cancer risks. Recently—after thirty years of complaints and more than a decade of pressure by a coalition of organizations and citizens—California passed Assembly Bill 1378, phasing out rice burning by the year 2000, with exemptions to be allowed to farmers who can prove financial hardship.

But the burning doesn't affect only human health. When crop residues go up in smoke, already depleted soils are robbed of invaluable organic matter. Fire may be a convenient and inexpensive way to clear a field, but it is also emblematic of a wasteful farming system that sees the land merely as a sterile medium that holds the roots and that can be artificially sanitized and then "pumped up" season after season.

In a timeless stance with a modern purpose, a farmer pours nitrogen fertilizer into furrows where irrigation water will carry it to the lettuce plants. Between 1950 and 1981 U.S. fertilizer use rose 195 percent, to fifty-four million tons annually.

Right and center:
In 1940 there were more than six million family farms in America; average size: 175 acres. By 1989 there were only one-third as many farms, yet the average size had tripled. According to the 1987 Census of Agriculture, *the total number of U.S. farmworkers has declined almost seventy percent since 1940.*

The fields roll out to the edges of the freeway. At this speed their enormity becomes a little more abstract. Food for a nation, it seems, is not grown in beautiful gardens. There is great beauty out here when the almond groves and fruit orchards are in blossom, but beautiful nature is incidental to the business of growing food. If researchers could get almond trees to produce more nuts for growers without flowering, they'd do it.

Industry, that's what this is. Out of step with traditional American farm culture, there is no self-sufficiency here; everything is shipped in, from seeds to petrochemicals to water. Just like factories. Quantity is the goal. Here are tomatoes, bred for shelf life and shippability—a trillion clones spread across the landscape. If you've ever bitten into a red, juicy tomato from your own garden, you know that these hard, pink, poisoned fruits are hardly worthy of the name. They have none of the fragrance and flavor of the real thing. And as long as consumers buy without complaint, the growers have no incentive to change their practices.

Left:
Sculpted beds carved out of a northern California hillside await a fall planting of commercial strawberries. Under a plastic cover the ground will be sterilized with fumigant, the contaminated plastic discarded, disposable irrigation tape laid down, granular fertilizers applied, and the seedlings planted into holes burned into a second covering of plastic. In the months until harvest, the plants and fruit may be treated with one or more of the sixty-five pesticides registered for use on strawberries.

Below:
To prepare for a season of mechanization, a laser-controlled land leveler scrapes the surface of a field. Clouds of topsoil blow away in the wind. The world has lost nearly one-fifth of the topsoil from its cropland since mid-century to wind and water erosion; the topsoil lost in the United States alone, if loaded into freight cars, would make a train that would encircle the planet twenty-four times.

There is a price to pay for all this cheap food—in money, in the health of a nation, and in the degradation of the planet. Take water. Before the great irrigation projects brought the water here, the Central Valley was arid much of the year. Then this parched land was flooded and planted with massive monocultures that bore fruit to feed the world. Three-quarters of a century later, the note is coming due.

Tom Harris, reporter for the *Sacramento Bee* and author of the book *Death in the Marsh* (Island Press, 1991), describes how decades of saturating this poorly drained valley have created an underground sea of salt and toxic trace elements dissolved by irrigation. This mix is so toxic it kills fish and waterfowl, poisons the soil, threatens residential drinking water, and may eventually mean desert days again for nearly a million acres of western San Joaquin farmland.

Harris further documents, as have others, including the U.S. Department of the Interior, the build-up of toxic levels of selenium—a compound resulting from salination—that has led directly to "death, deformity, and reproductive failure" of fish, waterfowl, and other wildlife not only in the Central Valley's Kesterson National Wildlife Refuge, but throughout the valley's drainage-saturated areas.

In his testimony before the Senate Committee on Agriculture and Forestry in 1976, William Brune of the Soil Conservation Service declared that the United States had already lost more than seventy-five percent of its original topsoil to erosion caused by unsound farming practices. Currently the national average is 8.1 tons lost per acre annually, equivalent to an area about the size of Connecticut. To be sustained farm fields must be rested, or fallowed, then planted in cover crops to sweeten the soil and improve its heart and productivity. These practices mean less erosion. But federal farm policies continue to push growers to go for higher and higher yields, rather than encouraging more sustainable approaches. To compete successfully, farmers must produce more. If you stop producing you'll be swept away.

"Get big or get out" was the message from agriculture secretary Earl Butz to America's farmers in the early 1970s. Farmers heeded the call. But the 1980s and '90s brought massive foreclosures on farms that had overextended themselves. In 1989 farmers owed the banks approximately $200 billion, more than the combined debts of Mexico and Brazil. By the

Left:
A solitary operator—six wheels and 175 horsepower between him and the land.

Below:
Exodus from the land. Food in industrialized countries is produced by only two percent of the population. More than 25 million Americans have left the land since 1940; in recent decades it has mostly been the young.

Below:
It takes two hundred to a
thousand years to create an inch
of topsoil, yet it can be degraded
in less than a decade through
compaction, erosion, and
chemical abuse. In 1947 Sir
Albert Howard, a British
agricultural researcher, was
ahead of his time when he wrote,
"Faced with the demand for
higher yields, the farmer has
grasped at the most desperate of
all methods: he has robbed the
future. He has provided the huge
output demanded of him, but
only at the cost of cashing in the
future fertility of the land
he cultivates."
Right:
After the harvest, cotton field.
Central Valley, California

thousands, smaller family farm operations are being swallowed up by the big growers, and the generation of would-be farmers who have seen their parents struggle against all odds to hold their land and fail now refuses to pick up the fallen standard.

The land is blackened and charred as far as you can see. Great expanses of unending desolation surround you. The wind kicks up eddies of silent ash; the air carries the acrid scent of spent fire. It feels like the aftermath of a war. Not far ahead, the plume of smoke from the fire hovers above the barren landscape.

A pickup is blocking the intersection. A man in a baseball cap motions you to turn right, away from the fire. "You can't go through. There's a fire in the fields. Just head west. Our people are positioned all through here. They'll get you around. No problem. No problem."

STEPPING

CHAPTER THREE

Dick Harter sits atop a grain bin and scans his rice fields. Surrounded on all sides by conventionally farmed orchards and rangeland, Harter's thriving nine-hundred-acre ranch in Chico, California, has become a haven for wildlife. "There's a creek that flows through the property, and big trees—habitat for deer, quail, pheasant; it's a happy place, birds chatter, there's little lizards and frogs dancing in the kiwis, the things that nature needs for balance. To my mind, if you have a food system that wipes out wildlife, ignores the ecosystem, ignores the way life works, you haven't got a life system."

Yams, black-eyed peas, okra, and corn flourish behind a row of dilapidated brick houses with missing windows. In this South Philadelphia neighborhood, where teenagers openly sell packages of crack on the street, residents have cleared trash and rubble from vacant lots and carved out food gardens of beauty and purpose—oases that lift the human spirit and provide real nourishment for themselves and their families.

Twelve hundred miles away, in Salina, Kansas, a team of plant breeders, using the native prairie as a model, works to develop a permanent, perennial agriculture that will produce a mix of high-protein, good-tasting grains. The goal: to eliminate the massive consumption of water, soil, chemicals, and energy usually associated with modern grain production.

Near Yokohama, Japan, a community-supported farm hums with activity on harvest day as people arrive to take their share of daikon, leeks, cabbage, persimmons, and pears from the produce piled high on tables. In a return to a form of social agriculture, the members of the community throw in their lot with the farmers by buying shares at the beginning of the season; good year or bad, those nourished by the farmer's labor also share in the farmer's risks.

In Gloucester, England, on what was once an old manor, the sound of milk tins and cowbells clinking signals the start of a new day. The milkers are disabled adults whose work with animals and the land develops skills and gives purpose to their lives.

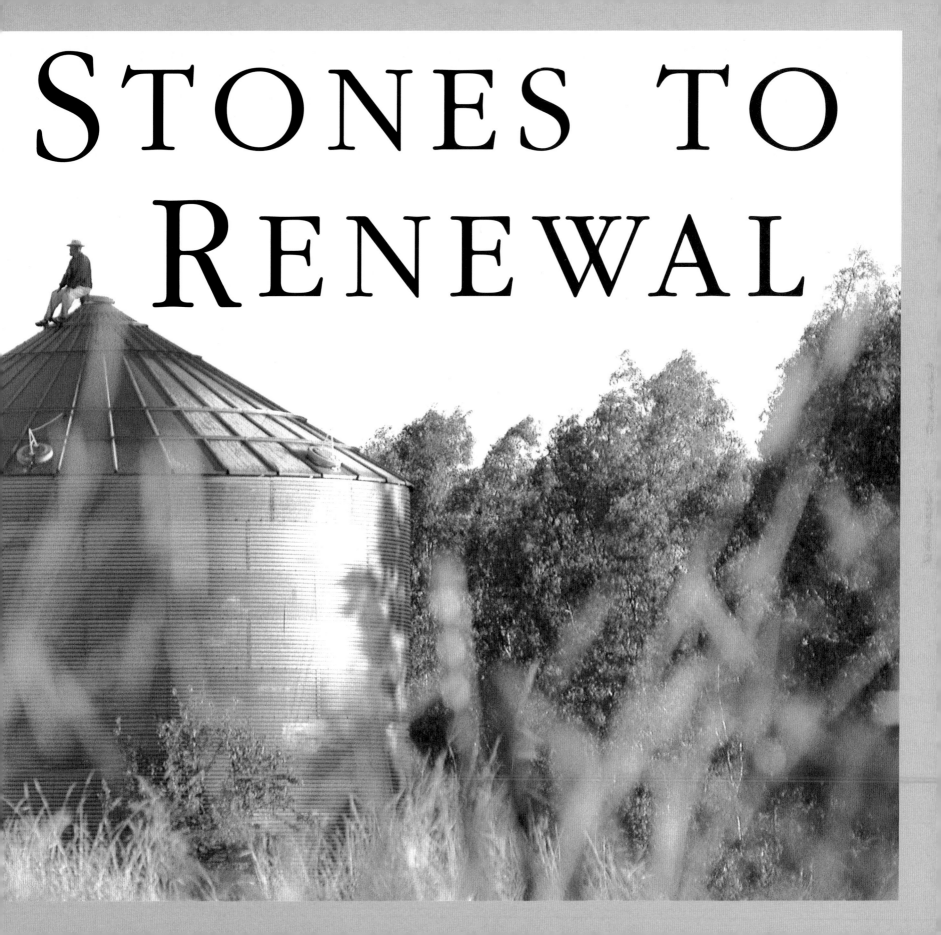

STONES TO
RENEWAL

In Zurich, Switzerland, a family leaves a high-rise apartment and travels by train to their allotment garden on the outskirts of the city. Leased to individuals, these one-eighth-acre plots form a patchwork of hundreds of small gardens—weekend farms for urbanites.

On a 140-acre farm in Iowa, a couple organizes a nation of immigrants to save the seeds descended from those their ancestors brought with them to America—seeds that bear the genes of traditional varieties, insurance against the genetic erosion of the world's food supply.

And in Goleta, California, a hundred-year-old farm, now an island among tract homes and shopping centers, provides organic food for its new suburban neighbors from orchards where avocados and peaches grow side by side and fields yield salad greens, corn, tomatoes, berries, melons, green beans, herbs, squash, and on and on.

———————

I began farming because I wanted to eat well and to tend the earth. I didn't know that I was part of a movement. It was years before I found others who were working in the same way, calling their practices "organic," "sustainable," "natural," and even "sensible" agriculture. They were growing food locally, close to home, applying techniques and philosophies as diverse as the climates and geographies where they lived. When I eventually visited them I found that, miles or continents apart, we shared similar goals: high-quality, safe food; a healthy environment; and strong local communities. More years passed before I sought out and discovered the literature, and it was a surprise to me in 1989 when the National Academy of Sciences in Washington, D.C., produced a scholarly looking volume approving what it called "alternative agriculture."

The academy defined this "alternative" approach not by the "conventional practices it rejects but by the innovative practices it includes," techniques that cooperate with, rather

Celery grows between the rows, and beneficial weeds cluster around the peach trees, creating a living mulch, nature's way of protecting the soil. Fairview

Gardens has flourished for one hundred years while suburban development claimed the surrounding neighborhood. Today, the twelve acres of diverse

organic food crops—a rich and fertile farm ecology—are bordered by housing developments on three sides and by a main thoroughfare on the fourth.

than subjugate nature, and "sustain and enhance rather than reduce and simplify biological interactions."

The authors concluded that "farmers successfully adopting these systems generally derive significant sustained economic and environmental benefits" and that "wider adoption of proven alternative systems would result in even greater economic benefits to farmers and environmental gains for the nation."

It seemed ironic that they called it "alternative." Before the 1940s everyone who farmed did so with little or no chemicals and without large-scale mechanization; the techno-chemical–based farming that many consider "conventional" agriculture is only two generations old. Although "alternative" methods are now gaining recognition, they are nothing new, only a continuation of something very old. They were simply overshadowed by the big-yield hoopla of the postwar modern agricultural revolution with its dramatic but costly results, its slogans, its proud conquest of nature, and its many miraculous products to buy.

Most people are now familiar with the term "organic" in its narrowest sense, which means "no chemicals." In response to the growing market demand for chemical-free food, the U.S. government, whose agriculture policies discourage even the most basic organic practices, passed a law—the Organic Foods Production Act of 1990—to regulate what materials will be allowed in organic production and to help the public be sure that if it says "organic," it is.

But there is more to good farming than the substances we *don't* use. Eliminating toxic chemicals is an important step, but a more complete farming approach goes further, seeking to grow a diversity of products, reduce external inputs, and become self-contained. It is concerned with the entire ecology of the farm from the tiniest soil microbes to the larger environment. Some of the practices might include crop rotations, careful timing of plantings, use of disease-resistant crop varieties and biological pest controls, new approaches to tilling the soil that preserve natural soil structure and prevent erosion and compaction, and particular attention to soil fertility. Rather than just substituting materials—a synthetic one for one from nature—the emphasis is on management and knowledge, knowledge acquired through experience, walking the fields and orchards every day, seeing and observing.

"What gardening is about is growing food, not about speculating. It's continuity, it's about always having something to eat, always having something from nature." California farmer Bob Cannard hand-cultivates with a wheel hoe just after sunrise.

*Farmer and "compost meister"
Peter Blaser uses a homemade
digital thermometer to test and
regulate piles of decomposing
straw and manure on his
farm in Switzerland.*

*On Cannard's farm in Sonoma,
California, weeds are honored as
guardians of the soil. They break
up compacted ground, bring
nutrients up from the subsoil, and
provide valuable organic matter.
In this field they envelop a healthy
crop of delicate lettuces.*

Cabbage and lettuce share a garden bed in Girenbad, Switzerland. The practices of intercropping and companion planting bring different crops together to confuse pests, make efficient use of space, and improve plant vitality. The Chinese developed techniques such as these thousands of years before the first synthetic chemicals were used on the land.

Like sentries among the vegetables, marigolds divert insect pests, and straw mulch holds in moisture and improves fertility. In an integrated system no single technique will dominate; instead a balance of complementary elements insures strength and vigor in the plants. The foundation of the whole system is healthy soil.

"The most important thing is mobilizing the elements that work behind the plants, behind life itself." Dutch farmers Willem and Joke Kips examine the soil for earthworms in their field, which only forty years ago was under the sea. "The earthworms are visual signs of the health of the system," Willem Kips says, evidence of the care invested in rebuilding this land.

Far right:
Compost piles shaded by a giant oak—some fresh with food scraps and weeds, others smoldering and breaking down, others settled and finished—accelerate nature's cycle of decay and fertility.

Bell beans grow tall, vetch crawls up their stalks, and Austrian peas cover the ground in a weave of organic material so dense that it is difficult to walk through. Green manure crops such as these nitrogen-fixing legumes are grown to flower and then turned under, planted solely to condition and add fertility to the soil.

"The best compost for the land is the wise master's feet and hands."
—Robert Herrick (1591–1674), "The Country Life"

A solitary gardener in a walled Victorian food garden in Dorset, England, embodies the sentiment of his 17th-century countryman.

The kitchen garden at Esalen Institute, an educational and spiritual community in Big Sur, California. Head gardener Steve Beck explains, "At Esalen, in the landscaping, gardens, and farm, we're attempting to align ourselves with nature, entering the system instead of trying to manipulate or control it. We find all of the opportunities for mindfulness that exist in the disciplines of yoga or meditation in plentiful supply in the garden."

Inherent in many of the practices of these "new" farmers are real environmental concern and creative and practical solutions. Going beyond the need to eliminate chemicals, they are beginning to question the need to disturb the soil with tilling at all, re-evaluating their dependency on mechanization and fossil fuel, finding ways to use less water, and recognizing the values of small-scale production.

Many small farms have created an interrelationship between themselves and their communities in which the products of the farm are sold within the community, and the resources, both financial and biological (waste materials for compost), are returned to or stay on the farm.

These are things that go beyond "organic" or "alternative," inspiring an agriculture that is truly sustainable.

The late author-publisher-teacher Robert Rodale, Jr., whose family has been one of the oldest champions of this movement, once said that the word *sustainable* should be seen as a question, the answer based on what farmers know about their land, gardeners about their communities, and families about their food.

I have seen this to be true. I remember visiting Bob Cannard on his farm in Sonoma, California. Everywhere I looked there seemed to be fields full of nothing but weeds. Puzzled when workers passed me carrying buckets of beautiful vegetables, I got down on my knees and parted the weeds. There before me were healthy rows of red and yellow peppers, squash, and tender lettuces. Cannard knows that weeds protect and nourish the soil and that he can grow a crop for nature together with the one for humanity. My friend Steve Beck, who years ago sought my advice on the classic art of pruning fruit trees, now shows me his orchard in Big Sur, California, filled with healthy, producing apple trees that have never been pruned.

No one would think these farmers could get away with such unorthodox practices, but they know their land, they know what sustainable means for them, and they've learned exactly how much of a helping hand to lend to nature, and when to leave well enough alone.

Like many of my friends in farming I've experimented with numerous techniques. Some failed, but many succeeded, and now there are places on my farm where I can thrust my arm into the soil up to my elbow and come up with dark, rich earth that is so alive that you can

*Making compost at Seven Stars
Farm, Phoenixville, Pennsylvania.
The* 1987 Census of Agriculture
*found that of 2.7 million farm
operators, 631,000—twenty-three
percent—were women.*

*"Rather than demonstrating
against things, I wanted to work
for something good." Birthe Hart
harvests red mustard on the
community farm where she lives
and works in Kimberton,
Pennsylvania. Once a nursing
student, Hart now says, "I realized
healing has to come from the
bottom up. I decided I had to grow
good food; through food you make
people healthy. Now the garden
is my home and my life."*

*Autumn brings the same workers
back year after year to René
Monier's vineyard in Provence,
France, where the fields are alive
with conversation and laughter,
and the tradition of sharing a
meal interrupts the harvest
for two hours each day.*

*On a communal farm near
Zulpich, Germany.*

see it move. This is the true measure of my success. It has taken time—nature's process is slow, deeply rooted, and with every cycle of the seasons the land grows a little fuller and stronger, and I grow a little wiser.

My inspirations do not come solely from my contemporaries or from two short decades of experience. For all of us, our role models can be found across continents and throughout the centuries.

The Chinese perfected a system of raised-bed, intensive agriculture during the Han dynasty. Two thousand years later researcher John Jeavons is using hand-dug, raised beds at his experimental garden in Willets, California. Jeavons, a former systems analyst at Stanford University, has proven that on a piece of land no larger than half an acre a family can provide much of its food, a small cash crop, and all the plant material necessary for composting.

Javanese perennial gardens and the agroforestry of the Chagga tribe in Tanzania contain the spark that may have inspired some of the concepts of "permaculture" and the "forest garden" developed by Robert De Hart in southern England. De Hart's one-eighth of an acre is a living

Far left:
Louis Savier supports his family and two hired workers by growing high-quality biodynamic vegetables on a three-acre market garden south of Paris. Greenhouses, cold frames (foreground), and meticulous management—as well as an inventive rail system to carry compost, irrigation, and harvested produce—make efficient use of every inch of space.

Left:
Near the freeway in Berkeley, California, Kona Kai Farms grosses an average of $225,000— and as much as $300,000—per year on this two-fifths of an acre. Gourmet-quality organic salad greens are produced on raised beds and in cold frames and air-freighted to restaurants around the country.

Above left:
In the Emmental Valley in Switzerland, land too steep for tractors is prepared and planted by a cable system: a winch at the top of the hill lowers and raises the guided farm implements. Just as the unique footplow used by Andean farmers allows them to cultivate their steep slopes, this cabling system is an ingenious adaptation to a vertical terrain.

Above:
Brian Leahy and his father-in-law, Dick Harter, check the rice harvest by their combine just outside Chico, California. Leahy's children will be the fourth generation to live off this ranch. For many farmers in this country, such a legacy is an impossible dream. "It's an incredible gift," Leahy says, "but you don't really own land, do you? You take care of it and pass it on."

Left:
The right tool for the job. On a dairy and mixed-cropping farm in Schwanden, Switzerland, horses pull a potato harvester while a tractor cuts silage for the cows.

example of agroforestry—tall apple trees form a canopy over nut and fruit trees on dwarf rootstock, currant and gooseberry bushes grow underneath, vegetables and herbs hug the ground, and climbing berries and vines trail upward.

When I visited De Hart's "forest garden" I was impressed by how little he had to do to produce such a volume and variety of foods, all in a space smaller than most suburban backyards. "Scientists seemed to be imbued with the idea that the whole of nature is competitive," De Hart told me, "that the forest is a continual battleground with plants and animals that are just struggling for themselves and killing all their rivals, but in fact the forest is far more a symbiotic organism, the forces of mutual aid are far more powerful. Conventional horticulture is constantly killing, killing weeds, killing insects; but from the organic point of view everything in nature has a positive role."

Before all this scientific killing began, another science had been evolving to meet the changing needs of farmers. In 1924 Rudolph Steiner, an Austrian philosopher, presented a series of seven lectures that became the foundation of biodynamic farming and gardening. Steiner's vision of the farm was as a self-contained "living organism." Influenced by traditional practices and philosophies—such as herbal wisdom—and a practical application of the lunar cycle and other cosmic influences, he challenged farmers to work with all the forces in play on the farm, from the purely physical to the spiritual. To this end he suggested a series of preparations made from herbs, minerals, and cow manure which, when introduced to the farm, help stimulate the life force in the soil, the plants, and the animals.

At about the same time, Sir Albert Howard, a British agricultural scientist doing field research in India, was inspired by some of the traditional practices there and defined the foundation of successful farming as humus: composted plant and animal matter. Howard, who is considered to be the father of modern organic farming, had a clear message: that the essential basis for healthy crops, animals, and therefore people was in the soil, and that this resource must not be squandered. "The real arsenal of democracy," he wrote in 1947, "is a fertile soil."

But another type of arsenal was already being built, based on the work of a German laboratory chemist, Baron Justus von Liebig, who was convinced that humus was not vital for soil health and that plant nourishment could be reduced to just three main elements: nitrogen,

Above:
Some one thousand varieties of organic fruits, vegetables, herbs, and edible flowers grow on the immaculately cultivated raised-bed garden at the Fetzer Winery in Mendocino County, California. The beds and experimental kitchens are what head gardener Michael Maltas calls "a kind of garden laboratory" to explore the link between food and wine "from the ground up."

Left:
The technique of using permanent raised beds originated two thousand years ago in China. "It produces a helluva lot more food on a small area," Maltas explains. "And it's classically the opposite of the wastefulness of the rototiller consciousness—smash everything down and start again, a vast energy input, like reinventing the wheel every year."

potassium, and potash. Although Liebig's theories were eventually disproved, his work and the research that proceeded from it unleashed an agricultural revolution of chemicals, technology, and fast fixes that by mid-century had pushed organic farming to the fringe, where it continued outside the mainstream.

———

On February 26, 1989, thirty million American households tuned into CBS' *60 Minutes* and heard with dismay and outrage that residues of the growth regulator Alar on apples and in apple products were seriously threatening the health of American children. The national response was swift. School boards across the country banned apple products. Orders for apple exports were canceled. While concerned parents created an instant demand for safe food, many conventional growers scrambled to "go organic."

The overwhelming attention to the "Alar problem" obscured more fundamental issues: we had not been poisoning just our food but the land and the water that produced that food as well. Technology had made us refugees from the land, and that same technology was destroying our global environment.

Later that year at the Asilomar Conference Center in Pacific Grove, California, more than a thousand people—farmers, scientists, gardeners, researchers, shopkeepers, food distributors, and concerned eaters—converged for the tenth annual conference on "sustainable agriculture," in part to ratify a new definition that would address the broader issues.

There was great enthusiasm—for many, a feeling that we were finally being validated, and for some, a desire to protect the essential philosophies of the movement from being watered down or co-opted by "agribusiness" to meet the sudden consumer demand. The "Asilomar Declaration" defined "sustainable agriculture" as "ecologically sound, economically viable, fair, and humane," and its practices as not only "efficient in their use of energy, biological sources of fertility, and pest management, but also that they enhance rural communities and encourage families to remain on the land."

But existing threats to the biosphere are such that we can no longer be content just to sustain. The "new" agriculture must also find ways to restore and renew. Wes Jackson contends in his book *New Roots for Agriculture* (University of Nebraska Press, 1985) that "the plowshare may well have destroyed more options for future generations than the sword" and "so destructive has the agricultural revolution been that, geologically speaking, it surely stands as the most significant and explosive event to appear on the face of the earth, changing the earth even faster than did the origin of life."

That there are problems *in* agriculture is clear, but that the practice *of* agriculture itself may be the problem challenges a number of assumptions many of us have. Agriculture is still held to be sacred. Its impact on the planet and the question of its ability to sustain itself may require the farmers of the future to look far beyond their fields and fencerows.

———————

Many believe the responsibility for feeding the world belongs wholly to farmers. Although good work toward this end is being done on farms, food gardens are having a profound impact as well. Individuals and communities are taking responsibility for their own nourish-

On a seed farm at Oberhofen, Switzerland, Andreas Ellenberger vigorously stirs a biodynamic preparation for one hour to potentize it. The preparations, derived from herbs, minerals, and cow manure, are an important part of a methodology that includes refined composting, nutrient recycling, and crop rotations. Biodynamics is based on a series of lectures presented in 1924 by Rudolph Steiner, an Austrian philosopher who believed that spiritual growth could not be attained without good food, alive and from living farms. Steiner developed this approach to help farmers reignite the vital force in their farms without the use of chemicals and other outside inputs.

ment, reclaiming it from distant farms, growing in backyards, neighborhoods, and towns, and in the process feeding more than just the body.

I think of the neighborhoods I visited in Philadelphia where the average household income is between $7000 and $8000 per year. I saw where neighbors had banded together and built productive food gardens in lots once filled with decaying garbage and rubble. Their inner-city renewal was rooted in that basic need all of us have, to touch the earth and to know our food. Alta Felton, eighty years old, tended her "Garden of Eatin'" and told me, "You work awful hard, and when the rewardin' time comes you find out it wasn't all in vain." Her rewards include sweet potatoes, lima beans, collards, melons, and blackberries—to name a few—a portion of which she gives to the homeless.

Perhaps one of the best examples of a population learning to feed itself is in the former Soviet Union, where farming and food distribution failed under centralized control. It is widely

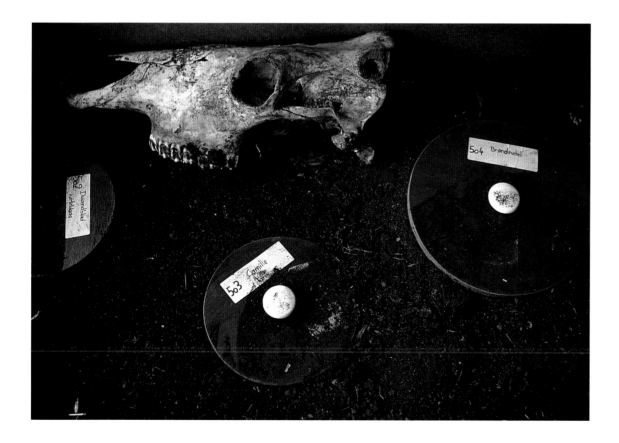

At a biodynamic farming school in the Netherlands, preparations made from potentized yarrow, chamomile, and stinging nettle are kept under carefully prescribed conditions before their use in the making of compost. An oak-bark preparation, stored in the cow's skull, is also introduced into the fields through compost. Each of these four elements represents an aspect of health and vigor that will then be replicated in the crops.

The Garden of Eatin' at 25th and Dickinson in South Philadelphia thrives near a decaying elevated railroad track where drugs are openly exchanged. A group of neighbors, mostly older black women, grow kale, cotton, black-eyed peas, okra, corn, lima beans, sweet potatoes, Jerusalem artichokes, and blackberries, as well as roses, calla lilies, and an occasional Christmas tree.

Alta Felton (above) founded the garden in 1979 and at eighty works in it every day. "Makes you feel kinda happy and good with all that beauty around. You know if you hadn't got out there and started something, and got the neighbors into it, then we couldn't stay here, because then there's nothing but rubbish," she says. "You take nothin' and just make beauty all around you."

claimed that families and individuals there are providing fifty percent of their own fruits and vegetables in small home gardens.

And lest anyone dismiss "gardens" as units too small to indicate any trend at all, consider the microfarms of an acre or less, such as Kona Kai Farms in Berkeley, California, which grows enough greens on two-fifths of an acre to make an average $225,000 a year.

Gene Logsdon, a noted farm writer, rightly contends that "gardens are acting as the incubators of the new farm ecology" where seeds are saved, biological relationships are explored, and new methods of soil fertility are practiced. While the exodus from conventional farms continues in record numbers, especially among the young, small farms resembling expanded gardens are springing up across the United States, redefining the future of growing food. The

The "garden goddess,"
Esalen Institute,
Big Sur,
California

Working with the earth, growing food as therapy, members of Camphill communities around the world seek social renewal through community living. Approximately fifty percent of the members are developmentally disabled. A young woman with Down's syndrome weeds an herb bed at Camphill Village, Kimberton Hills, Pennsylvania.

number of organic farms, for example, grew by four hundred percent between 1988 and 1990 in this country, and every region reports an increase of small farms and gardens.

Production on these farms not only shows a reduction in costs both financial and environmental but, in many cases, yields that exceed those of many conventional farms.

————————

Masanoba Fukuoka has not disturbed the soil with a plow or used fertilizers on his small farm in southern Japan for almost forty years, yet his yields of rice are comparable with the

Right and below:
A Waldorf school biodynamic gardening program, near Kreuzlingen, Switzerland. To "teach the whole child—head, heart, and hands" is the basis of Waldorf education. The garden gives the children a better sense of themselves, their place in the natural world, and where their food comes from. Biology, earth sciences, chemistry, and even math take on real meaning for children learning about plants and animals, soils and nutrient cycles.

Left:
Beneath the flight path of Heathrow Airport in an unmistakably suburban neighborhood, Chris Algar transformed a standard backyard plot into an organic food garden paradise lush with brussels sprouts, cabbages, beans, chard, cauliflower, and corn.

Above:
In 1990 Americans spent $6.4 billion on lawn-care products, many of which were pesticides applied in concentrations three to six times higher per acre than commercial farmers use. Where others might grow a green lawn, California architect Stephen Berman has planted half an acre in corn, beans, squash, tomatoes, salad greens, and herbs surrounding his contemporary Mayan-style home.

Right:

Horticulture project, San Bruno Jail, California. Founder Cathy Sneed Markum says, "Because it's an organic garden, I am able to say, 'Well, we could take this chemical here and spray it on this stuff. But what's it going to do to us? What's it going to do to the other plants? It's just like you. When you shoot up heroin, what does it do to you? What does it do to your family? What does it do to society? It's the same thing.' It's the clearest way I've found to help them think about what's happening in their lives. I think it changes the way they see the world, or it can."

Far right:

"No one has nurtured these guys," says Markum, "and they haven't seen a lot of nurturing around them. You know, I've had these big bad tough guys say to me, 'Oh Cathy, this is girls' work. I don't want to do nothin' with these plants.' And two weeks later the same macho giant with the tattoos and the tracks down his arm is out there saying, 'Hey, don't step on my babies!'"

most productive of Japanese farms. Fukuoka states, "Ever since I began proposing a way of farming in step with nature, I have sought to demonstrate the validity of five major principles: no tillage, no fertilizer, no pesticides, no weeding, and no pruning. I practice what I call 'do nothing' farming here, yet each year I harvest close to 5200 pounds of winter grain and 4000 pounds of rice per acre."

In a good year on my twelve-acre farm in Golcta, California, we harvest over 30,000 pounds of peaches, plums, and citrus, 25,000 pounds of avocados, and tons of fresh vegetables,

Left:

The Bartol Intergenerational
Garden at the On Lok Senior
Center in San Francisco started
life on a ground-floor lot. When a
proposal to build a high rise on
the site was made, residents
protested. The building was built,
but the garden was moved up
eight stories to the roof, where it
produces an array of Chinese
vegetables and fruits for the
residents who tend it.

Above:

Dona Valentina Ríos shows off
peppers in her garden in
Philadelphia, Pennsylvania. "My
mother has a beautiful green
thumb," Marcy Díaz says. "She
makes her gardens something of
her homeland. It's something to
grab onto from her culture, there's
a place for tropical as well as
American vegetables. She's a
person who likes to give, and she
doesn't have money, so she always
grows extra and gives what
she can."

"The garden, to me and others in our group, is our 'safe' haven. We go there to gather socially, argue emotionally, and to discuss eggplants," writes one New York City urban gardener, Julie Kirkpatrick. "We struggle to work cohesively as a group. Without 'our' garden? What would we do on summer nights when no breeze is passing through our tiny boxes? We have shaped a little corner of our world into something to which we feel connected. The garden makes our lives here more bearable and more enriched." By 1992 community gardens like this one at 6th Street and Avenue B in the East Village had reclaimed more than twelve hundred of New York City's vacant lots—an estimated twenty thousand remain unused.

"Once a garden has been a success, you go on to tackle other community problems—success breeds success—it empowers people," says Jane Weissman of a New York City urban gardening program, Operation GreenThumb. Across the country, the sun sets on a community garden in San Francisco.

Marina La Pinia (center) remembers that eight years ago, "the lot behind our house was a dumping ground, all garbage, dead rats, dead dogs, dead cats, anything you could imagine; we could not open our backdoors for the smell." Now, she and her husband, Adariano (right), grow bitter melons, nine kinds of squash, and yard-long beans for their Filipino friends, and for their Puerto Rican neighbors, hot peppers. Fairhill Community Garden, Philadelphia

Our future depends on reconnecting with the natural world: knowing our food, regenerating our land, and strengthening our communities. "We cannot isolate one aspect of life from another," wrote farmer-writer Wendell Berry. "When we change the way we grow our food, we change our food, we change society, we change our values."

Occidental, California

berries, and herbs. Although good production is a key to financial viability, success must be measured in other terms as well. I see it in the children who have never been on a farm before as they leave after a tour with carrots or strawberries in their hands and memories of goats and geese. I like knowing that even here, surrounded by roads and suburban development, a family of red-tailed hawks lives in our orchard and that our neighbors stroll through the farm, reconnecting with a distant part of themselves. As our soil grows rich and strong, it's good to know there's no debt to the bank for fertilizers and pesticides and that our land improves every year. This is our investment and a savings we know we can depend on.

Dick Harter and his son-in-law Brian Leahy grow rice on their nine-hundred-acre farm near Chico, California, a piece of land that looks more like a wildlife reserve than the successful farm that it is.

"Very few farmers farm from the heart," Harter says, "they farm from the pocketbook. These things that they do, all the inputs they think that it takes—chemicals, machines—it's a trap. There's nothing in technological systems that can perpetuate itself the way life can—to recycle, purify, heal. Nature's got everything it needs to produce food."

Zulpich, Germany

Below:
Hombrechtikon,
Switzerland

Right:
Near Lake Constance,
Switzerland

O F MARKET

CHAPTER FOUR

*Right: Marketplace.
Chincheros, Peru*

My grandmother always greeted me with a hug and kiss. My foot would be barely inside the door, and in one mysterious move I'd be seated at her kitchen table. Within moments piles of food would appear. She always put out enough for the whole family and could never understand why one small boy couldn't consume it all. I tried to, for I knew that her gift of food was Nanna's ultimate expression of love. The hugs and kisses were a mere formality.

Years later I find myself echoing my grandmother's offering in a daily ritual that begins in the fields and orchards of our farm, and eventually blesses the table, the plate, and the palate.

No one knows for sure how the word "farm" came into our language. For me the Old English source seems most appropriate: *feorm*, "a provision of food; hence a banquet or feast."

At our farm, harvesting before a meal often leads spontaneously to that feast. A short trip from the kitchen to the fields for a handful of tomatoes can yield armloads of bounty: the tomatoes border the peppers, where reds entice you into golds; the basil spills over into the melon patch; and, after getting lost in the tall, dense rows of sweet corn, one gets drawn into the peach orchard or down the rows of berries. It is always a surprise what varied—and how much—food the earth will yield if properly tended.

Often after sitting down we hold hands in silent reverence for the bounty the earth has provided. A gathering of friends and family around a meal has become a favorite ritual. In this time together nothing else exists, only the sharing and the talk and the joyful noises accompanying each bite. The unparalleled pleasure and nourishment we experience together goes beyond words. It is as if millions of messages are carried in

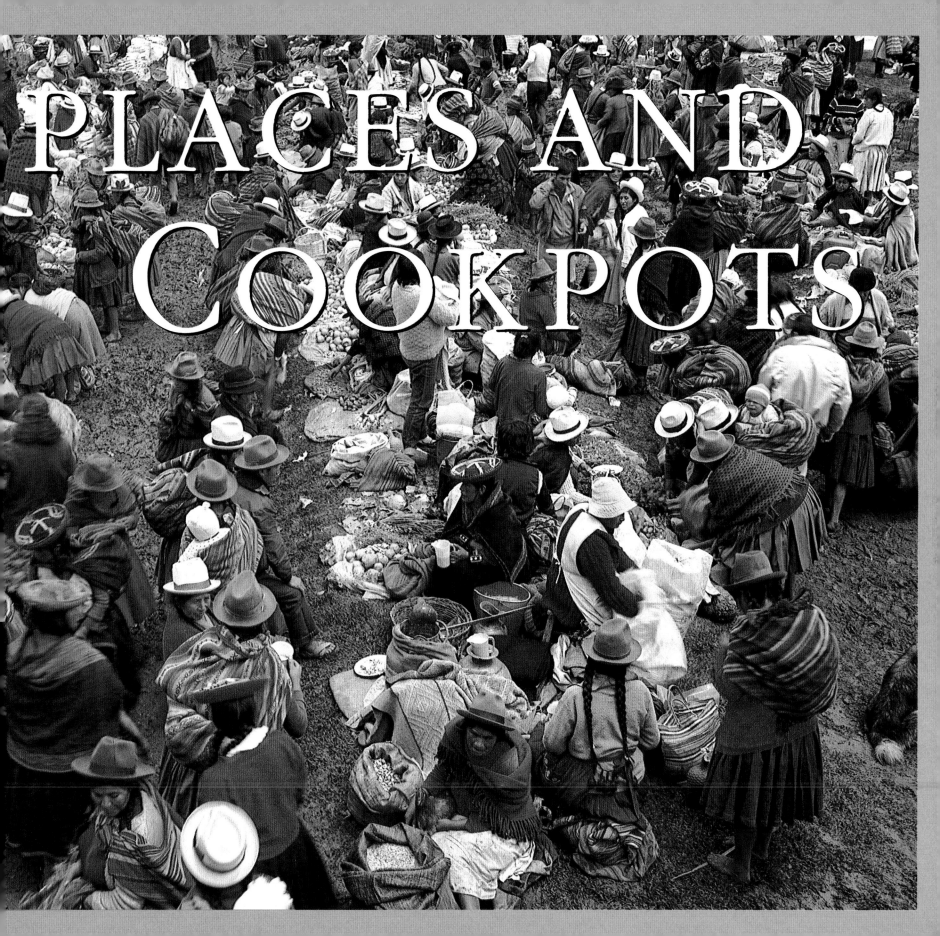

PLACES AND COOKPOTS

Right:
Fruit vendor.
Urubamba,
Peru

Far right:
Early morning.
Piazza Centrale,
Siena, Italy

the cells of our food, silent reminders of our roots and connections to each other and to the earth that provides.

I can remember vividly the many times I have shared a meal with people with whom I could not speak. In a small village in China a chicken was butchered in honor of my presence, and its head offered to me in a gesture of respect and supreme hospitality.

In Africa, in the mountains of Burundi, I ate in a small round hut with a family of ten. We shared from one large plate, our hands used as utensils. They fretted when I stopped eating to make some photographs, afraid that I might miss a beat and fall behind, that I might go hungry.

In Sicily a brief stop to speak with farmers along any road would always land me in their homes and kitchens. Hours later, almost immobile from vast quantities of homemade pasta and wine, I would stagger to my car, arms loaded with gifts of olives, wine, breads, and cheese. My rental car, laden with what my new friends had produced with their hands and from their land, smelled like an Italian delicatessen.

The language of food is universal; the impulse to feed is common to all cultures, rich or poor. Yet for many in our modern world the relationship with food has become a marginal one at best. We have become disconnected from the most intimate act on earth: the procuring and consuming of food, that which nourishes our bodies, our minds, and our spirits.

Saturday morning. Union Square, New York City

Bolzano, Italy

Water chestnuts. Anning county,
Yunnan, China

Potatoes and tomatoes. Gap,
Provence, France

Marketplace.
Mwaro,
Burundi

Gap,
Provence,
France

Fruit vendor.
Amsterdam,
the Netherlands

Eager crowds build around our stand at the farmer's market with curiosity and anticipation as I husk an ear of corn, remove the worm that is a sign that no poisons have been used, and break the ear in half. Some hesitate at first to accept my offering—is it the worm or the new experience of eating corn raw? "We don't charge extra for the worms," I quip, and remind them of the saying that "the corn is too old if the picker stumbles on the way back from the field."

Every home gardener and every farmer knows the pride and gratification of having people exclaim over the quality of food he or she has raised. I am certainly no exception. There is an

135

Hot peppers, daikon, beans, carrots, ginger. Northern Burma

Catania, Sicily

Catania, Sicily

incredible pleasure in watching people discover, for example, that sweet corn does not need to be boiled and then coated with butter and salt, that fruits do not need sugar, and that potatoes are delicious in and of themselves, not merely a tasteless utensil to convey salt and catsup to the mouth. Many for the first time can experience the true beauty of food—its taste, color, texture, and smell. This time at least, the food is alive with health, purity, and an enrichment that is more than physical. Not only are they eating the actual body of the food; they also consume the care and energy that went into producing it.

Equally important, they are savoring it at the time nature intended. With convenient, year-round access to foods grown far away, it is easy to forget that corn does not ripen in

Endive. Gap, Provence, France

137

Right:
Tree tomatoes.
Mwaro, Burundi

Far right:
Native maize.
Pisac, Peru

December or melons in February. It is easy to lose touch with the unique pleasure each season provides: the anticipation of peaches brought on by summer's heat, the last apples of winter, or the first tender asparagus shoots that signal the arrival of spring.

The simple offering of a tree-ripened peach, or a carrot dug only hours before, can create a revolution among eaters. It can inspire changes in the way we think about food and how we obtain it. When we begin to see our part in the food cycle—that we are more than just "consumers"—food becomes more than just another commodity for consumption.

The idea of "cheap" food has become an emblem in our culture; America spends a smaller percentage of per capita income on food than any other country in the world. Our government promotes a cheap food policy: subsidizing large-scale farms with discount water, paying growers not to market surplus crops, favoring chemical-supported high-yield monoculture, and penalizing farmers who want to diversify by restricting their eligibility for government programs. Those who would try more sustainable practices are discouraged by policies designed to insure that the dollar amount Americans pay at the supermarket remains low.

But what is the true cost of food? Is the bill being paid well beyond the checkout counter? Who pays for the subsidies farmers receive to produce this food? And what is the cost to our

health as soils become exhausted and produce depleted food, and poisons find their way to our kitchen tables and into our bodies? How about the farm workers whose hands do the hoeing and harvesting—what toxic materials are they exposed to? Perhaps the greatest debt in this spiraling bill is being paid by the earth. It is being eroded, compacted, and polluted.

We are part of this process, and we can be part of the solution—each time we make a purchase we contribute to a whole chain of food consequences extending from the intimate to the global environments. Active participation in that food process challenges us to see beyond the cold, neat rows of the supermarket, where digital displays, studio lighting, and triple-layer, four-color packaging create the illusion of bounty, security, and unlimited choice.

I think of the markets in Peru or in Africa, where abundant colors flood together in living, moving masses of humanity and goods—where the foods are alive and culturally connected to each pueblo or tribe that produced them, where markets are as much gathering places for social exchange as they are for food. One old woman in Burundi told me she had come some thirty kilometers to the market not to shop but to see her friends and to exchange gossip.

Right:
Paris, France

Below right:
Grapes.
Provence, France

Far right:
Chengdu, Szechwan, China

Below:
Bolzano, Italy

Left:
Marketplace.
Chincheros, Peru

Right:
Catania,
Sicily

I remember seeing a group of women crowded around a blanket where beans were for sale. The attention was not on the beans, but directed into folds of colorful cloth where a newborn baby rode on its mother's back.

In the south of France I observed the seriousness with which people consider their food. Each selection was scrutinized for freshness, and a purchase was made only after a careful consultation with the grower. It was there that I realized the preparation of food did not begin in the kitchen but in the marketplace with the conscious knowing that it was the ingredients themselves that would determine the outcome of the final dish.

My sense of responsibility as farmer has heightened seeing the faces of those who will eat my food—no intermediary, no package to hide behind, no truck to load for distant ports.

Left:
Measuring sorghum. Mwaro,
Burundi

Above:
Loquats. Catania,
Sicily

145

Peach harvest. Fairview Gardens Farm

Goat cheese. Near Noto, Sicily

146

Community garden. Chelsea,
New York City

Fava beans. Sicily

In this relationship nurturing replaces factory production. Knowing and seeing those I am feeding humanizes the process, returning life to the fields and real care to every step. I can tell the person who is buying my corn that we just picked it hours before, that this year melons or tomatoes will be late due to the cool temperatures, that all our food is grown with compost and free of chemicals.

Little questions—"Where was this grown?" "When was it picked?" "What materials were used on it?" "How is the land where it grew being cared for?"—can start a profound change

within ourselves and within a system that removes everything that is real and basic from our lives. Small steps like putting in a garden can change a neighborhood, and then a whole town. When everyone starts asking and taking responsibility, then greater changes begin to happen.

The problems of our farmland and production of our food no longer belong to the two percent of the population we call farmers. When we rejoin the food process we begin to see ourselves as farmers, and the whole planet as our farm to be nurtured and cared for. And when we rejoin the food process we rejoin the environmental process as well: we begin to understand more precisely what part of our planet belongs to us for food, for fiber, and for fuel—and what part must be left sacred to nature.

We must bring the interconnection among our food, our health, our communities, and our environment into view for the worst of reasons—that we may not survive if we do not—and for the best of reasons—that we might embark on the wonderful adventure of creating a society in which the beauty of our food is felt in every aspect of our lives.

By the simple act of reconnecting with our food, we will nourish and revitalize ourselves and our earth. The act of eating then becomes an act of caring—for our bodies and those of our families, and for the body of the earth of which we partake.

Right:
Garlic.
Enna, Sicily

Far right:
Farmers' lunch:
homemade
pasta, wine,
bread, cheese,
and olive oil.
Sicily

Harvesters' lunch.
Provence, France

Apple season. Hombrechtikon,
Switzerland

Chefs. Siena, Italy

From the field to the table:
ornamental kale with romanesco,
beets, chard, and spinach.
Occidental, California

Chef. Xiamen, Fujian, China

Day's meal cooking. Ijenda, Burundi

味道鮮美 經濟實惠

沅湯水餃

小收糧票 每碗兩角

Streetside soup. Chengdu,
Szechwan, China

Dim sum. Guangzhou, China

159

Below:
Lunch from
the garden.
Occidental,
California

Right:
Autumn.
Northern
California

WHAT YOU CAN DO

EAT RESPONSIBLY

Buy locally grown foods, directly from the source, if possible. Develop a relationship with a farmer's market or a local fruitstand, farm, or orchard.

Buy unprocessed organically and biodynamically grown foods, read labels carefully, and ask your retailers to substantiate the sources and growing methods of the products they carry.

Eat seasonally. Reconnect with the seasons and learn what local foods are available at what times.

Learn the art of food preserving. Freeze, dry, or can the summer's bounty for use over the rest of the year.

Buy by mail order or join or form a food-buying co-op to obtain organic foods wholesale and in bulk, particularly when they are are not available locally or seasonally.

Eat lower on the food chain—fewer meat and animal products and more grains and fresh fruits and vegetables.

Eat at home more often. Spend an afternoon or evening with a friend or a family member planning a meal. Select the raw ingredients, prepare them in a healthy and attractive way, and take your time eating together.

ACT LOCALLY

Learn more about farming and food gardening. Understand the food cycle, from preparing the soil to the harvest.

Create a food garden of your own, even if you have only a small backyard, a few square feet, a small greenhouse, or just a window box. Use only natural techniques for fertility and to control weeds and pests.

Redesign and convert your landscaping using both ornamental and edible plants.

Substitute natural methods for the use of pesticides, chemical fertilizers, and herbicides in your home, yard, and gardens.

Recycle your food scraps and other biodegradable products into compost, which can then be used to fertilize your garden and returned to the earth.

Conserve and recycle water. Find out which varieties require less water; install a simple gray-water system to recycle household wastewater onto your garden.

Save seeds. Preserve and propagate any traditional, non-hybrid seeds that may have been passed on to you by friends or family.

Teach your children where their food comes from and what foods are beneficial to their health and to the health of the earth.

RESPOND POLITICALLY

Find out about the origins of your food. Don't purchase products that have been produced by exploiting the environment, animals, or other human beings. These may include coffee, tea, bananas, and veal, for example.

Urge your elected officials to support legislation that lessens our dependency on the chemical treadmill, encourages farming practices that preserve and rebuild natural resources, protects the health and rights of farm workers both at home and abroad, keeps families on the land, and regenerates rural communities.

RESOURCES: WHERE TO BEGIN

Here are just a few examples of a range of organizations and publications.

ORGANIZATIONS

American Community Gardening Association, 325 Walnut St., Philadelphia, PA 19106; (215) 625–8280. Information about member gardens nationwide

American Horticultural Therapy Association, 326A Christopher Ave., Gaithersburg, MD 20879; (301) 869–2397/948–3010

Biodynamic Agricultural Association/UK, Woodman Lane, Clent, Stourbridge, West Midlands DY9 9PX, England; (0562) 884933

Biodynamic Farming Association, Box 550, Kimberton, PA 19442. Publishes a list of member Community Supported Agriculture farms and training opportunities throughout the U.S. and Canada

Committee for Sustainable Agriculture, P.O. Box 1300, Colfax, CA 95713; (916) 346–2777. Educational, networking organization. Puts on annual Ecological Farming Conference; publishes *Organic Food Matters* newspaper

Henry Doubleday Research Association/Ryton Gardens, Ryton-on-Dunsmore, Coventry CV8 3LG, England; (0203) 303517. Education and research organization; demonstration gardens and heirloom seed bank; publishes newsletter and books

National Federation of City Farms and Community Gardens, AMF House, 93 Whitby Rd., Brislington, Bristol BS4 3QF, England; (0272) 719109

National Gardening Association, 180 Flynn Ave., Burlington, VT 05401; (802) 863–1308. Grow-lab for schools, educational curriculum for children; publishes *Youth Gardening Book*

Pesticide Action Network, North American Regional Center, 965 Mission St., Suite 514, San Francisco CA 94103; (415) 541–9140. Provides research services, resource lists; publishes *Global Pesticide Campaigner* newsletter

Rodale Institute, 33 E. Minor St., Emmaus, PA 18098; (215) 683–6383. Research, experimental gardens through Rodale Research Center; publications include *Organic Gardening* magazine

Soil Association/Organic Food and Farming Centre, 86–88 Colston St., Bristol BS1 5BB, England; (0272) 290661. Campaigns for sustainable farming policy worldwide; publishes *Living Earth* magazine

BOOKS, DIRECTORIES, AND OTHER PUBLICATIONS

Alternative Farming Systems Information Center. *Educational and Training Opportunities in Sustainable Agriculture, 1991.* National Agricultural Library, Rm. 111, Beltsville, MD 20705; (301) 504–5755

Campbell, Stu. *Let It Rot.* Pownal, VT: Garden Way, 1990. A guide to composting

Coleman, Eliott. *The New Organic Grower.* Post Mills, VT: Chelsea Green, 1989. Manual of tools and techniques for the home and market gardener

Conford, Philip, ed. *A Future for the Land: Organic Practice from a Global Perspective,* Devon, England: Resurgence/Green Books, 1992

Creasy, Rosalind. *Cooking from the Garden.* San Francisco: Sierra Club Books, 1988. Recipes for seasonal and ancient variety produce

Fukuoka, Masanobu. *The One-Straw Revolution, An Introduction to Natural Farming.* Emmaus, PA: Rodale Press, 1978

Gear, Alan. *New Organic Food Guide.* London: Dent, 1990

Hamilton, Geoffrey. *Successful Organic Gardening: The Complete Guide to Growing Flowers, Fruit and Vegetables Naturally.* London: Dorling Kindersley, 1991

Hart, Robert. *Forest Gardening.* Devon, England: Resurgence Books, 1991

Healthy Harvest—A Global Directory of Sustainable Agriculture and Horticultural Organizations. Washington, DC: Potomac Valley Press, 1993

Heifetz, Jeanne. *Green Groceries.* New York: HarperCollins, 1992. Mail-order sources for organic foods

Howard, Sir Albert. *An Agricultural Testament.* Emmaus, PA: Rodale Press, reprint 1979

Jeavons, John. *How to Grow More Vegetables.* Berkeley, CA: Ten Speed Press, revised 1991

Kourik, Robert. *Designing and Maintaining Your Edible Landscape Naturally.* Santa Rosa, CA: Metamorphic Press, 1986

Mollison, Bill, with Reny Slay. *Introduction to Permaculture.* Tyalgum, Australia: Tagari, 1991

Mott, Lawrie, and Karen Snyder. *Pesticide Alert: A Guide to Pesticides in Fruits and Vegetables.* San Francisco: Sierra Club Books, 1987

Olkowski, William, Sheila Daar, and Helga Olkowski. *Common Sense Pest Control.* Newtown, CT: The Taunton Press, 1991

The Organic Directory Yearbook. Birmingham, England: Wham Marketing, 1993; (021) 449–6691

Rodale, Robert. *Save Three Lives, A Plan for Famine Prevention.* San Francisco: Sierra Club Books, reprint 1991. Why traditional farming methods may be superior to Western innovations

Seed Savers Exchange. *Garden Seed Inventory.* R.R. 3, Box 239, Decorah, IA 52101; (319) 382–5990. Directory of seed company catalogs listing non-hybrid vegetable seeds offered in the U.S. and Canada

Strange, Marty. *Family Farming.* Lincoln: University of Nebraska Press, 1988. Cultural and historical context for the current American farm situation

Teitel, Martin. *Rainforest in Your Kitchen.* Washington, DC: Island Press, 1992. A practical step-by-step guide to creating environmental change through how you eat

Wright, Angus. *The Death of Ramon Gonzales: A Modern Agricultural Dilemma.* Austin: University of Texas Press, 1990

Summer harvest. Fairview Gardens Farm

INDEX

*Numbers in italics refer to
captions and/or photographs.*

ACKNOWLEDGMENTS

This book took me almost ten years to complete and involved the help of individuals and organizations on five continents. Without them it simply would not have been possible. My thanks go to all the people listed below and others too numerous to mention.

Patrick Gallagher, who from the beginning encouraged me to write this book, who devoted endless hours to planning, research, and fieldwork, and whose friendship was unwavering throughout. For the work in China, Tang Shiwei for his companionship and help with translation; Kun Li for acting as our guide; Cindy Walsh and John Schneller, fellow travelers; and Lin Bo for his contacts. In Kenya, the Oatways for their hospitality before and after several intense sojourns; and Jacob Talaam for guiding us into the remote Kerio Valley and introducing us to his tribe in the Elgeyo Marakwet district. In Burundi, to Jacques Lonhienne for managing the impossible by helping with permits and for providing incredible hospitality and assistance in Bujumbura; Lucy Harris Hall for her miracle in obtaining appropriate government permission; André and Chantal Schmidt for opening up their home in Bujumbura; and Jean Rutembesa for guiding me throughout the Ijenda region of Burundi and faithfully translating. In Sicily, Vittorio Turco for appearing out of nowhere and in short order organizing an itinerary and contacts that opened many doors; the Furnari family for their hospitality and assistance in Catania; and Salvatore Leanti La Rosa and Salvina Testo for translations. All my Peruvian friends in Santa Barbara for contacts in their homeland; the Maruy family for their support and hospitality in Lima; Narcisso in Cuzco for his guidance, support, and translations; David Espejo for trekking to Colquepata and beyond and translating Quechua. Among the Hopi, Caroline for her simplicity, strength, and hospitality in allowing Aaron and me to stay with her on many visits and share in her life; Titus and Little Dan for their wisdom and inspiration; and David Ortiz, who died before this project was completed. Sally McCabe from Philadelphia Greens; Jane Weissman at Operation GreenThumb; and Sandi Anderson at Green Guerrillas for introducing me to the world of urban gardens. For their generous financial support, Gary and Charlene Peters; Margaret Carswell and Robert Engle; Jim Hagen; Emanuel and Jacqueline Weintraub; Mark and Rochelle Bookspan; Bernard Ableman; A&I Color Labs in Los Angeles for donating the processing for the Peru section; and Randy Wright at Color Services in Santa Barbara for donations of color printing. Bob Wilkinson for his help and encouragement during the project's inception; Miguel Ordonez for valuable assistance during its early stages; Richard Cravens for his help in conceptualizing the text; Michael Katz for his guidance and assistance; John Collier, who twenty years ago nurtured me as a student of photography and more recently strongly supported this book and its message; Malcolm Collier for his time and encouragement in working through the direction for the book; Michael Hoffman, whose advice forced me to adopt a more contemporary approach; Steve Berman for his personal friendship and financial support; Arianna Huffington for introducing me to Paul Gottlieb, who believed in this project enough to publish it; my editor at Abrams, Sharon AvRutick, who very patiently walked me through the process of my first book, and Bob McKee, the designer, for putting all the pieces together; David Brower, whose friendship to me and encouragement of my work helped me to believe in myself; Earth Island Institute for providing the sponsorship for this project; and Selma Rubin for her support, both financial and personal. Cornelia Chapman and her late husband, Roger, for their patience and constant support and for providing the land that has nurtured both myself and hundreds of others; Steve Soderquist, Bill Fleming, and Salvador Gomez, whose work, commitment, and care for the farm made it possible for me get away to travel and photograph. Elias and Donna Chiacos for their friendship and support and for reading various drafts of the text; Cynthia Wisehart, who stood by me during the last year, editing, brainstorming, counseling, and basically living this work (without her contribution its completion would not have been possible); Sam Bittman for his very creative work on chapter two; and Wes Jackson for his contribution of the foreword and for his long-term commitment to sustainable agriculture. My father for getting me interested in photography at a very young age; my mother for being a mom and worrying about me each time I went off to remote places; my grandparents for instilling in me a sense of the earth that their generation knew so well; Donna for the gift of our son and for her loving support during all the trials and tribulations of this process; Jeanne Marie for her love and companionship during my travels and for putting up with me while I was consumed with endless hours of finishing this work; and my son, Aaron. All the farmers and gardeners I visited who shared with me their fields and their harvests and whose stewardship of the land provided the real foundation for this book. And the land I work, from which all this has come.